TABLE OF CONTENTS

Chapter 1
Introduction to Financial Reporting

QUESTIONS

1- 1. a. The AICPA is an organization of CPAs that prior to 1973 accepted the primary responsibility for the development of generally accepted accounting principles.

   b. The Financial Accounting Standards Board replaced the Accounting Principles Board as the primary rule-making body. It is an independent organization and includes members other than public accountants.

   c. The SEC has the authority to determine generally accepted accounting principles and to regulate the accounting profession. The SEC has elected to leave much of the determination of generally accepted accounting principles and the regulation of the accounting profession to the private sector.

1- 2. Consistency allows for the same accounting principle from period to period. A change in principle requires statement disclosure.

1- 3. The concept of historical cost determines the balance sheet valuation of land. The realization concept requires that a transaction has occurred for the profit to be recognized.

1- 4. a. Entity

   b. Realization

   c. Materiality

   d. Conservatism

   e. Historical cost

   f. Historical cost

   g. Disclosure

1- 5. Entity concept

1- 6. Generally accepted accounting principles do not apply when a firm does not appear to be a going concern. In this case the liquidation values are the appropriate figures.

1- 7. With the time period assumption, inaccuracies of accounting for the entity, short of its complete life span, are accepted. The assumption is made that the entity can be accounted for reasonably accurately for a particular period of time. In other words, the decision is made to accept some inaccuracy because of incomplete information about the future in exchange for more timely reporting. The statements are considered to be meaningful because material inaccuracies are not acceptable.

1- 8. It is true that the only accurate way to account for the success or failure of an entity is to accumulate all transactions from the opening of business until the business eventually liquidates. But it is not necessary that the statements be completely accurate in order for them to be meaningful.

1- 9. a. Natural business year

   A year that ends when operations are at a low ebb for the year.

   b. Calendar year

   The accounting time period is ended on December 31.

   c. Fiscal year

   A twelve-month accounting period that ends at the end of a month other than December 31.

1-10. Money.

1-11. When money does not hold a stable value, the financial statements can lose much of their significance. To the extent that money does not remain stable, it loses usefulness as the standard for measuring financial transactions.

1-12. No.

There is a problem with determining the index in order to adjust the statements. The items that are included in the index must be representative and the price of items change because of various factors, such as quality, technology, and inflation.
Yes.

A reasonable adjustment to the statements can be made for inflation.

1-13.   False.

An arbitrary write-off of inventory cannot be justified under the conservatism concept. The conservatism concept can only be applied where there are alternative measurements and each of these alternative measurements has reasonable support.

1-14.   Yes, inventory that has a market value below the historical cost should be written down in order to recognize a loss. This is done based upon the concept of conservatism. Losses that can be reasonably anticipated should be taken in order to reflect the least favorable effect on net income of the current period.

1-15.   End of production

The realization of revenue at the completion of the production process is acceptable when the price of the item is known and there is a ready market.

Receipt of cash

This method should only be used when the prospects of collection are especially doubtful at the time of sale.

During production

This method is allowed for long-term construction projects because recognizing revenue on long-term construction projects as work progresses tends to give a fairer picture of the results for a given period in comparison with having the entire revenue realized in one period of time from a project.

1-16. It is difficult to apply the matching concept when there
      is no direct connection between the cost and revenue.
      Under these circumstances, accountants often charge off
      the cost in the period incurred in order to be
      conservative.

1-17. If the entity can justify the use of an alternative
      accounting method on the basis that it is preferable, then
      the change can be made.

1-18. The accounting reports must disclose all facts that may
      influence the judgment of an informed reader. Usually
      this is a judgment decision for the accountant to make.
      Because of the complexity of many businesses and the
      increased expectations of the public, the full disclosure
      concept has become one of the most difficult concepts for
      the accountant to apply.

1-19. There is a preference for the use of objectivity in the
      preparation of financial statements, but financial
      statements cannot be completely prepared based upon
      objective data; estimates must be made in many situations.

1-20. This is a true statement. The concepts of materiality
      allow the accountant to handle immaterial items in the
      most economical and expedient manner possible.

1-21. Some industry practices lead to accounting reports that do
      not conform to generally accepted accounting principles.
      These reports are considered to be acceptable, but the
      accounting profession is making an effort to eliminate
      particular industry practices that do not conform to the
      normal generally accepted accounting principles.

1-22. Events that fall outside of the financial transactions of
      the entity are not recorded. An example would be the loss
      of a major customer.

1-23. True. The accounting profession is making an effort to
      reduce or eliminate specific industry practices.

1-24. The entity must usually use the accrual basis of
      accounting. Only under limited circumstances can the
      entity use the cash basis.

1-25.   There is no one source or list of accounting principles
        that has substantial authoritative support; therefore, the
        accountant must be familiar with acceptable sources to
        refer to in order to decide whether any particular
        accounting principle has substantial authoritative
        support. The ultimate responsibility is with the
        accountant to prove that generally acceptable accounting
        principles have been followed.

1-26.   The separate entity concept directs that personal
        transactions of the owners not be recorded on the books of
        the entity.

1-27.   At the point of sale.

1-28.   a. The building should be recorded at cost, which is
            $50,000.

        b. Revenue should not be recorded for the savings between
            the cost of $50,000 and the bid of $60,000. Revenue
            comes from selling, not from purchasing.

1-29.   The materiality concept supports this policy.

1-30.   The Securities and Exchange Commission (SEC).

1-31.   The basic problem with the monetary assumption when there
        has been significant inflation is that the monetary
        assumption assumes a stable dollar in terms of purchasing
        power. When there has been inflation, the dollar has not
        been stable in terms of purchasing power and, therefore,
        dollars are being compared that are not of the same
        purchasing power.

1-32.   The matching principle deals with the costs to be matched
        against revenue. The realization concept has to do with
        the determination of revenue. The combination of revenue
        and costs determine income.

1-33.   The term "generally accepted accounting principles" is
        used to refer to accounting principles that have
        substantial authoritative support.

1-34.   The process of considering a Statement of Financial
        Accounting Standards begins when the Board elects to add a
        topic to its technical agenda. The Board only considers
        topics that are "broke" for its technical agenda.

        On projects with a broad impact, a Discussion Memorandum
        or an Invitation to Comment is issued. The Discussion
        Memorandum or Invitation to Comment is distributed as a
        basis for public comment. After considering the written
        comments and the public hearing comments, the Board
        resumes deliberations in one or more public Board
        meetings. The final Statement on Financial Accounting
        Standards must receive a majority affirmative vote of the
        Board.

1-35.   The FASB Conceptual Framework for Accounting and Reporting
        is intended to set forth a system of interrelated
        objectives and underlying concepts that will serve as the
        basis for evaluating existing standards of financial
        accounting and reporting.

1-36.   a. Committee on Accounting Procedures:

            A committee of the AICPA that played an important role
            in the determination of generally accepted accounting
            principles in the United States between 1939 and 1959.

        b. Committee on Accounting Terminology:

            A committee of the AICPA that played an important role
            in the defining of accounting terminology between 1939
            and 1959.

        c. Accounting Principles Board:

            An AICPA board that played a leading role in the
            development of generally accepted accounting
            principles in the United States between 1959 and 1973.

        d. Financial Accounting Standards Board:

            The Board that has played the leading role in the
            development of generally accepted accounting
            principles in the United States since 1973.

1-37.   Concepts Statement No. 1 indicates that the objectives of
        general-purpose external financial reporting are primarily
        for the needs of external users who lack the authority to
        prescribe the information they want and must rely on
        information management communicates to them.

1-38.   Financial accounting is not designed to measure directly
        the value of a business enterprise. Concepts Statement
        No. 1 indicates that financial accounting is not designed
        to measure directly the value of a business enterprise,
        but the information it provides may be helpful to those
        who wish to estimate its value.

1-39.   According to Concepts Statement No. 2, to be relevant,
        information must be timely and it must have predictive
        value or feedback value or both. To be reliable,
        information must have representational faithfulness and it
        must be verifiable and neutral.

1-40.   1. Definition
        2. Measurability
        3. Relevance
        4. Reliability

1-41.   1. Historical cost
        2. Current cost
        3. Current market value
        4. Net realizable value
        5. Present value

1-42.   The accrual basis income statement recognizes revenue when
        it is realized (realization concept) and expenses
        recognized when they are incurred (matching concept). The
        cash basis recognizes revenue when the cash is received
        and expenses when payments are made.

1-43.   True. Usually the cash basis does not indicate when the
        revenue was earned and when the cost should be recognized.
        The cash basis recognizes cash receipts as revenue and
        cash payments as expenses.

1-44.   When cash is received and when payment is made is
        important. For example, the timing of cash receipts and
        cash payments can have a bearing on a company's ability to

1. a. The Board follows certain precepts in the conduct of its activities. They are:

    1. *To be objective in its decision making* and to ensure, insofar as possible, the neutrality of information resulting from its standards. To be neutral information must report economic activity as faithfully as possible without coloring the image it communicates for the purpose of influencing behavior in Any particular direction.

    2. *To weigh carefully the views of its constituents* in developing concepts and standards. The ultimate determinant of concepts and standards, however, must be the Board's judgment, based on research, public input, and careful deliberation, about the usefulness of the resulting information.

    3. *To promulgate standards only when the expected benefits exceed the perceived costs.* While reliable quantitative cost-benefit calculations are seldom possible, the Board strives to determine that a proposed standard will fill a significant need and that the costs it imposes, compared with possible alternatives, are justified in relation to the overall benefits.

    4. *To bring about needed changes in ways that minimize disruption to the continuity of reporting practice.* Reasonable effective dates and transition provisions are established when new standards are introduced. The Board considers it desirable that change be evolutionary to the extent that can be accommodated by the need for relevance, reliability, comparability, and consistency.

    5. *To review the effects of past decisions* and interpret, amend, or replace standards in a timely fashion when such action is indicated.

b. Financial Accounting Standards Advisory Council

An Overview

The Financial Accounting Standards Advisory Council, FASAC or "the Council" for short, was formed in 1973 concurrent with the establishment of the Financial Accounting Standards Board (the FASB or the Board).

The primary function of FASAC is to advise the Board on issues related to projects on the Board's agenda, possible new agenda items, project priorities, procedural matters that may require the attention of the FASB, and other matters as requested by the chairman of the FASB. FASAC meetings provide the Board with an opportunity to obtain and discuss the views of very diverse group of individuals from varied business and professional backgrounds.

The members of FASAC are drawn from the ranks of CEOs, CFOs, senior partners of public accounting firms, executive directors of professional organizations, and senior members of the academic and analyst communities, all with an interest in the integrity of full and complete financial reporting and disclosure.

Carrying Out the Mission

It is the job of the FASB to establish the "generally accepted accounting principles," or GAAP, to which public financial reporting by U.S. corporations must conform and to keep those principles current.

In conducting its activities, the Board strives to carefully weigh the views of its constituents, who include all those with an interest in financial reporting, including users, preparers, and auditors of financial reports. The Council provides an important sounding board to help the FASB understand what constituents are thinking about a wide range of issues.

FASAC's role is *not* to reach a consensus or to vote on the issues that it considers at its meetings. Rather, FASAC operates as a window through which the Board can obtain and discuss the representative views of the diverse groups the FASB affects. Thus, FASAC provides the forum for two-way communication. While it is important to convene the Council members as a group, that is so that the Board can hear the individual views of those members and so that the members can hear and respond to each other's views.

Members of FASAC are urged to speak out publicly on matters before the FASB and also to be supportive of the Board's process, and the principle of private-sector standard setting. Individual Council members are not expected to agree with the Board's decisions on all of the technical aspects of the projects on the Board's agenda, but it is important that FASAC members support the institution and its due process.

PROBLEMS

PROBLEM 1-1

1. __b__   6. __i__
2. __a__   7. __e__
3. __h__   8. __f__
4. __c__   9. __g__
5. __d__

PROBLEM 1-2

1. __o__   6. __e__   11. __h__
2. __a__   7. __f__   12. __k__
3. __b__   8. __j__   13. __c__
4. __l__   9. __i__   14. __m__
5. __d__   10. __g__   15. __n__

PROBLEM 1-3

a. __2__   Typically, much judgment and estimates go into the preparation of financial statements.

b. __4__   Financial accounting is not designed to measure directly the value of a business enterprise. The end result statements can be used as part of the data to aid in estimating the value of the business.

c. __4__   FASB Statement of Concepts No. 2 lists timeliness, predictive value, and feedback value as ingredients of the quality of relevance.

d. __2__   The Securities and Exchange Commission has the primary right and responsibility for generally accepted accounting principles. They have primarily elected to have the private sector develop generally accepted accounting principles and have designated the Financial Accounting Standards Board as the primary source.

e. __4__   The concept of conservatism directs that the measurement with the least favorable effect on net income and financial position in the current period be selected.

f.   _3_   The Internal Revenue Service deals with Federal tax law, not generally accepted accounting principles.

g.   _5_   Opinions were issued by The Accounting Principles Board.

PROBLEM 1-4

a.   _1_   Statements of Position are issued by the AICPA.

b.   _2_   This is the definition contained in SFAC No. 6

c.   _2_   This is the definition contained in SFAC No. 6.

d.   _5_   Comparability is not one of the criteria for an item to be recognized.

e.   _2_   Future cost is not one of the measurement attributes recognized in SFAC No. 5.

f.   _1_   Revenue is usually recognized at point of sale.

g.   _1_   Financial accounting is not designed to measure directly the value of a business enterprise.

PROBLEM 1-5

a. Sales on credit $ 80,000
    Cost of inventory sold on credit   <65,000>
    Payment to sales clerk   <10,000>
    Income $ 5,000

b. Collections from customers $ 60,000
    Payment for purchases   <55,000>
    Payment to sales clerk   <10,000>
    Loss $< 5,000>

CASES

CASE 1-1 STANDARDS OVERLOAD?

(As more financial accounting standards were issued, a charge of standards overload emerged. This issue took many forms, including the issue of different accounting standards for nonpublic companies than for public companies. Another form of this issue was whether different accounting standards should apply to small vs. large companies.)

Note: The standards overload issue has been reviewed extensively in the literature since approximately 1980.

Excellent material for reviewing the standards overload issue are:

1.   Mosso, David "Standards Overload - No Simple Solution," Journal of Accountancy, November 1983, pg. 120-122.

2.   News Report "Standards overload relief requires top priority, says AICPA Committee report," Journal of Accountancy, May, 1983, pg. 18-22.

3.   Abdel-halik, Rashad "Financial Reporting by Private Companies: Diagnosis and Analysis," Management Accounting, October, 1983, pg. 80-81. (The entire study was published by the Financial Accounting Standards Board.)

a.   This is an opinion question:

The Financial Accounting Standards Board published a report entitled "Financial Reporting by Private Companies: Diagnosis and Analysis".

This research report supports that GAAP financial statements for private companies are perceived to benefit managers and bankers. Managers and bankers tend to find a single set of GAAP financial statements to be useful.

b.   The research report, "Financial Reporting by Private Companies: Diagnosis and Analysis," indicates that there is a reasonable amount of support by CPAs for a distinction in GAAP between public and nonpublic companies. This support from the CPAs may be because of billing problems with the nonpublic companies, which would tend to be smaller companies. It could also be that the smaller CPA firms work extensively with nonpublic companies. The smaller CPA firms would tend to have more problems than the big CPA firms in keeping up with changing standards.

c. Most small business owner-managers would likely object to continually increased reporting requirements. They see them as increased costs without improved benefits, since their user groups tend to be confined to owners and bankers.

Although most small business owner-managers would prefer to have fewer standards, they do not favor a distinction between financial reporting standards for small and large companies. They do not want their statements to be viewed as inferior.

d. CPAs in a small CPA firm are likely to view standards overload as a bigger problem than do CPAs in a large CPA firm. Likely reasons for this are the problems of keeping up with GAAP, lack of specialization in a small firm, and small CPA firms work more with small businesses. Therefore, they are more likely to experience fee resistance than are large firms.

e. Standards overload does not appear to be a major problem from the viewpoint of the objectives of financial reporting. Providing information useful to present and potential investors and creditors and other users in making rational investment, credit, and similar decisions may require many standards and somewhat complicated standards.

CASE 1-2 STANDARD-SETTING: "A POLITICAL ASPECT"

a. The hierarchy of accounting qualities in SFAC No. 2 includes neutrality as one of the ingredients. SFAC indicates that, to be reliable, the information must be verifiable, subject to representational faithfulness, and neutral.
    To quote from the Beresford letter: "If financial statements are to be useful, they must report economic activity without coloring the message to influence behavior in a particular direction."

b. Costs of transactions do exist whether or not the FASB mandates their recognition in financial statements. The markets may not be able to recognize these costs in the short run if they are not reported. Thus investors, creditors, regulators, and other users of financial reports may not be able to make reasonable business and economic decisions if the costs are not reported.

c. Much of the standard setting in the U.S. is in the private sector. A major role in the private sector has been played by The American Institute of Certified Public Accountants. Since 1973 the primary role in the private sector has been played by The Financial Accounting Standards Board.

It should be noted that the Securities Act of 1934 gave the SEC the authority to determine generally accepted accounting principles and to regulate the accounting profession. The Beresford letter recognizes that the SEC and congressional committees maintain an active oversight of the FASB.

d. True. Quoting from the letter: "We expect that changes in financial reporting will have economic consequences, just as economic consequences are inherent in existing financial reporting practices."

CASE 1-3 STANDARD-SETTING: "BY THE WAY OF THE UNITED STATES CONGRESS"

a. This is an opinion question. It is the opinion of the author that the United States Congress is not well qualified to debate and set generally accepted accounting principles. Very few in the United States Congress have a financial or accounting background.

b. Under the Securities Act of 1934, the Securities and Exchange Commission (SEC) was created. In effect, the SEC was given the authority to determine generally accepted accounting principles and to regulate the accounting profession.

With these bills the Senate and the House are going around the SEC in determining the generally accepted accounting principles for stock option compensation.

CASE 1-4 RECOGNIZING REVENUE AND RELATED COSTS - CONSIDER THESE SITUATIONS (PART I)

A. General Motors Corporation

   a. Title apparently passes to the dealer at the time of shipment.

   Yes, this method does resemble point of sale.

   b. Sales are generally recorded when products are shipped to independent dealers. Therefore there would be no time lag between recognizing sales and the reduction for these items.

   No.
   Apparently a time lag is not a problem. There is a problem of estimating for normal dealer sales incentives, returns and allowances, and GM Card rebates.

   c. Costs related to special sales incentive programs are recognized as reductions to sales after the sale has been recorded. This does present a matching problem. Estimating for special sales incentive would be too subjective at the time of sale.

B. Kodak

   a. Title apparently passes when the product is shipped.

   b. Recognizing revenue from contractional situations over the contractual period appears to be reasonable. It does present a matching problem in that the maintenance and service may not be spread evenly over the period.

   Recognizing revenue from noncontractional situations as services are performed is reasonable. In this case the revenue and the related cost are recognized at the same time.

C. Compaq

   a. Point of sale.
   b. Matching
      Related costs to the revenue are being recognized at the time of sale.

c. This policy appears to be appropriate. Related costs to the revenue are being recognized at the time of sale.

d. This policy appears to be appropriate. To be conservative revenue is recognized only after significant obligations are fulfilled.

CASE 1-5 RECOGNIZING REVENUE AND RELATED COSTS - CONSIDER THESE SITUATIONS (PART II)

A. UAL Corporation

   a. This procedure does appear to be appropriate. Collection is made in advance. Revenue is not recognized until transportation is furnished.

   b. Collections in advance of service are considered to be a liability. The time period between collection and providing the service would be relatively short. Therefore it should be considered a current liability.

B. Peco Energy

   a. A reasonable estimate for service or energy delivered could be made at the end of each month.

   b. A reasonable estimate for service or energy delivered could be made at the end of each month.

C. Osmonics

   a. $4,750,000   (1988-1992)
      (2,342,000)   (1992)
      $2,408,000

   b. 1993

   c. There is not a good matching of embezzlement losses and recoveries. Sometimes accountants are presented with difficult situations. In these cases, disclosure becomes important.

CASE 1-6 CASH BASIS - ACCRUAL BASIS?

a.   Cash basis

b.   Accrual basis

c.   To conform to Statement of Financial Accounting Standard No. 106.

d.   A company on the accrual basis could report an item on the cash basis if the effect of the item on the statements was immaterial. This could also happen if an accounting standard allowed or required the item to be reported on the cash basis.

CASH 1-7 GOING CONCERN?

a.   The going-concern assumption is that the entity in question will remain in business for an indefinite period of time.

b.   Yes.

      The potential problem is that the firm may not be able to continue in business as a going concern. This puts into question the recoverability and classification of assets or the amounts and classification of liabilities.

c.   This disclosure puts the user of the statements on warning that the statements may be misleading if the company cannot continue as a going concern.

CASE 1-8 ECONOMICS AND ACCOUNTING: THE UNCONGENIAL TWINS

a.   Per Kenneth E. Boulding:

      "Ritual is always the proper response when a man has to give an answer to a question, the answer to which he cannot really know. Ritual under these circumstances has two functions. It is comforting (and in the face of the great uncertainties of the future, comfort is not to be despised) and it is also an answer sufficient for action."

b.   No.

Per Kenneth E. Boulding:
"The wise businessman will not believe his accountant
although he takes what his accountant tells him as important
evidence. The quality of that evidence, however, depends in
considerable degree on the simplicity of the procedures and
the awareness which we have of them."

c.   Per Kenneth E. Boulding:

"It is the sufficient answer rather than the right answer
which the accountant really seeks."

Boulding indicates that accounting does not need to be
accurate in order to serve a useful function.

CASE 1-9 I OFTEN PAINT FAKES

(This case is intended to serve as a forum for discussing the
accuracy of financial statements prepared using generally
accepted accounting principles.)

a.   Accounting reports prepared using generally accepted
     accounting principles are not exactly accurate. They are
     intended to be sufficient to aid in making informed
     decisions.

b.   No, accountants do not paint fakes. But, it may take an
     understanding of generally accepted accounting principles to
     reasonably comprehend the significance of the statements.

Chapter 2
Introduction to Financial Statements and Other
Financial Reporting Topics

<u>QUESTIONS</u>

2- 1.   a.   Unqualified opinion with explanatory paragraph
          b.   Unqualified opinion with explanatory paragraph
          c.   Unqualified opinion
          d.   Adverse opinion
          e.   Qualified opinion

2- 2.   The responsibility for the preparation and integrity of financial statements rests with management. The auditor simply examines them for fairness, conformity with GAAP, and consistency.

2- 3.   The basic purpose of the integrated disclosure system is to achieve uniformity between annual reports and SEC filings. It is hoped that this will improve the quality of disclosure and lighten the disclosure load for the companies reporting.

2- 4.   The explanatory paragraphs explain important considerations that the reviewer of the financial statements should be aware of. An example would be a doubt as to going concern ability.

2- 5.   A review consists principally of inquiries of company personnel and analytical procedures applied to financial data. It is substantially less in scope than an examination in accordance with generally accepted auditing standards.

2- 6.   No. The accountant's report will indicate that they are not aware of any material modifications that should be made to the financial statements in order for them to be in conformity with generally accepted accounting principles, and the report will indicate departures from generally accepted accounting principles.

2- 7.   The accountant does not express an opinion or any other form of assurance.

2- 8.   No. Some statements have not been audited, reviewed, or compiled. These statements are presented without being accompanied by an accountant's report.

2- 9.   Balance Sheet
        The purpose of a balance sheet is to show the financial position of an accounting entity as of a particular date.

        Income Statement
        The income statement summarizes the results of operations for an accounting period.

        Statement of Cash Flows
        The statement of cash flows details the inflows and outflows of cash during a specified period of time.

2-10.   Footnotes increase the full disclosure of the statements by providing information on inventory and depreciation methods, subsequent events, contingent liabilities, etc.

2-11.   Contingent liabilities are dependent on an occurrence to determine if payment will be necessary. Liabilities from lawsuits are dependent on the outcome of the cases; they therefore represent contingent liabilities.

2-12.   a, c.

2-13.   A proxy is the solicitation sent to stockholders for the election of directors and for the approval of other corporation actions. The proxy represents the shareholder authorization regarding the casting of that shareholder's vote.

2-14.   A summary annual report is a condensed annual report that omits much of the financial information included in a typical annual report.

2-15.   The firm must include a set of fully audited statements and other required financial disclosures in the proxy materials sent to shareholders. The 10-K is also available to the public.

2-16.   There is typically a substantial reduction in non-financial pages and financial pages. The greatest reduction in pages is usually in the financial pages.

2-17.   Cash flows from operating activities, cash flows from investing activities, and cash flows from financing activities.

2-18.   The income statement and the statement of cash flows.

2-19.   Assets, liabilities, and owners' equity.

2-20.   No. Cash dividends are paid with cash.

2-21.   Footnotes are an integral part of financial statements. A detailed review of footnotes is absolutely essential in order to understand the financial statements.

2-22.   APB Opinion No. 22 requires disclosure of accounting policies as the first footnote to financial statements or just prior to the footnotes.

2-23.   They are interchangeable terms referring to ideals of character and conduct. These ideals, in the form of codes of conduct, furnish criteria for distinguishing between right and wrong.

2-24.   Law can be viewed as the minimum standard of ethics.

2-25.   Assets = Liabilities + Stockholders' equity (capital).

2-26.   The scheme of the double-entry system revolves around the accounting equation:

         Assets = Liabilities + Stockholders' Equity

         With double-entry, each transaction is recorded with the total dollar amount of the debits equal to the total dollar amount of the credits. Each transaction affects two or more asset, liability, or owners' equity accounts (including the temporary accounts).

2-27.   a. Assets, liabilities, and stockholders' equity accounts are referred to as permanent accounts because the balances in these accounts carry forward to the next accounting period.

         b. Revenue, expense, gain, loss, and dividend accounts are not carried into the next period. These accounts are closed to Retained Earnings.

22

2-28.   Because the employee worked in the period just ended, the salary must be matched to that period's revenue.

2-29.   Most of the accounts are not up to date at the end of the accounting period. These accounts need to be adjusted so that all revenues and expenses are recognized and the balance sheet accounts have a correct ending balance.

2-30.   Companies use a number of special journals to improve record keeping efficiency that could not be obtained by using only the general journal.

2-31.   The SEC requires foreign registrants to conform to U.S. GAAP, either directly or by reconciliation. This approach presents a problem to the U.S. Securities exchanges, such as the NYSE. This is because the U.S. standards are perceived to be the most stringent. This puts exchanges like the NYSE at a competitive disadvantage with foreign exchanges that have lower standards.

2-32.   Sole Proprietorship
        A sole proprietorship is a business entity owned by one person.

        Partnership
        A partnership is a business owned by two or more individuals.

        Corporation
        A corporation is a legal entity incorporated in a particular state. Ownership is evidenced by shares of stock.

2-33.   The use of insider information could result in abnormal returns.

2-34.   In an efficient market the method of disclosure is not as important as whether or not the item is disclosed.

2-35.   Abnormal returns could be achieved if the market does not have access to relevant information or if fraudulent information is provided.

2-36.   Pooling of interests — With the pooling method, the
         recorded assets and liabilities of the firms involved
         in the combination are carried forward to the combined
         entity at their previous recorded amounts. Income of
         the combined firm includes income of the constituents
         for the entire period.

         Purchase — With the purchase method the firm doing the
         acquiring records the identifiable assets and
         liabilities at fair value at the date of acquisition.
         The difference between the fair value of the
         identifiable assets and liabilities and the amount paid
         is recorded as goodwill (an asset).

2-37.   Consolidated statements reflect an economic, rather
         than a legal, concept of the entity.

2-38.   The financial statements of the parent and the
         subsidiary are consolidated for all majority-owned
         subsidiaries unless control is temporary or does not
         rest with the majority owner.

TO THE NET

1. The article selected will be different for each student.

2. Calls for discussion of "A vision for the Future - Report of the FASB."

PROBLEMS

PROBLEM 2-1

	Cash		
Dec 6	2,500	Dec 10	500
Dec 14	3,000	Dec 17	6,000
Dec 24	1,200	Dec 28	700

	Sales		
		Dec 2	4,000
		Dec 6	2,500

	Accounts Receivable		
Dec 2	4,000	Dec 24	1,200
Dec 21	900		

	Office Salaries		
Dec 10	500		

	Land		
		Dec 14	2,200

	Gain on Sale of Land		
		Dec 14	800

	Equipment		
Dec 17	6,000		

	Services		
		Dec 21	900

PROBLEM 2-2

	Cash		
July 15	500	July 1	10,000
		July 20	300
		July 24	400

	Revenue		
		July 8	3,000

	Accounts Receivable		
July 8	3,000	July 15	500

	Land		
July 1	10,000		

	Repair Expense		
July 12	600		

	Accounts Payable		
July 20	00	July 12	600

	Wages Expense		
July 24	400		

PROBLEM 2-3

Insurance Expense		
(1)	600	

Prepaid Insurance		
	(1)	600

Supplies Expense		
(2)	300	

Supplies		
	(2)	300

Revenue		
(3)	1,000	

Unearned Revenue		
	(3)	1,000

Interest Expense		
(4)	200	

Interest Payable		
	(4)	200

Salaries Expense		
(5)	500	

Salaries Payable		
	(5)	500

Revenue		
	(6)	400

Accounts Receivable		
(6)	400	

PROBLEM 2-4

Prepaid Insurance		
(1)	640	

Insurance Expense		
	(1)	320

Supplies Expense		
(2)	100	

Supplies Expense		
	(2)	100

Interest Receivable		
(3)	100	

Interest Income		
	(3)	100

Salaries Expense		
(4)	800	

Salaries Payable		
	(4)	800

Unearned Revenue		
	(5)	600

Revenue		
(5)	600	

Accounts Payable		
	(6)	400

Advertising Expense		
(6)	400	

27

PROBLEM 2-5

a. __4__ The balance sheet equation is defined as assets are equal to liabilities plus owners' equity.

b. __1__ Assets ($40,000) = liabilities? + owners' equity ($10,000).

c. __3__ Assets ($100,000) = liabilities ($40,000) + owners' equity?

d. __3__ Accounts receivable is a balance sheet account and therefore a permanent account.

e. __3__ Insurance expense is an income statement account and therefore a temporary account.

f. __4__ Expenses, assets, and dividends all have a normal balance of a debit.

PROBLEM 2-6

a. __1__ All-purpose statement is not a classification for an audit opinion.

b. __1__ An unqualified opinion usually has the highest degree of reliability.

c. __5__ The typical unqualified opinion has three paragraphs.

d. __4__ All of the above.

e. __4__ Two years of audited balance sheets and three years of audited statements of income and three years of statements of cash flows.

f. __1__ Lack of harmonization of international accounting standards is thought to have a negative effect on international trade of accounting practice and services.

g. __2__ The Internal Revenue Service deals with U.S. federal taxes.

h. __2__ Form 10-K is the annual financial report submitted to the Securities and Exchange Commission.

PROBLEM 2-7

	Permanent (P) or Temporary (T)	Normal Balance Dr. (Cr.)
Cash	P	Dr.
Accounts receivable	P	Dr.
Equipment	P	Dr.
Accounts payable	P	Cr.
Common stock	P	Cr.
Sales	T	Cr.
Purchases	T	Dr.
Rent expense	T	Dr.
Utility expense	T	Dr.
Selling expenses	T	Dr.

PROBLEM 2-8

c	1
d	2
b	3
a	4

PROBLEM 2-9

c	1
b	2
a	3.
d	4

CASES

CASE 2-1 THE CEO RETIRES

Teaching Note: The CEO Retires (Teaching note prepared by the American Accounting Association)

PURPOSE: This case is meant to illustrate that the accounting choices available can be used by management to manipulate the reported financial results of the company.

CONTENT: The CEO of a company is entering the last year of his employment. For reasons of enhanced reputation, maximum compensation in his final year, and maximum compensation through the years via his pension, he has the incentive to manipulate the financial results of the company. Since this is his last year with the company, any long-term effects of the decisions he may make are not considered relevant. Furthermore, there are numerous directions the CEO can take: changing accounting estimates, deferring investing decisions, or changing accounting methods.

After consideration of a variety of alternatives, the CEO meets with the CFO to get his response to the CEO's proposed options.

Decision Model

a. Determine the Facts

Work through the case, identifying essential facts, especially those included in the contents section above.

Known facts should be listed first; then determine what one would want to know if possible. NOTE: Make the point to students that we never have all the facts; decisions are almost always made on incomplete information.

b. Define the Ethical Issues

(1) List all stakeholders - be sure that the class is thorough in this step -- the ethical issues will most likely arise out of conflicting interests between and among the stakeholders.

the CEO, Dan Murphy

the CFO, Mike Harrington

the other members of top management

30

the members of the Board of Directors

the company's auditors

the company's employees (i.e., if inventory builds, it may lead to later layoffs; a lack of repair work may create dangers in the workplace)

the company's customers (i.e., if inventory builds, it may lead to obsolescence; lack of repair work may lead to product quality problems)

(2) List the ethical issues

The CEO's compensation	vs.	The integrity of the company's financial statements
The CFO's loyalty to his superior	vs.	The CFO's responsibility to his job
The CFO's loyalty to his superior	vs.	The CFO's responsibility to protect the interests of the company and its employees
Top management's responsibility to represent the interests of the shareholders	vs.	Each individual's desire for promotion and advancement
The Board of Directors' duty to provide oversight on the behalf of the shareholders	vs.	Rewarding the CEO for a job well done
The auditor's duty to ensure that the financial statements present fairly the condition of the company	vs.	The auditor's desire to remain engaged as the auditor of the company

(This list can be extended, but you should be sure that these issues are identified)

c. **Identify Major Principles, Rules, and Values**

(Here you will repeat some of the above, e.g. integrity, but you will translate others into ethical language, e.g., fairness, obligation, rights)

Integrity (of the CEO and of the financial statements)

Equity

Fairness

Credibility

Protection of the business

d. **Specify the Alternatives**

Identify major options: encourage creative solutions that may be closer to win-win if possible.

The CFO could support a favorable plan for the CEO

The CFO could object to the proposals and refuse to sign off on them

The CFO could object to the proposals and threaten to go to the Board if the CEO persists

The CFO could communicate his concerns to the outside auditors

Note: *At this point, or even earlier, some students will have begun to take a position. The instructor should be aware of these positions and challenge students to be open to questioning their position, as well as to be open to similar questioning by others. You may want to return to this "position taking" in the discussion over Step g, the decision.*

e. **Compare Norms, Principles, and Values with the Various Alternatives**

See how many of the class members will move to a decision at this point, based on the force or strength of a norm or principle. In some cases, a principle is so strong or the harm so egregious that some will decide now.

For example, the concern for integrity of the financial statements may lead to strong resistance by the CFO to the CEO's proposals.

Regardless of whether a decision is reached, work through Steps f and g as if such steps were still required.

f. **Assess the Consequences**
Take two or three differing alternatives and examine the long- and short-range consequences.

The CFO could support a favorable plan for the CEO

The CEO benefits from enhanced retirement benefits (if the outside auditors sign off)

The CFO may be rewarded by the CEO with increased salary or bonus

The firm, including successor leaders and employees, may suffer from reduced earnings in the years following the CEO's retirement

The CFO may have problems with successor leaders if his agreement to the CEO's plan is discovered

The CFO's integrity will be compromised

The CFO could object to the proposals and refuse to sign off on them

The CEO may drop his plans to enhance his retirement

The CEO may threaten to penalize the CFO's job security or income

The CEO may take his plan to the Board without concurrence of the CFO

The CFO's integrity will be intact

The CFO could object to the proposals and threaten to go to the Board if the CEO persists

The CEO may drop his plans to enhance his retirement

The CEO may threaten to penalize the CFO's job security or income

The CFO may stand fast or may capitulate and agree

The CEO may persist and the CFO may go to the Board

The Board may reject the CEO's plans

The Board may agree with the CEO

The Board may seek the advice of the outside auditors

The CFO's integrity is intact

The CFO could communicate his concerns to the outside auditors

The outside auditors may agree with the CFO and indicate that they will refuse to issue an unqualified report

The outside auditors may support the CEO's plan

The CFO will then have to drop the matter or decide whether to go to the Board

The CFO's integrity will be intact

(There may be additional consequences to alternatives reviewed. There may also be other alternatives. The task now is to weigh or evaluate the consequences of the various alternatives. Some kind of numerical weighting, like a +3, -3 scale, can be used to determine comparative value of alternatives. Point out to the class the difficulty of assigning numerical values, but also note that we do compare, routinely, the significance of various consequences, although not always quantitatively.)

(If a decision was not reached in Step e above, then no principle or value was determinative. Now the consequence with the highest numerical value should be the choice *if it squares with one of the basic listed principles and values.*)

g. **Make Your Decision**

Take a vote; insist that everyone choose.

Examine the outcome and rationale for different positions, if there is time.

TIME ALLOCATION

A full discussion and analysis of the case will take approximately an hour. If you are interested in focusing on the identification of ethical issues at various points in the course, you could deal with the identification of stakeholders and defining of the ethical issues in 15-20 minutes.

<u>CASE 2-2   THE DANGEROUS MORALITY OF MANAGING EARNINGS</u>

a. According to the article, "most managers and their accountants know otherwise - that managing short-term earnings can be part of a manager's job."

b. "It seems many managers are convinced that if a practice is not explicitly prohibited or is only a slight deviation from rules, it is an ethical practice regardless of who might be affected either by the practice or the information that flows from it."

c. "A major finding of the survey was a striking lack of agreement. None of the respondent groups viewed any of the 13 practices unanimously as an ethical or unethical practice."

d. 1. On average, the respondents viewed management of short-term earnings by accounting methods as significantly less acceptable than accomplishing the same ends by changing or manipulating operating decisions or procedures.

   2. The direction of the effect on earnings matters. Increasing earnings is judged less acceptable than reducing earnings.

   3. Materiality matters. Short-term earnings management is judged less acceptable if the earnings effect is larger rather than smaller.

   4. The time period to the effect may affect ethical judgments.

   5. The method of managing earnings has an effect.

e. Management does not have the ability to manage earnings in the long run by influencing financial accounting.

a. Yes

   SFAC No. 6, "Elements of Financial Statements:" "Liabilities
   are probable future sacrifices of economic benefits arising
   from present obligations of a particular entity to transfer
   assets or provide services to other entities in the future as
   a result of past transactions or events."

b. The airlines had millions and millions of miles accumulated
   in unused miles. Thousands of these accounts are inactive
   and will never accumulate adequate miles for a flight or any
   award. In addition, the airlines apparently have the right
   to change the terms for granting a flight or an awards.

c. 1. A contingent liability is dependent upon the occurrence
      or non-occurrence of one or more future events to confirm
      the liability.

   2. Yes

      In practical terms, the unused miles represent a
      contingent liability. The situation is complicated by
      the fact that the airlines apprently have the right to
      make changes to their frequent-flier programs.

   3. Recommend that the contingent liability be recorded and
      the accounting policy be disclosed.

      In practice, the airlines record this liability and
      briefly describe their policy. Seldom is the dollar
      amount of the liability disclosed.

      Most airlines use the incremental method to account for
      their frequent flier awards. Once a program member
      accumulates the required number of miles to qualify for
      free travel, then the liability is recorded. The dollar
      amount of the liability is estimated at the incremental
      cost of providing the free transportation.

      The incremental cost may be computed differently by
      each airline. Examples of cost factors to be considered
      are costs of food, additional fuel, issuing the ticket
      and handling of baggage.

CASE 2-4 INTERNATIONAL ACCOUNTING - HARMONIZATION IN PRACTICE

a. The comments of Dennis R. Beresford indicate a very positive trend in harmonization of international accounting.

b. No

   The meeting described represents a positive trend towards harmonization, but a very preliminary effort when viewed in the big picture. Approximately only a dozen countries were represented and they apparently have somewhat similar economic systems.

CASE 2-5 MATERIALITY: IN PRACTICE

(This case provides the opportunity to review the application of the materiality concept.)

a. Professional standards require auditors to make a preliminary judgment about materiality levels during the planning of an audit. Therefore it would be prudent for auditors to give careful consideration to planning materiality decisions.

b. SAS No. 47 recognizes that it ordinarily is not practical to design procedures to detect misstatements that could be qualitatively material.

c. It is difficult to design procedures to detect misstatements that could be quantitatively material. Although difficult to design these procedures a number of "rule of thumb" materiality calculations have emerged. A difficulty with these "rule of thumb" materiality calculations is that sizeable differences can result depending on the "rule of thumb."

d. Because of the difficulty of applying the materiality concept it is often an issue in court cases involving financial statements.

<u>CASE 2-6 WHO IS RESPONSIBLE?</u>

a. The official position as presented by the accounting
    profession is that the financial statements are the
    responsibility of the Company's management.

b. The accountant (auditor) expresses an opinion on the
    financial statements based on the audit. The audit is to be
    conducted in accordance with generally accepted auditing
    standards.

c. Society appears to focus on the role of the independent
    auditor as a public watchdog. This includes taking
    responsibility for the financial statements. This role is
    broader than the official position as to the responsibility
    of the accountant (auditor).
        Another factor is that the accountant (auditor) is
    perceived as having the ability to pay, either directly, or
    by way of insurance.

d. Unqualified opinion.

e. No. We would expect these audited financial statements to be
    free of material misstatement.

<u>CASE 2-7 SAFE HARBOR</u>

(This case provides the opportunity for the student to express
opinions as to any benefits to users of financial reports from
forward-looking statements.)

a. Management is in an ideal position to project financial
    results. Users of financial reports will likely be aided in
    making decisions by the forward-looking statements of
    management.

b. Yes.
    Investors will be aided in making decisions because of the
    forward-looking statements of management.
        Abusive litigation is probably of little benefit to
    investors, since the lion's share of recoveries under the
    litigation may go to the attorneys who brought the suit than
    to the investors.

Chapter 3
Balance Sheet

<u>QUESTIONS</u>

3- 1.   Assets - Resources of the firm
        Liabilities - Debts of the firm - Creditors' interest
        Owners' Equity - Owners' interest in the firm

3- 2.   a. L   e. A   i. A   m. A   q. A
        b. L   f. A   j. E   n. L   r. A
        c. A   g. L   k. E   o. L   s. A
        d. A   h. A   l. E   p. A   t. A

3- 3.   a. TA   c. IA   e. IA   g. TA   i. TA   k. IV
        b. CA   d. CA   f. CA   h. CA   j. CA   l. TA

3- 4.   They are listed in order of liquidity, which is the ease
        with which they can be converted to cash.

3- 5.   Marketable securities are held as temporary investments
        or idle cash. They are short-term, low risk, highly
        liquid, low yield. Examples are treasury bills and
        commercial paper. Investments are long-term, held for
        control or future use in operations. They are usually
        less liquid and expected to earn a higher return.

3- 6.   Accounts receivable represents the money that the firm
        expects to collect; accounts payable represents the
        debts for goods purchased by a firm.

3- 7.   A retailing firm will have only finished goods and
        supplies. A manufacturing firm will have raw materials,
        work in process, finished goods, and supplies.

3- 8.   Depreciation measures the wearing away of the usefulness
        of the asset. Tools, machinery, and buildings are
        depreciated because they wear out. Land is not
        depreciated, since its value typically does not decline.
        If the land has minerals or natural resources, it may be
        subject to depletion.

3- 9.   Straight-line depreciation is better for reporting, since
        gives higher profits than does accelerated depreciation.
        Double-declining balance is preferable for tax purposes,
        since it allows the highest depreciation and, thereby,
        lower taxes in the early years of the life of the asset.
        Using double-declining balance for taxes increases the
        firm's cash flow in the short run.

3-10.   The rent is treated as a liability because it is
        unearned. The rental agency owes the tenant the use of
        the property until the end of the term of the agreement.
        The rent should be recognized as income over the period
        covered by the rent.

3-11.   a.   A bond will sell at a discount if its stated rate of
             interest is less than the market rate. It sells to
             yield the market rate. It might also sell low if
             there were a great deal of risk involved.

        b.   The discount is shown as a reduction of the
             liability.

                    Bonds payable $1000
                    Less: bond discount   170 $830

             The bond discount is amortized, with the amortization
             shown as interest expense on the income statement.

3-12.   Include minority interest as a long-term liability for
        primary analysis.

3-13.   Historical cost causes difficulties in analysis because
        cost does not measure the current worth or value of the
        asset.

3-14.   At the option of the bondholder (creditor), the bond is
        exchanged for a specified number of common shares (and
        the bondholder becomes a common stockholder). Often
        convertible bonds are issued when the common stock price
        is low, in the opinion of management, and the firm
        eventually wants to increase its common equity. By
        issuing a convertible bond, the firm may get more for the
        specified number of common shares. When the common stock
        price increases sufficiently, the bondholder will convert
        the bond to common stock.

3-15.

a.	CA	f.	CA	k.	CL	p.	NA
b.	CA	g.	E	l.	NL	q.	CA
c.	CL	h.	NA	m.	CL	r.	CL
d.	CL	i.	CA	n.	CA	s.	CA
e.	E	j.	E	o.	E		

3-16.   a.   Accumulation of dividends. With the cumulative
             feature, if a corporation fails to declare the usual
             dividend on the cumulative preferred stock, the
             amount of passed dividends becomes dividends in

40

arrears. Common stockholders cannot be paid any dividends until the preferred dividends in arrears and the current preferred dividends are paid.

b. Participation in excess of stated dividend rate. When preferred stock is participating, preferred stockholders may receive an extra dividend beyond the stated rate. The terms of the participation depend on the terms included with the stock certificates.

c. Convertibility into common stock. Convertible preferred stock contains a provision that allows the preferred stockholders, at their option, to convert the share of preferred stock at a specific exchange ratio into another security of the corporation.

d. Callability by the corporation. Callable preferred stock may be retired (recalled) by the corporation at its option.

e. Preference in liquidation. Should the corporation liquidate, the preferred stockholders normally have preference to have their claims settled prior to any payment to common stockholders.

3-17. The account unrealized exchange gains or losses is an owners' equity account that is used to record gains or losses from translating foreign currency financial statements incorporated into the financial statements of an enterprise by consolidation, combination, or the equity method of accounting.

3-18. Treasury stock represents the stock of the company that has been sold, repurchased, and not returned. It is subtracted from stockholders' equity so that net stockholders' equity is for shares outstanding only.

3-19. The $60, or any portion, will occur as cost of sales if the goods are sold and as inventory if they are not sold.

3-20. These subsidiaries are presented as an investment on the parent's balance sheet.

3-21. Minority interest is presented on a balance sheet when an entity in which the parent company has less than 100% ownership is consolidated.

3-22.   If DeLand Company owns 100% of Little Florida, Inc., it
        will not have a minority interest, since minority
        interest reflects ownership of minority shareholders in
        the equity of consolidated subsidiaries that are not
        wholly owned. If it only owns 60%, then there would be a
        minority interest. Little Florida would not be
        consolidated when control is temporary or does not rest
        with the majority owner.

3-23.   The account unrealized decline in market value of
        noncurrent equity investments is an owners' equity
        account that is used to record unrealized losses on
        long-term equity investments.

3-24.   Redeemable preferred stock is subject to mandatory
        redemption requirements or has a redemption feature that
        is outside the control of the issuer. Coupled with the
        typical characteristics of no vote and fixed return, this
        security is more like debt than equity for the issuing
        firm.

3-25.   Donated capital results from donations to the company by
        stockholders, creditors, or other parties.

3-26.   The land account under assets would be increased and the
        donated capital account in stockholders' equity would be
        increased. The donated land would be recorded at the
        appraisal amount.

3-27.   A quasi-reorganization is an accounting procedure
        equivalent to an accounting fresh start. A quasi-
        reorganization involves the reclassification of a deficit
        in retained earnings to paid-in capital. It changes the
        carrying values of assets and liabilities to reflect
        current values.

3-28.   The unearned compensation is presented as a reduction in
        stockholders' equity and the offsetting amount is
        presented as a liability.

3-29.   An ESOP is a qualified stock-bonus, or combination stock-
        bonus and money-purchase pension plan designed to invest
        primarily in the employer's securities.

3-30.   These institutions are willing to grant a reduced rate of
        interest because they are permitted an exclusion from
        income for 50% of the interest received on loans used to
        finance an ESOP's acquisition of company stock.

3-31. Some firms do not find an ESOP attractive because it can result in a significant amount of voting stock in the hands of employees. This will likely dilute the control of management.

3-32. This firm records the commitment as a liability and as a deferred compensation deduction within stockholders' equity.

3-33. Depreciation is the process of allocating the cost of building and machinery over the periods of benefit. Spreading the cost of an intangible asset is called amortization, while spreading the cost of a natural resource is called depletion.

3-34. The three factors usually considered when computing depreciation are asset cost, length of the life of the asset, and the salvage value when it is retired from service.

3-35. A firm will often want to depreciate slowly for the financial statements because this results in the highest immediate income. The same firm would want to depreciate at a fast pace for income tax returns because this results in the lowest immediate income and thus lower income taxes.

3-36. Over the life of an asset, the total depreciation will be the same, regardless of the depreciation method selected.

3-37. Yes. Depreciation is the process of allocating the cost of buildings and machinery over the periods of benefit.

3-38. <u>Accumulated Other Comprehensive Income</u>
Conceptually, this account balance represents retained earnings from other comprehensive income.

Categories of other comprehensive income are:
1. foreign currency translation adjustments.
2. unrealized holding gains and losses on available-for-sale marketable securities.
3. changes to stockholders equity resulting from additional minimum pension liability adjustments.
4. unrealized gains and losses from derivative instruments.

TO THE NET

1. a. Total stockholders' equity $3,624,000,000.

    b. Cost of treasury shares $1,243,000,000.

    c. The shares have been issued and paid for. Subsequently the shares were bought back and not retired.

2. a. "A quasi-reorganization is an accounting procedure that eliminates an accumulated deficit in retained earnings and permits the company to proceed on much the same basis as if it had been legally reorganized. A quasi-reorganization involves restating a company's assets and liabilities to their fair values, with the net amount of these adjustments added to or deducted from the deficit. Any remaining deficit in retained earnings is then eliminated by a transfer from paid-in capital, giving the company a "fresh start" with zero balance in retained earnings."

    b. The board voted to exit a nuclear power plant (Clinton). This would result in a substantial write down.
        With this is mind the board wanted an accounting fresh start.

PROBLEMS

PROBLEM 3-1

Airlines International
Balance Sheet
December 31, 2000

ASSETS:

Current assets:

Cash	$ 28,837	
Marketable securities		10,042
Accounts receivable	$ 67,551	
Less: Allowance for doubtful accounts	248	67,303
Inventory		16,643
Prepaid expenses		3,963
Total current expenses		$126,788
Investment and special funds		11,901
Property, plant, and equipment:		
Property, plant, and equipment	$809,980	
Less: Accumulated depreciation	220,541	589,439
Other assets		727
Total assets		$728,855

LIABILITIES AND STOCKHOLDERS' EQUITY

Current liabilities:		
Accounts payable	$ 77,916	
Accrued expenses	23,952	
Unearned transportation revenue	6,808	
Current installments of long-term debt	36,875	
Total current liabilities		$145,551
Long-term debt, less current portion		393,808
Deferred income taxes		42,070
Stockholders' equity:		
Common stock	$ 7,152	
Capital in excess of par	72,913	
Retained earnings	67,361	
Total stockholders' equity		147,426
Total liabilities and stockholders' equity		$728,855

PROBLEM 3-2

Lukes, Inc.
Balance Sheet
December 31, 2000

ASSETS

Current assets:
Cash $ 3,000
Receivables, less allowance
   of $3,000   58,000
Inventories   54,000
Prepaid expenses   2,000
   Total current assets $117,000
Plant and equipment:
Buildings $ 75,000
Machinery and equipment   300,000
                                                   375,000
Less: accumulated depreciation   200,000   175,000
Land   11,000
Other assets   7,000
         Total assets $310,000

LIABILITIES AND STOCKHOLDERS' EQUITY

Current liabilities:
Accounts payable $ 35,000
Accrued income taxes   3,000
Other accrued expenses   8,000
Current portion of long-term debt   7,000
   Total current liabilities $ 53,000
Long-term liabilities:
Long-term debt, less current portion   99,870
Deferred income tax liability   24,000
   Total long-term liabilities   123,870

Stockholders' equity:
Common stock, no par value 10,000
   shares authorized, 5,724 shares
   issued   3,180
Retained earnings   129,950
Total stockholders' equity   133,130
Total liabilities and stockholders' equity $310,000

Alleg, Inc.
Balance Sheet
December 31, 2000

ASSETS

Current assets:
Cash	$ 13,000
Marketable securities	17,000
Accounts receivable	26,000
Inventories	30,000
Total current assets	86,000

Plant and equipment:
Land and buildings	57,000
Machinery and equipment	125,000
Less: Accumulated depreciation	182,000
Total plant and equipment	61,000
	121,000

Intangibles:
Goodwill	
Patents	
	8,000
Other assets	18,000
Total assets	50,000
	$275,000

LIABILITIES AND STOCKHOLDERS' EQUITY

Current liabilities:
Accounts payable	$ 15,000
Current maturities of long-term debt	11,000
Total current liabilities	26,000

Long-term liabilities:
Mortgages payable	80,000
Bonds payable	70,000
Deferred income taxes	18,000
Total long-term liabilities	168,000

Stockholders' equity:
Common stock, no par value
21,000 shares authorized at $1 par value,
10,000 shares issued
Additional paid-in capital	10,000
Retained earnings *	38,000
Total stockholders' equity	33,000
Total liabilities and stockholders' equity	81,000
	$275,000

PROBLEM 3-4

a. Restricted cash in sinking fund should be classified as long-term investment.

b. Investment in Subsidiary Company is long-term.

c. Measurement basis of marketable securities should be disclosed.

d. Preferable to show land and buildings separately, since land is not depreciable.

e. Treasury stock should be deducted from stockholders' equity.

f. Discount on bonds payable is a contra liability and should be classified as a deduction from bonds payable.

g. Prepaid expenses should be classified as a current asset.

h. For most industries, liabilities should be classified as current and long-term.

i. Preferred and common stock should be separated, as should capital in excess of par.

j. Net income and dividends are usually shown on a separate statement of retained earnings.

PROBLEM 3-5

a. Heading date is wrong. It should read December 31, 2000.

b. Disclose allowance for doubtful accounts.

c. Treasury stock should be deducted from stockholders' equity.

d. Land and building are disclosed net. Accumulated depreciation should be disclosed.

e. Short-term U.S. Notes should be classified under current assets.

f. Supplies should be classified under current assets.

g. Bonds payable should be under long-term liabilities.

h. Premium on bonds payable should be presented with bonds payable under long-term liabilities.

i. Minority interest should be presented before stockholders' equity.

j. Redeemable preferred stock should be presented before stockholders' equity.

PROBLEM 3-6

a. Balance sheet should be in the heading.

b. $10,000 cash should be classified under "other assets" (restricted for payment of long-term note).

c. Disclose accumulated depreciation related to building.

d. Patent should be classified under intangibles.

e. Organizational costs should be disclosed under intangibles.

f. Prepaid insurance should be under current assets.

g. Dividends payable should be classified as a current liability.

h. Notes payable and bonds payable due in the years 2000 and 2010 respectively, should not be classified as a current liability.

PROBLEM 3-7

a. The dividends would reduce retained earnings on the balance sheet.

b. You would disclose a contingent liability in footnote format.

c. No accounting recognition is given for possible general business risks for which losses cannot be estimated.

d. This subsequent event requires a footnote.

e. Restricted cash should be classified as a long-term asset.

f. Securities held for control should be classified as long-term investments.

g. Land must be listed at cost. It will have to be written back down.

h. This would be disclosed in a footnote. (Also on the income statement, the loss will be disclosed as an extraordinary item.)

PROBLEM 3-8

a. Minority interest will be 20% of the total equity of $300,000, or $60,000. Minority interest should be classified as a liability for purposes of financial analysis.

b. The minority share of earnings will be 20% of $50,000, or $10,000.

PROBLEM 3-9

		Preferred	Common
a.	Year 1	0	0
	Year 2		
	Preferred		
	Cumulative from year 1		
	10,000 shares x $100 par value =		
	$1,000,000 x 10%	$100,000	
	Year 2 dividend		
	10,000 shares x $100 par value =		
	$1,000,000 x 10%	$100,000	
	Total	$200,000	0
	Year 3		
	Preferred		
	Year 3 dividend		
	10,000 shares x $100 par value =		
	$1,000,000 x 10%	$100,000	
	Common		
	The common gets the remaining dividends because the preferred is nonparticipating		$120,000
	Total	$100,000	$120,000

		Preferred	Common
b.	Year 1	0	0
	Year 2		
	Preferred		
	Arrears (see computation in a.)	$100,000	
	Year 2 dividend		
	(See computation in a.)	<u>$100,000</u>	
	Total	<u>$200,000</u>	0
	Year 3		
	Preferred		
	Year 3 dividend		
	(See computation in a.)	$100,000	
	Common		
	80,000 shares x $5 = $400,000		
	x 10% = 40,000		40,000
	2% to preferred		
	(2% x $1,000,000)	20,000	
	2% to common		
	(2% x $400,000)		8,000
	Remaining dividend to common		<u>52,000</u>
	Total	<u>$120,000</u>	<u>$100,000</u>

		Preferred	Common
c.	Year 1	0	0
	Year 2		
	Preferred		
	Arrears (see computation in a.)	$100,000	
	Year 2 Dividend		
	(See computation in a.)	<u>$100,000</u>	
	Total	<u>$200,000</u>	0

Year 3
  Preferred
      Year 3 dividend
        (See computation in a.) $100,000

  Common
    80,000 shares x $5 = $400,000
            x 10% = 40,000   40,000

Fully participating; therefore, the
remaining dividend will be split
between preferred and common in
proportion to their outstanding
stock at total par value.

Total par value of preferred
                $1,000,000   71.43%
Total par value of common
                $ 400,000   28.57%
    Total $1,400,000   100.00%

Preferred 71.43% x $80,000 = $ 57,144
Common 28.57% x $80,000   = $ 22,856
    Total $157,144 $ 62,856

	Preferred	Common
d.		
Year 1	0	0

Year 2
 Preferred
 Year 2 dividend
   (See computation in a.) $100,000

   Common
    Remainder to common $100,000
        Total $100,000 $100,000

Year 3
 Preferred
 Year 3 dividend
   (See computation in a.) $100,000
 Common
  Remainder to common $120,000
        Total $100,000 $120,000

52

PROBLEM 3-10

a.
   Year 1
      Preferred
         5,000 x $100 x 9% = $45,000   <u>$ 40,000</u>   <u>0</u>
   Year 2
      Preferred
         Cumulative $ 5,000
         5,000 x $100 x 9% = $45,000   45,000

      Common
         10,000 x $10 x 9% = $9,000   9,000

      Fully participating; therefore, the
      remaining dividend will be split
      between preferred and common in
      proportion to their outstanding
      stock at total par value.

      Total par value of preferred
                  $ 500,000   83.3%
      Total par value of common
                 $ <u>100,000</u>   <u>16.7%</u>
         Total $ <u>600,000</u>   <u>100.0%</u>

      $65,000 - $5,000 - $45,000 - $9,000
              = $6,000   <u>5,000</u>   <u>1,000</u>
                              <u>$55,000</u> <u>$10,000</u>

b.   Preferred Common
   Year 1
      Preferred
         5,000 x $100 x 9% = $45,000   <u>$ 40,000</u>   <u>0</u>
   Year 2
      Preferred
         5,000 x $100 x 9% = $45,000 $45,000

      Common $20,000
         Remaining dividend to common
          ($65,000 - $45,000)

c.
    Year 1
        Preferred
            5,000 x $100 x 9% = $45,000 $ 40,000   0
    Year 2
        Preferred
            Cumulative $ 5,000
            5,000 x $100 x 9% = $45,000   45,000
        Common
            10,000 x $10 x 9% = $ 9,000

    Additional % to preferred and common:

    Preferred: 5,000 x $100 x 1%   5,000
    Common   : 10,000 x $10 x 1%   1,000
                                                    $ 55,000 $ 10,000
d.
    Year 1
        Preferred
            5,000 x $100 x 9% = $45,000 $ 40,000   0
    Year 2
        Preferred
            Cumulative $ 5,000
            5,000 x $100 x 9% = $45,000   45,000
        Remaining to common $ 15,000
                                                    $ 50,000 $ 15,000

PROBLEM 3-11

a.
    Straight-line method   = $100,000 - $10,000   = $9,000
                                      10   per year

b.
    Declining-balance method
                    Year 1
                        1/10 x 2 x $100,000 = $20,000

                    Year 2
                        1/10 x 2 x $ 80,000   = $16,000

                    Year 3
                        1/10 x 2 x $ 64,000   = $12,800

c.

Sum-of-the-years'-digits method

Year 1	10/55 x $90,000	=	$16,363.63
Year 2	9/55 x $90,000	=	$14,727.27
Year 3	8/55 x $90,000	=	$13,090.91

PROBLEM 3-12

$$\frac{\$60,000 - \$10,000}{25,000 \text{ hrs.}} = \$2.00 \text{ per hour}$$

Year 1	5,000 x $2.00	=	$10,000
Year 2	6,000 x $2.00	=	$12,000
Year 3	4,000 x $2.00	=	$ 8,000

PROBLEM 3-13

a.   The straight line method will result in the lowest
depreciation in the first year. With the depreciation
being the lowest for straight line, the income will be the
highest using the straight-line method. The straight-line
method should be used for the financial statements. The
declining-balance method will result in the maximum
depreciation in the first year. With the depreciation
being the highest, the income will be the lowest. The
declining-balance method should be used for taxes.

Straight-line ($50,000 - $10,000)/5 = $8,000

Declining-balance method = 1/5 x 2 x $50,000

= $20,000

Sum-of-the-years'-digits = 5/15 x ($50,000 - $10,000)

= $13,333

b.   It is permissible to use different depreciation methods in
financial statements than in tax returns.

CASES

CASE 3-1 BALANCE SHEET REVIEW

(This case provides an opportunity to review a moderately
complicated balance sheet.)

a. 1. The financial statements of the parent and the
        subsidiary are consolidated for all majority-owned
        subsidiaries, unless control is temporary or does not
        rest with the majority owner.

    2. No.
        For one or more of the subsidiaries there is less than
        100% ownership. The minority interest is on the balance
        sheet, prior to stockholders' equity.

    3. No.
        These affiliates have been accounted for using the
        equity method. (See footnote 5.)

    4. No.
        These affiliates are included in other assets. The
        assets of the affiliates are not included on the
        consolidated balance of Merck.

b. 1. The gross receivables cannot be determined from the
        published balance sheet. (Allowance for doubtful
        accounts is not disclosed.)

    2. $3,374,100,000

c. 1. $2,623,900,000

    2. This cannot be determined.
        "The majority of domestic inventories are valued at the
        lower of last-in, first-out (LIFO) cost or market.
        Remaining inventories are valued at the lower of first-
        in, first-out (FIFO) cost or market.

3. Inventories at December 31 consisted of:

	(In Millions)		(In Percentage)	
	1998	1997	1998	1997
Finished goods	$1,701.2	$1,230.6	64.8%	57.4%
Raw materials and work in process	851.6	849.7	32.5	39.6
Supplies	71.1	64.8	2.7	3.0
			100.0%	100.0%
	$2,623.9	$2,145.1		

Potentially this is a negative trend. Inventory has increased in finished goods.

d. 1. $7,843,800,000

2. $11,886,600,000

3. Depreciation is provided over the estimated useful lives of the assets, principally using the straight-line method.

4. For tax purposes, accelerated methods are used.

5.

Buildings	$3,664,000,000
Machinery, equipment and office furnishings	6,211,700,000
	$9,875,700,000
Allowance for depreciation	$4,042,800,000

Allowance is approximately 41% of the total for buildings, machinery, equipment and office furnishings. Thus, property, plant, and equipment is moderately old.

There is $1,782,100,000 in construction in progress. Thus, there appears to be substantial additions in progress.

e. $10,228,500,000

f. 1. $8,287,200,000, net
     1,123,900,000, accumulated amortization
   $9,411,100,000

2. $8,287,200,000

g. 1. Treasury stock -- A firm creates treasury stock when it repurchases its own stock and does not retire it. Since treasury stock lowers the stock outstanding, it is subtracted from stockholders' equity.

2. 607,399,428 shares

h. 1. 2,967,851,980 shares

2.
2,967,851,980	shares issued
(607,399,428)	treasury shares
2,360,452,552	

i. 1. $31,853,400,000

2,
```
$ 6,068,800,000
  3,220,800,000
  6,057,000,000
  3,705,000,000
$19,051,600,000
```

3. $12,801,800,000

4.
```
Assets          = Liabilities + Stockholders' Equity
$31,853,400,000 = $19,051,600,000 + $12,801,800,000
```

CASE 3-2 INSIGHT ON LIABILITIES AND SHAREHOLDERS' EQUITY

(This case provides the opportunity to review the presentation of liabilities and shareholders' equity of Motorola.)

a. 1. The financial statements of the parent and the subsidiary are consolidated for all majority-owned subsidiaries, unless control is temporary or does not rest with the majority owner. Such statements reflect an economic rather than a legal concept of the entity.

2. Yes. There is no minority interest disclosed on the consolidated balance sheet.

b. Deferred taxes are caused by using different accounting methods for tax and reporting purposes. Any situation where revenue or expense is recognized in the financial statements in a different time period than for the tax return will create deferred tax situations.

c. 1. This describes a long-term liability for a borrowing due in a period exceeding one year or operating cycle, whichever is longer.

2. The current part of long-term debt is disclosed under current liabilities because it is due within one year or operating cycle, whichever is longer. Thus it is part of current liabilities.

d. Retained earnings are the undistributed earnings of the corporation – that is, the net income for all periods minus the dividends (both cash and stock) that have been declared.

e. 1. 601,100,000

   2. 1,400,000,000

f. 1. $11,440,000,000
      2,633,000,000
      1,188,000,000
      1,245,000,000
   $16,506,000,000

   2. $12,222,000,000

   3. $28,728,000,000 ($16,506,000,000 + $12,222,000,000)

CASE 3-3 INSIGHT ON SHAREHOLDERS' INVESTMENT

(This case provides the opportunity to review shareholders' investment in some detail.)

a. 1. Shareholders' investment represents the residual ownership interest in the assets of an entity after deducting liabilities.

   2. Equity – oriented deferred compensation is the amount of compensation costs deferred and amortized to future periods as the services are provided.

   3. Donated capital represents the capital donated to the firm.

   4. Accumulated other comprehensive income represents retained earnings from other comprehensive income. Categories of other comprehensive income are: (1) foreign currency translation adjustments, (2) unrealized holding gains and losses on available-for-sale marketable securities, (3) changes to stockholders equity resulting from additional pension liability adjustments, and (4) unrealized gains and losses from derivative instruments.

5. Retained earnings represent the undistributed earnings of the corporation - that is, the net income for all past periods minus the dividends that have been declared.

6. Treasury stock represents the firm's stock that has been issued and repurchased but not retired.

b. 1. Common stock issued at January 29, 1999; 40,221,000 shares.

2. Common stock outstanding at January 29, 1999
    Issued   40,221,000
    Treasury stock   (10,317,000)
    Outstanding   29,904,000

c. 1. $242,503,000

2. No.
   The market value of the stock is arrived at by investors buying and selling the stock.
      The dollar amount in shareholders' investment is arrived at considering past transactions.

CASE 3-4 INSIGHTS ON ASSETS

(This is a moderately complicated case. The major emphasis is on assets.)

a. The financial statements of the parent and the subsidiary are consolidated for all majority-owned subsidiaries, unless control is temporary or does not rest with the majority owner.

b. $57,826,000

c. 1. $35,488,000

2. $20,838,000

3. Accumulated depreciation represents the total depreciation taken for all prior periods for the depreciable assets on hand as of the balance sheet date.

4. None.
   Land is not depreciated.

5. Total cost - January 2, 1999   (A) $35,488,000
   Accumulated depreciation - January 2, 1999 (B) $14,650,000

   B ÷ A

$$\frac{\$14,650,000}{\$35,488,000} = 41.3\%$$

Based on the accumulated depreciation in relation to the cost it appears that the property, plant and equipment is not relatively old as of January 2, 1999.

6. For financial reporting they want to report the highest income in the early years of using the assets. For tax purposes they want to report the maximum expense in the early years of using the assets.

d. 1. $195,006,000

    2. $141,354,000

e. Converse's fiscal year end is the Saturday closest to December 31 in each year. Occasionally the fiscal year will consist of 53 weeks, the other fiscal years will have 52 weeks.

f. "The preparation of financial statements in conformity with generally accepted accounting principles requires management to make estimates and assumptions that affect the reported amounts of assets and liabilities and disclosure of contingent assets and liabilities at the date of the financial statements and the reported amounts of revenues and expenses during the reporting period. Actual results could differ from those estimates.

CASE 3-5 OUR PRINCIPAL ASSET IS OUR PEOPLE

a. It would be very subjective to identify which payments relating to people would be considered an asset and which would be considered an expense. Also, if considered an asset, the subsequent using up would be difficult to determine. The legal implications likely also have a bearing on not considering people as an asset; but it should be noted that accountants use an economic definition of an asset.

b. They are using a broad definition of an asset, recognizing the importance of people to the firm.

CASE 3-6 BRANDS ARE DEAD?

a. SFAC No. 6:

   "Assets are probable future economic benefits obtained or controlled by a particular entity as a result of past transactions or events."

b. As a practical matter brands would represent a valuable asset. Brands also appear to fall within the definition of an asset presented in SFAC No. 6.

c. Brands appear to fall within the definition of an asset presented in SFAC No. 6. But in practice, generally accepted accounting principles in the United States do not recognize brands as an asset when internally generated. This apparent inconsistent position is likely rationalized by conservatism.

d. A brand purchased would be recognized as an asset. This would be considered to be objective.

CASE 3-7 ADVERTISING - ASSET?

a. SFAC No. 6:

   "Assets are probable future economic benefits obtained or controlled by a particular entity as a result of past transactions or events."

b. To be conservative, advertising is not usually recognized as an asset in the United States. Identifying the future benefits of advertising is usually considered to be too subjective. Examples of advertising being presented as an asset can be found in United States accounting. When it is recognized as an asset, it may be presented under other assets and possibly disclosed in a footnote.

Chapter 4
Income Statement

QUESTIONS

4- 1. Extraordinary items are events or transactions that are distinguished by their unusual nature and infrequency of occurrence. They might include casualty losses or losses from expropriation or prohibition. They must be shown separately, net of tax, in order that trend analysis can be made of income before extraordinary items.

4- 2. d, f

4- 3. Examples include sales of securities, write-down of inventories, disposal of a product line not qualifying as a segment, gain or loss from a lawsuit, etc. They are shown separately because of their materiality and the desire to achieve full disclosure. They are not given net-of-tax treatment because they are included in income before the income tax is deducted. Also, net-of-tax treatment would infer that these items are extraordinary.

4- 4. Under the equity method, equity in earnings of nonconsolidated subsidiaries is a problem in profitability analysis because the income recognized is not a cash inflow. The cash inflow is only the amount of the investor share of dividends declared and paid. Further, equity earnings do not come directly from the operations of the business in question, but rather from a subsidiary.

4- 5. It would appear that this is the disposal of a product line that is specifically separate from the dairy products line. The disposal of the vitamin line should be identified as discontinued operations and be presented after income from continuing operations on the income statement.

4- 6. Unusual or infrequent items relate to operations. Examples are write-downs of receivables and write-downs of inventory.

4- 7. In 2000, the cumulative effect of the new change would be presented on the income statement as a reduction, net of tax, after any extraordinary items and just before net income.

4- 8.   The declaration of a cash dividend reduces retained
        earnings and increases current liabilities. The payment
        of a cash dividend reduces current liabilities and cash.

4- 9.   First, a stock split is usually for a larger number of
        shares. Secondly, a stock dividend reduces retained
        earnings and increases paid-in capital. A stock split
        merely increases the shares and reduces the par value,
        leaving the capital stock account intact. Both require
        restatement of any per share items.

4-10.   If a firm consolidates subsidiaries that are not wholly
        owned, the total revenues and expenses of the subsidiaries
        are included with those of the parent. To determine the
        income that would accrue to the parent, however, it is
        necessary to deduct the portion of income that would
        belong to the minority owners.

4-11.   The statement of retained earnings summarizes the changes
        to retained earnings. Retained earnings represents the
        undistributed earnings of the corporation. The income
        statement net income is added to retained earnings. A
        loss is deducted from retained earnings.

4-12.   1. Appropriations as a result of a legal requirement.
        2. Appropriations as a result of a contractual
            agreement.
        3. Appropriations as a result of management discretion.

        Appropriations as a result of management discretion are
        not likely a detriment to the payment of a dividend.

4-13.   The balance sheet shows the account balances as of a
        particular point in time. The income statement shows the
        revenues and expenses resulting from transactions for the
        period of time.

4-14.   a. Minority share of earnings is an income statement
            item that represents the minority owners' share of
            consolidated earnings.

        b. Equity in earnings is the proportionate share of the
            earnings of the investor that relate to the investor's
            investment.

4-15. The two traditional formats for presenting the income statement are the multiple-step and single-step. The multiple-step is preferable for analysis because it provides intermediate profit figures that are useful in analysis.

	2001	2000	1999
	1997	1996	1995
4-16. Earnings per share	$1.40	$1.00	$.80

4-17. Accountants have not accepted the role of disclosing the firms capacity to make distributions to stockholders. Therefore, the firms capacity to make distributions to stockholders cannot be determined using published financial statements.

4-18. Management does not usually like to tie comprehensive income closely with the income statement because the items within accumulated other comprehensive income have the potential to be volatile.

1. a. **COMPANY MISSION:**
      Coachmen Industries, Inc. is a leading manufacturer of
      recreational vehicles, modular homes, and related
      products. Our mission is to design, market and
      continually advance our products to be the value leader
      in the industries we serve. This, in turn, allows us to
      prosper as a business and to offer opportunities to our
      employees as well as provide a reasonable return to our
      shareholders.

   b.

	1998	1997	1996
Income before cumulative effect of accounting change	$33,062,608	$24,762,624	$27,336,830
Cumulative effect of accounting change for Company - owned life insurance policies			2,293,983
Net income	$33,062,608	$24,762,624	$29,630,813

   Income before cumulative effect of accounting change is
   the better number for viewing a trend and consistency.
   This number has been prepared using consistent accounting
   principles.

2. a. A Style of Management

   Dana people are our most important asset. Dana's growth
   is dependent on People Finding a Better Way™ to improve
   continuously through concentration on idea generation
   (minimum of two ideas per person per month, 80%
   implemented education (minimum of 40 hours per person per
   year) and cooperation among Dana people globally.

   More than 60 years ago, Charles A. Dana said, "There is
   only one thing really worthwhile about an organization,
   and that is its men and women." The belief that Dana's
   people are its greatest asset is the cornerstone of the
   Dana Style. Ongoing education, employee empowerment and
   innovation, promotion from within – at Dana, these aren't
   goals or concepts. They are realities.

b.

| | Year Ended December 31 | | |
	1996	1997	1998
	(In Millions)		
Income before minority interest and equity in earnings of affiliates	$470.3	$310.4	$504.6
Minority interest	(32.8)	(22.4)	(7.9)
Equity in earnings of affiliates	13.4	32.1	37.4
Net income	$450.9	$320.1	$534.1

Equity in earnings of affiliates represents Dana's share of earnings in companies in which Dana has an investment, but does not have control.

PROBLEMS

PROBLEM 4-1

a.

Decher Automotives
Income Statement
For the Year Ended December 31, 2000

Sales		$1,000,000
Cost of sales		
Beginning inventory	$ 650,000	
Purchases	460,000	
Merchandise available for sale	$1,110,000	
Less: Ending inventory	440,000	
Cost of sales		670,000
Gross profit		330,000
Operating expense:		
Selling expenses	$ 43,000	
Administrative expenses	62,000	105,000
Operating income		225,000
Other income:		
Dividend income		10,000
		235,000
Other expense:		
Interest expense		20,000
Income before taxes and extraordinary items		215,000
Income taxes		100,000
Income before extraordinary items		115,000
Extraordinary items: flood loss, net of tax		(30,000)
Net income		$ 85,000

b.   Earnings per share:

Before extraordinary items		$ 1.15
Extraordinary items (loss)		(.30)
Net income		$ .85

c.

Decher Automotives
Income Statement
For the Year Ended December 31, 2000

Revenue:		
Sales		$1,000,000
Other income		10,000
Total revenue		1,010,000
Expenses:		
Cost of sales	$670,000	
Operating expenses	105,000	
Interest expense	20,000	795,000
Income before taxes and extraordinary items		215,000
Income taxes		100,000
Income before extraordinary items		115,000
Extraordinary items, flood loss, net of tax		30,000
Net income		$85,000

PROBLEM 4-2

Lesky Corporation
Income Statement
For the Year Ended December 31, 2000

Revenue from sales		$362,000
Cost of products sold		242,000
Gross profit		120,000
Operating expenses:		
Selling expenses	$47,000	
Administrative and general expenses	11,400	58,400
Operating income		61,600
Other items:		
Other income:		
Rental income	$1,000	
Interest income	2,400	3,400
Other expense:		
Interest expense		(2,200)
Income before tax		62,800
Federal and state income taxes		20,300
Net income		$42,500

PROBLEM 4-3

Consolidated Can
Income Statement
For the Year Ended December 31, 2000

Sales	$480,000
Cost of products sold	410,000
Gross profit	70,000
Selling and administrative expenses	42,000
Operating income	28,000
Other income	1,600
	29,600
Interest expense	8,700
Income before tax and extraordinary items	20,900
Income tax	9,300
Income before extraordinary items	11,600
Extraordinary gain, net of tax	1,000
Net income	12,600
Retained earnings 1/1	270,000
	282,600
Less: dividends	3,000
Retained earnings	$279,600

PROBLEM 4-4

a.

Taperline Corporation
Income Statement
For the Year Ended December 31, 2000

Revenues:		
Sales		$670,000
Rental income		3,600
Gain on the sale of fixed assets		3,000
Total revenues		676,600
Expenses:		
Cost of sales	$300,000	
Selling expenses	97,000	
General and administrative		
expenses	110,000	
Depreciation	10,000	
Interest expense	1,900	518,900
Income before extraordinary items		
and taxes on income		157,700
Income tax		63,080
Earnings before extraordinary item		94,620
Casualty loss	$ 30,000	
Less: Tax saving	12,000	18,000
Net income		$ 76,620

Earnings per share on common stock:
(30,000 shares outstanding)
Income before extraordinary items $3.15
Net income $2.55

b.

Taperline Corporation
Income Statement
For the Year Ended December 31, 2000

Sales		$670,000
Cost of sales		300,000
Gross profit		370,000
Operating expenses:		
Selling expenses	$ 97,000	
General and administrative		
expenses	110,000	
Depreciation	10,000	217,000
Operating income		153,000
Other revenue:		
Rental income	$ 3,600	
Gain on the sale of fixed assets	3,000	6,600
		159,600
Other expenses:		
Interest expense		1,900
Income before extraordinary items		
and taxes on income		157,700
Income tax		63,080
Income before extraordinary item		94,620
Casualty loss	$ 30,000	
Less: Tax saving	12,000	18,000
Net income		$ 76,620

Earnings per share on common stock:
(30,000 shares outstanding)
Income before extraordinary items $3.15
Net income $2.55

PROBLEM 4-5

$$\text{Tax Rate} = \frac{\text{Taxes}}{\text{Income Before Taxes}} = \frac{\$20,000}{\$40,000} = 50\%$$

Provision for unusual write-offs	$50,000
Less: tax effects (50% x $50,000)	25,000
Net item	$25,000
Extraordinary charge, net of tax of $10,000	$50,000
Net earnings (loss)	(30,000)
Net earnings with nonrecurring items removed ([$30,000)+$25,000+$50,000]	$45,000

PROBLEM 4-6

Sales		$4,000,000
Cost of sales		2,000,000
Gross profit		2,000,000
Operating expenses		
Administrative expenses	$400,000[1]	
Selling expense	600,000[2]	1,000,000
Operating income		1,000,000
Interest expense		110,000[3]
Earnings before tax		890,000
Income tax (48%)		427,200
Net income		$ 462,800
Earnings per share $9.26		

[1]Administrative expenses are 20% of $2,000,000. This is 10% of sales. Therefore, sales are $4,000,000.

[2]150% times $400,000

[3]$1,000,000 x 11% = $110,000

PROBLEM 4-7

Total revenues from regular operations	$832,000
Total expenses from regular operations	776,000
Income from operations	56,000
Extraordinary gain, net of tax	30,000
Net income	$ 86,000

Earnings per share:
Before extraordinary items	$56,000/10,000 = $5.60
Extraordinary gain	$30,000/10,000 = $3.00
Net income	$86,000/10,000 = $8.60

72

PROBLEM 4-8

Victor, Inc.
Partial Income Statement
For the Year Ended December 31, 2000

Income from continuing operations, unadjusted (a)		$400,000
Adjustments:		
Settlement of lawsuit		(10,000)
Gain on sale of securities		30,000
Income from continuing operations, adjusted, before tax		420,000
Income tax (30%)		126,000
Income from continuing operations		294,000
Discontinued operations:		
Loss on operations of consumer products division	$ 60,000	
Loss from disposal of assets	90,000	
	150,000	
Tax effect (30%)	45,000	
Loss from discontinued operations		105,000
Income before extraordinary item		189,000
Extraordinary item:		
Loss from hailstorm	$ 20,000	
Tax effect (30%)	6,000	14,000
Income before cumulative change in accounting principle		175,000
Cumulative change in accounting principle from average cost to FIFO	$ 30,000	
Tax effect (30%)	9,000	
Increase in income from change in accounting principle		21,000
Net income		$196,000

Earnings per share:	
Income from continuing operations	$ 2.94
Discontinued operations	(1.05)
Extraordinary loss	(.14)
Cumulative change in accounting principle	.21
Net income	$ 1.96

73

PROBLEM 4-9

a.	A	h.	B	p.	A
b.	A	i.	C	q.	A
c.	A	j.	B	r.	A
d.	B	k.	B	s.	A
e.	B	l.	B	t.	B
f.	A	m.	A	u.	B
g.	A	n.	B	v.	A
		o.	B		

PROBLEM 4-10

a.	C	h.	B	o.	A
b.	B	i.	B	p.	B
c.	A	j.	A	q.	A
d.	B	k.	B	r.	B
e.	A	l.	A	s.	B
f.	B	m.	B		
g.	C	n.	B		

PROBLEM 4-11

a. Net income $ 20,000
    Plus: Extraordinary loss from flood   120,000
                                                            $140,000

b. $60,000

c. $60,000

d. $40,000

e. $100,000 - $50,000 = $50,000

PROBLEM 4-12

a. Net income from operations $146,000

b. $20,000 Loss

c. $94,000
    -30,000
    -50,000
    +25,000
    $39,000

PROBLEM 4-13

a. 1. Receipt of cash:

Sales, 210,000 ounces x $300 = $63,000,000

Cost of goods sold (1),
    210,000 ounces x $250   =   52,500,000
Gross profit $10,500,000

Selling expenses   2,000,000
Administrative expenses   1,250,000
Profit before taxes   7,250,000
Taxes   3,625,000
Net income $ 3,625,000

(1) $50,000,000   = $250 per ounce
     200,000

2. Point of sale:

Sales, 230,000 ounces x $300 = $69,000,000

Cost of goods sold,
    230,000 ounces x $250   =   57,500,000
Gross profit $11,500,000

Selling expenses   2,000,000
Administrative expenses   1,250,000
Profit before taxes   8,250,000
Taxes   4,125,000
Net income $ 4,125,000

3. End of production:

Sales, 200,000 ounces x $300 = $60,000,000

Cost of goods sold,
    200,000 ounces x $250   =   50,000,000
Gross profit $10,000,000

Selling expenses   2,000,000
Administrative expenses   1,250,000
Profit before taxes   6,750,000
Taxes   3,375,000
Net income $ 3,375,000

4. Based on delivery:

Sales, 190,000 ounces x $300 = $57,000,000

Cost of goods sold,	
190,000 ounces x $250 =	47,500,000
Gross profit	$ 9,500,000
Selling expenses	2,000,000
Administrative expenses	1,250,000
Profit before taxes	6,250,000
Taxes	3,125,000
Net income	$ 3,125,000

b.

1. Receipt of cash

   This method should only be used when the prospects of collection are especially doubtful at the time of sale.

2. Point of sale

   In practice, the point of realization usually is the point of sale. At this point, the earnings process is virtually complete and the exchange value can be determined.

3. End of production

   The realization of revenue at the completion of the production process is acceptable when the price of the item is known and there is a ready market.

   This method should receive strong consideration in this case. The question that needs to be resolved is how fixed is the price of uranium. Since the price has gone from $150 per ounce in 1961 to $300 per ounce in 1977, the price does not appear to be fixed.

4. Based on delivery

   This is not usually an acceptable realization point. Delivery is an objective guideline, but delivery does not usually represent a significant event.

PROBLEM 4-14

a. No. This loss does not relate to the cost of goods sold. It is likely an extraordinary loss meeting the criteria of being of unusual in nature and infrequent in occurrence.

b. No. Land is carried at historical cost.

c. Yes. The cost of machinery and equipment should be charged to a fixed asset account.

d. No. Depreciation should be recognized over the period of use.

e. Yes. Some loss to employees would be expected, and it is immaterial in relation to the cost of goods sold.

f. No. This car should not be recorded on the company's books, unless it is to be used for company business.

PROBLEM 4-15

a. Comprehensive income will tend to be mere volatile than net income because the items within other comprehensive income tend to be more volatile than net income.

b. The standard directs that earnings per share be computed based on net income.

c. $30,000
       5,000
       3,000
    $38,000

d. No.
    These items could net out as an addition to net income, or a deduction from net income.

CASES

CASE 4-1 ELECTRONIC SOLUTIONS

(This case provides the opportunity to review the statements of
consolidated earnings of Motorola. Emphasis is on multiple-step
and single-step income statements.)

a. Yes
    The statement does not present minority interest in net
    income of subsidiaries.

b. No
    Using the equity method, income related to unconsolidated
    subsidiaries would be booked as income from unconsolidated
    subsidiaries (equity income).

c. (In Millions)

Motorola, Inc. and Consolidated Subsidiaries

Years Ended December 31	1998	1997	1996
Net sales	$29,398	$29,794	$27,973
Manufacturing and other costs of sales	20,886	20,003	18,990
Gross profit	8,512	9,791	8,983
Operating expenses:			
Selling, general and administrative expenses	5,493	5,188	4,715
Restructuring and other charges	1,980	327	–
Depreciation expense	2,197	2,329	2,308
Operating expenses	9,670	7,844	7,023
Operating income (loss)	(1,158)	1,947	1,960
Other expense - interest expense, net	216	131	185
Income before taxes	(1,374)	1,816	1,775
Income tax provision (benefit)	(412)	636	621
Net earnings	$(962)	$1,180	$1,154

d.

		1998	1997	1996
(a)	Restructuring and other charges	$1,980	$327	-
(b)	Restructuring and other charges, net of tax benefit (a) x (e)	1,386	212	-

Computation of tax benefit:

		1998	1997	1996
(c)	Income tax provision (benefit)	$(412)	$636	$621
(d)	Earnings (loss) before income taxes (c) ÷ (d)	(1,374) 29.99%	1,816 35.02%	1,775 34.99%
(e)	(1 - tax rate)	70.01%	64.98%	65.01%
	(f) Net earnings (loss)less restructuring and other charges (f + b)	$424	$1,392	$1,154

CASE 4-2   CONVENIENCE

(This case provides the opportunity to review consolidated statements, nonrecurring items, and change in accounting principle.)

a. Financial statements of legally separate entities may be issued to show income as it would appear if the companies were a single entity (consolidated). Such statements reflect an economic, rather than a legal, concept of the entity. This is the usual case when the parent company has control.

b. No.
    Minority income was not reported.

c. No.
    Income from nonconsolidated subsidiaries is not reported on the statement (equity income).

d.   1997   1996   1995   ____
    $564,000,000 $531,000,000 $490,300,000

    Unusual or infrequent items are typically left on primary analysis because they relate to operations.

e.

	1997	1996	1995
Non-recurring changes (A)	$184,000,000	$136,100,000	$421,800,000
1 - Tax Rate * (B)	62.35%	61.75%	61.60%
(A) x (B)	$114,724,000	$84,041,750	$259,828,800

Estimate of tax rate:

	1997	1996	1995
Income taxes (A)	$340,500,000	$328,900,000	$305,700,000
Earnings Before Income Taxes (B)	$904,500,000	$859,900,000	$796,000,000
(A)/(B)	37.65%	38.25%	38.40%
* (1 - Tax Rate)	62.35%	61.75%	61.60%

f.   1.   No.
A different accounting principle was used for 1997 than was used in prior years.

2.   Cannot be determined based on published financial statements.

3.   No.
The cumulative effect of accounting change (net of tax) in 1997 was ($18,000,000). This relates to years prior to 1997. It does not appear to be material enough to negate comparisons with prior years.

CASE 4-3   RUN

(This case provides the opportunity to review the consolidated statements of income for Reebok. Emphasis on consolidated statements and minority interest).

a.   Financial statements of legally separate entities may be issued to show income as it would appear if the companies were a single entity (consolidated). Such statements reflect an economic, rather than a legal, concept of the entity.

b.   Yes.
The presence of minority interest indicates that subsidiaries have been consolidated in which Reebok has less than 100% ownership.

c.   Computation of tax rate:

	1998	1997	1996
Income before income taxes and minority interest (A)	$37,030,000	$158,085,000	$237,668,000
Income taxes (B)	11,925,000	12,490,000	84,083,000
Tax rate (B ÷ A) (C)	32.20%	7.90%	35.38%
Special charges (d)	$35,000,000	$58,161,000	–
Special charges, net of tax (e) $35,000,000 (1 - 32.20%) $58,161,000 (1 - 35.38%)	$23,730,000	$37,583,648	
Income before minority interest with special charge removed ($25,105,000 - $23,730,000) ($145,595,000 - $37,583,648) ($153,585,000 - 0)	$1,375,000	$108,011,352	$153,585,000

CASE 4-4 THE BIG ORDER

a. United Airlines should record the purchase of these planes when a plane is delivered.

b. In general, revenue recognition is being made at the completion of production. Under summary of significant accounting policies in the notes to the 1990 financial statements, Boeing describes its revenue recognition with this statement.

   "Sales under commercial programs and U.S. Government and foreign military fixed-price type contracts are generally recorded as deliveries are made."

c. The case indicates that the order was equally split between firm orders and options. This would lead us to believe that the firm orders were "firm" and that United Airlines would be committed to accept delivery of these planes.

   In reality, the orders may not be firm in the sense that Boeing may be willing to negotiate a reduction if United Airlines were in financial trouble or if the need for the planes had substantially declined.

In the 1990 annual report of Boeing, in the section Management's Discussion and Analysis of Financial Condition and Results of Operations, a section on backlog had this comment:

"In evaluating the Company's firm backlog for commercial customers, certain risk factors should be considered. Approximately 55% of the firm backlog for commercial airplanes is scheduled to be delivered beyond 1992. An extended economic downturn could result in less than currently anticipated airline equipment requirements resulting in requests to negotiate the rescheduling, or possible cancellation, of firms orders."

d. 1. There would not necessarily be disclosure in the financial statements and footnotes. This was not a transaction that was recorded.

    There was disclosure of credit agreements in a footnote "long-term debt." This footnote did not specifically refer to this order.

    2. Disclosure would likely be found in the president's letter and the section Management's Discussion and Analysis. In fact, extensive disclosure was located in these sections.

e. 1. There would not necessarily be disclosure in the financial statements and footnotes. This was not a transaction that was recorded. A review of the financial statements and footnotes did not turn up disclosure.

    2. Disclosure would likely be found in the president's letter and the section Management's Discussion and Analysis. In fact, extensive disclosure relating to orders was found. Some of this disclosure specifically commented on the United Airlines order, while some was general on orders.

CASE 4-5 CELTICS

(This case provides the opportunity to review the statements of income of the Boston Celtics.)

a. Franchise and other intangible assets were recognized as intangible assets on the balance sheet. These costs are now being amortized (expensed) on the statement of income.

b. No.
   Since these operations were discontinued they would not be included in projecting the future.

c. Apparently there was a new contract with players that called for substantial increases.

d. Revenues from ticket sales and television and radio broadcast rights fee increased substantially between 1997 and 1998.

e. Much of the income in 1996 came from discontinued operations. The board would typically not want to consider the income from discontinued operations when setting the distribution.

CASE 4-6 GROWTH

(This case provides the opportunity to review the consolidated statements of income for Wal*Mart for 1996, 1997, and 1998. Emphasis is on minority interest, equity in unconsolidated subsidiaries, and multiple-step statement of income.)

a. 1. If a firm consolidates subsidiaries not wholly owned, the total revenues and expenses of the subsidiaries are included with those of the parent. However, to determine the income that would accrue to the parent, it is necessary to deduct the portion of income that would belong to the minority owners. This is described as minority interest.

   2. When a firm accounts for its investments in stocks using the equity method (the investment is not consolidated), the investor reports equity earnings (losses). Equity earnings (losses) are the investor's proportionate share of the investee's earnings (losses).

   3. No.
      They are both related to investments, but in one case our company has control while in the other case our company does not have control. The answers to part 1 and 2 describe the difference in the accounting.

b.

Wal*Mart
Consolidated Statements of Income
(Amounts in millions except per share data)
Fiscal years ended January 31

	1998	1997	1996
Net sales	$117,958	$104,859	$93,627
Cost of sales	93,438	83,510	74,505
Gross profit			
Operating, selling and general	24,520	21,349	19,122
Operating income	19,358	16,946	15,021
Other income (expense)			
Other income - net	5,162	4,403	4,101
Interest costs:			
Debt	1,341	1,319	1,146
Capital leases			
Income before income taxes,	(555)	(629)	(692)
minority interest and equity	(229)	(216)	(196)
in unconsolidated subsidiaries			
Provision for income taxes	5,719	4,877	4,359
Current			
Deferred	2,095	1,974	1,530
Income before minority interest	20	(180)	76
and equity in unconsolidated			
subsidiaries			
	3,604	3,083	2,753
Minority interest and equity			
in unconsolidated subsidiaries			
Net income	(78)	(27)	(13)
Net income per share - basic			
and dilutive	$3,526	$3,056	$2,740
	$1.56	$1.33	$1.19

CASE 4-7   PREPARING FOR THE FUTURE

(This case provides an opportunity to review multiple issues.
This includes pooling of interest vs. purchase, materiality, net
of tax treatment, research and development, and special income
statement items.)

a.   Purchase method

The special charges include a $23.9 million charge to
operating expense for purchased research and development
related to the MSI and Membrex acquisitions. This
indicates that the accounts were not carried forward to the
combined entity at their previous recorded amounts.

b.   1. $27,706,000

2. $2,000,000

3. $25,706,000
No. A special charge is considered to be an unusual or
infrequent item. Unusual or infrequent items do not
qualify for net of tax treatment.

4.   Material
Examples to support the conclusion that the special
charge was material.

a. Income (loss) before income taxes for second quarter
ended June 30, 1998 - $24,120,000 loss. Special
charge $25,706,000

b. Special charge before taxes $25,706,000 for the second
quarter ended June 30, 1998. Common shareholders'
equity June 30, 1998, $85,784,000.

c.   1.   Expense

2.   The special charges include a $23.9 million charge to
operating expense for purchased research and development
to the MSI and Membrex acquisitions.

3.   Benefit expected in the future. Based on the amount
Osmonics paid for the purchased research and development
they apparently expected a substantial amount of future
benefit.

d.   1.   Unusual or infrequent items are considered to be part of
operations.

2.   No.   Unusual or infrequent items do not qualify for net
      of tax tretament.
e.   This is an opinion question.

Your text states that unusual or infrequent items are
typically left in primary analysis because they relate to
operations.   In supplementary analysis, unusual or infrequent
items should be removed net after tax.

This indicates to review earnings with and without unusual or
infrequent items.   It does indicate that typically unusual or
infrequent items are included in primary analysis.

In the Osmonics situation to include the unusual or
infrequent items in primary analysis gives a distorted view.
judgement must be used when reviewing financial reports.

Chapter 5
Basics of Analysis

<u>QUESTIONS</u>

5- 1.   A ratio is a fraction comparing two numbers. Ratios make
        the comparisons in relative, rather than absolute, terms,
        which helps alleviate the problem of size difference.

5- 2.   a.   Liquidity is the ability to meet current obligations.
             Short-term creditors such as banks or suppliers would
             be particularly interested in these ratios.

        b.   Borrowing capacity measures the protection of
             long-term creditors. Long-term bond holders would be
             particularly interested.

        c.   Profitability means earning ability. Investors would
             be particularly interested.

5- 3.   Comparisons of historical data, industry average,
        earnings of competitors, etc.

5- 4.   An absolute change would be -+ X dollars; a percentage
        change would be -+ X percent of the base. Percentage
        changes usually give better measures because they
        recognize the difference in the size of the base.

5- 5.   Horizontal analysis expresses an item in relation to that
        same item for a previous base year. This analysis
        measures over time.

        <u>Example</u>
        In 2000, sales were $750,000; in 1997, they were
        $500,000. Horizontal analysis shows 2000 sales as 150% of
        those in 1997.

        Vertical analysis compares one item with another base
        item for that same year.

        <u>Example</u>
        In 2000, selling expenses were $75,000 and sales were
        $750,000. Vertical analysis would show selling expenses
        as 10% of 2000 sales.

5- 6.   Trend analysis involves comparing the past to the
        present. It can be used both for ratios and absolute
        figures.

`5- 7. When comparing two firms of different size, relative figures are most meaningful. These include ratios and common-size analysis. The relative amounts of sales, assets, profits, or market share help evaluate relative size.

5- 8. While managers make great use of financial reports, investors, creditors, employers, suppliers, and consumers also use financial reports.

5- 9. Managers analyze data to study profitability and the overall financial position of the firm. Investors study profitability and the chance to earn on their investment. Creditors study the ability of the firm to handle debt.

5-10. a. GAP Inc.

Property and equipment is the single largest asset followed by merchandise inventory. These would normally be very large assets for a merchandising firm.

The Interpublic Group of Companies

Accounts receivable represents the largest asset. This seems reasonable since, there is no inventory and a somewhat limited investment in fixed assets. This would be typical of this type of firm.

Intel Corporation

The largest asset category is property, plant and equipment. This would be typical of a manufacturing firm.

b. Intel Corporation

It would not be unusual that a manufacturing firm has a large amount in current assets in relation to current liabilities because of receivables and inventory.

5-11. A manufacturing firm will have raw materials, work in process, finished goods, and supplies. A retail firm will only have finished goods and supplies. It will not have raw materials and work in process.

5-12. Some types of products must be processed and immediately packaged for sale. They cannot be held in the processing state. Each night, all raw materials must be converted to finished goods. Cosmetics, such as nail polish, would dry up overnight. Foods might spoil. They, therefore, cannot be left in a semifinished state.

5-13. Median 10.5%; upper quartile 13%; lower quartile 9.3%.

5-14. Reference Book of Corporate Managements

5-15. a. Eleven. (Not including zero assets.)

    b. Manufacturing, wholesaling, construction, mining, utilities, financial institutions, insurance, and real estate.

5-16. a. Yes. The Department of Commerce Financial Reports includes industry sales. We could relate the sales of the firm in question to the total industry amount.

    b. Yes. The Department of Commercial Financial Report includes total assets for the total industry. We could relate the total assets of the firm in question to the total in the industry.

5-17. The SIC is the Standard Industrial Classification. It was developed for use in the classification of establishments by type of activity in which they are engaged.

    Determining a company's SIC is a good starting point in your search of a company, industry, or product. Many library sources use the SIC number as a method of classification. Thus, knowing a company's SIC will be necessary in order to use some library sources.

5-18. Standard & Poor's Register of Corporations, Directors and Executives, Volume 3, Section 5, lists the officer deaths that have been reported to the publisher

5-19. Standard & Poor's Analyst's Handbook.

5-20. Value Line Investment Survey.

5-21. The Securities Owner's Stock Guide.

5-22.   The F & S Index of Corporations and Industries includes a
comprehensive index to articles on a corporation.

5-23.   A weekly newspaper, The Wall Street Transcript, provides
        access to corporate management presentations to financial
        analysts.

5-24.   The Standard & Poor's Register of Corporations, Directors
        and Executives, Volume 2, contains information on
        principal business affiliations of officers.

5-25.   1. Standard & Poor's Industry Survey
        2. Value Line Investment Survey

5-26.   The Wall Street Transcript contains brokerage house
        assessment reports.

1.

Novell
Consolidated Statement of Operations (Partial)
Horizontal Common-Size

Fiscal year ended	October 31 1998	October 31 1997	October 26 1996
Net sales	78.84	73.27	100.00
Cost of sales	77.87	90.44	100.00
Gross profit			
Operating expenses	79.14	68.33	100.00
Sales and marketing			
Product development	74.42	85.48	100.00
General and	81.72	102.56	100.00
administrative	92.61	101.45	100.00
Restructuring charges	–	300.05	100.00
Total operating expenses			
	77.86	96.95	100.00

Novell
Consolidated Statement of Operations (Partial)
Vertical Common-Size

Fiscal year ended	October 31 1998	October 31 1997	October 26 1996
Net sales	100.00	100.00	100.00
Cost of sales	22.02	27.54	22.31
Gross profit			
Operating expenses	77.98	72.46	77.69
Sales and marketing			
Product development	35.62	44.03	37.74
General and	20.78	28.06	20.05
administrative	12.49	14.73	10.64
Restructuring charges	–	5.49	1.34
Total operating expenses			
	68.90	92.31	69.76

<u>Comment</u>
Net sales declined substantially in 1997. Novell was not able to control expenses in 1997 in relation to the decline in sales. Some expenses actually increased in 1997, especially restructuring charges.

In 1998 cost of sales and sales and marketing were in control in relation to net sales. Product development and general and administrative expenses were high in 1998 in relation to the decline in sales.

2. a. Retail - variety store

 b. Natural business year.
    The natural business year ends when sales activities are at their lowest point during the year. Many retailers select a date around January 31.

 c. Cost of sales, buying and occupancy. This would be normal for this type of business.

 d. Merchandise inventories.
    Property and equipment, net.
    This would be normal for this type of business.

 e. Trade accounts payable
    This would be normal for this type of business.

PROBLEM 5-1

Gap Inc.

a. Vertical Common-Size Balance Sheet
January 30, 1999 and January 31, 1998

	(In Percentage)	
	January 30,	January 30,
ASSETS	<u>1999</u>	<u>1998</u>
Current assets:		
Cash and equivalents	14.3	27.4
Merchandise inventory'	26.7	27.0
Other current assets	<u>6.3</u>	<u>5.5</u>
Total current assets	47.2	54.9
Property and equipment:		
Leasehold improvements	26.3	25.4
Furniture and equipment	40.4	37.0
Land and buildings	4.1	4.6
Construction-in-progress	<u>6.2</u>	<u>2.0</u>
	76.9	69.0
Accumulated depreciation and	<u>29.6</u>	<u>28.1</u>
amortization	47.3	40.9
Property and equipment, net	<u>5.4</u>	<u>4.2</u>
Lease rights and other assets	<u>100.0</u>	<u>100.0</u>
Total assets		

Problem 5-1 (continued)

| | (In Percentage | |
	January 30, 1999	January 31, 1998
LIABILITIES AND SHAREHOLDERS' EQUITY		
Current liabilities		
Notes payable	2.3	2.5
Accounts payable	17.3	12.5
Accrued expenses and other current	16.5	12.2
liabilities	3.1	2.5
Income taxes payable	39.2	29.7
Total current liabilities		
LONG-TERM LIABILITIES		
Long-term debt	12.5	14.9
Deferred lease credits and other liabilities	8.6	8.0
Total long-term liabilities	21.1	22.8
SHAREHOLDERS' EQUITY		
Common stock	.8	1.0
Additional paid-in capital	9.2	6.6
Retained earnings	78.7	71.7
Accumulated other comprehensive earnings	(.3)	(.5)
Deferred compensation	(.8)	(1.1)
Treasury stock at cost	(48.0)	(30.3)
Total shareholders' equity	39.7	47.5
Total liabilities and shareholders'equity	100.0	100.0

b.   Gap Inc.

Horizontal Common-Size
January 30, 1999, January 31, 1998

	(In Percentage)	
	1998	1997
ASSETS		
Current Assets:		
Cash and equivalents	61.9	100.0
Merchandise inventory	144.1	100.0
Other current assets	135.5	100.0
Total current assets	102.2	100.0
Property and equipment:		
Leasehold improvements	122.9	100.0
Furniture and equipment	129.5	100.0
Land and buildings	104.3	100.0
Construction-in-progress	368.0	100.0
	132.3	100.0
Accumulated depreciation and amortization	124.8	100.0
Property and equipment, net	137.4	100.0
Lease rights and other assets	152.7	100.0
Total assets	118.8	100.0
LIABILITIES AND SHAREHOLDERS' EQUITY		
Current Liabilities:	107.0	100.0
Notes payable	164.1	100.0
Accounts payable	161.4	100.0
Accrued expenses and other current liabilities	146.6	100.0
Income taxes payable	156.6	100.0
Total current liabilities		
Long-Term Liabilities:		
Long-term debt	100.1	100.0
Deferred Lease credits and other		
liabilities	128.1	100.0
Total long-term liabilities	109.9	100.0
Shareholders' Equity:		
Common stock	100.8	100.0
Additional paid-in capital	164.8	100.0
Retained earnings	130.5	100.0
Accumulated other comprehensive earnings	82.2	100.0
Deferred compensation	83.0	100.0
Treasury stock, at cost	188.3	100.0
Total shareholders' equity	99.3	100.0
Total liabilities and shareholders' equity	118.8	100.0

c.   <u>Vertical Common-Size</u>

<u>Assets</u>
- Significant decrease in cash and equivalents
- Substantial increase in construction-in-progress

<u>Liabilities</u>
- Substantial increase in accounts payable
- Substantial increase in accrued expenses and other current liabilities

<u>Shareholders' Equity</u>
- Substantial increase in retained earnings
- Significant increase in treasury stock

<u>Horizontal Common-Size</u>

<u>Assets</u>
- Significant decrease in cash and equivalents
- Significant increase in merchandise inventory
- Significant increase in other current assets
- Significant increase in leasehold improvements
- Significant increase in furniture and equipment
- Substantial increase in construction-in-progress
- Significant increase in accumulated depreciation
- Significant increase in property and equipment
- Significant increase in lease rights and other assets

c.

<u>Liabilities and Shareholders' Equity</u>
- Significant increase in accounts payable
- Significant increase in accrued expenses and other current liabilities
- Significant increase in deferred lease credit and other liabilities
- Significant increase in additional paid-in capital
- Significant increase in retained earnings
- Substantial increase in treasury stock

PROBLEM 5-2

a. Gap Inc.
Vertical Common-Size Analysis
Statements of Earnings

(In Percentages)	1998	1997	1996
Net sales	100.0	100.0	100.0
Costs and expenses			
Cost of goods sold and occupancy expenses	58.7	61.8	62.2
Operating expenses	26.5	25.1	24.0
Net interest expense (income)	0.2	0.0	(0.4)
Earnings before income taxes	14.6	13.1	4.2
Income taxes	5.5	4.9	5.6
Net earnings	9.1	8.2	8.6

Note: Gap presented a vertical common-size analysis.

b. Gap Inc.
Horizontal Common-Size Analysis
Statements of Earnings

(In Percentages)	1998	1997	1996
Net sales	171.3	123.2	100.0
Costs and expenses			
Cost of goods sold and occupancy expenses	161.9	122.4	100.0
Operating expenses	189.2	128.7	100.0
Net interest expense (income)	N/A	N/A	100.0
Earnings before income taxes	176.2	114.1	100.0
Income taxes	167.3	108.3	100.0
Net earnings	182.1	117.9	100.0

c. <u>Vertical Common-Size</u>

- A decrease in cost of goods sold and occupancy expenses
- An increase in operating expenses

Note: Cost of goods sold decrease and occupancy expenses was
more than the increase in operating expenses.

<u>Horizontal Common-Size</u>
All items, except for net interest expense (income), has very
substantial increases.

PROBLEM 5-3

a.   The Interpublic Group of Companies
                          Vertical Common-Size Balance Sheets

		(In Percentages)
December 31	1998	1997
Assets		
Current Assets:		
Cash and cash equivalents	11.6	12.3
Marketable securities	.5	.5
Receivables, net	50.7	51.9
Expenditures billable to clients	3.9	4.1
Prepaid expenses and other current assets	2.0	1.9
Total current assets	68.8	70.8
Other Assets:		
Investment in unconsolidated affiliates	.7	.8
Deferred taxes on income	1.4	1.3
Other investments and miscellaneous assets	4.3	3.7
Total other assets	6.4	5.8
Fixed Assets, at Cost:		
Land and buildings	1.4	1.4
Furniture and equipment	9.4	9.3
	10.7	10.7
Less accumulated depreciation	6.1	6.1
	4.7	4.6
Unamortized leasehold improvements	1.7	1.7
Total fixed assets	6.3	6.3
Intangible assets, net	18.5	17.2
Total Assets	100.0	100.0

b.   The Interpublic Group of Companies
          Horizontal Common-Size Balance Sheets

	(In Percentages)	
December 31	1998	1997
Assets		
Current Assets:	109.6	100.0
Cash and cash equivalents	99.3	100.0
Marketable securities	113.5	100.0
Receivables, net	113.8	100.0
Expenditures billable to clients	118.4	100.0
Prepaid expenses and other current assets		
Total current assets	112.8	100.0
Other Assets:		
Investment in unconsolidated affiliates	101.9	100.0
Deferred taxes on income	128.7	100.0
Other investments and miscellaneous assets	134.0	100.0
Total other assets	128.5	100.0
Fixed Assets, at Cost:		
Land and buildings	113.9	100.0
Furniture and equipment	117.2	100.0
	116.8	100.0
Less accumulated depreciation	115.0	100.0
	119.1	100.0
Unamortized leasehold improvements	111.3	100.0
Total fixed assets	117.0	100.0
Intangible Assets	124.7	100.0
Total assets	116.0	100.0

b. continued

	(In Percentages)	
	1998	1997
Liabilities and Stockholders' Equity		
Current Liabilities:		
Payable to banks	3.1	3.1
Accounts payable	52.0	53.3
Accrued expenses	9.0	8.0
Accrued income taxes	3.0	2.7
Total current liabilities	67.1	67.1
Noncurrent Liabilities:		
Long-term debt	4.3	5.3
Convertible subordinated debentures and notes	3.0	3.4
Deferred compensation and reserve for termination		
allowances	4.6	4.6
Accrued postretirement benefits	.7	.8
Other noncurrent liabilities	1.3	1.2
Minority interests in consolidated subsidiaries	.8	.5
Total noncurrent liabilities	14.6	15.8
Stockholders' Equity:		
Preferred stock	–	–
Common stock	.2	.2
Additional paid-in capital	9.4	8.6
Retained earnings	16.1	14.8
Adjustments for minimum pension liability	(.5)	(.2)
Net unrealized gain on equity securities	.1	.2
Cumulative translation adjustment	(1.9)	2.7)
	23.4	21.0
Less:		
Treasury stock	(4.17)	(2.9)
Unearned ESOP compensation	–	(.1)
Unamortized expense of restricted stock grants	(1.07)	(.9)
Total stockholders' equity	18.2	17.0
Commitments and contingencies	–	–
Total liabilities and stockholders' equity	100.0	100.0

c. <u>Vertical Common-Size</u>
No substantial changes

<u>Horizontal Common-Size</u>
Material increase in all major sections (total current
assets, total other assets, total fixed assets, and
intangible assets).

The biggest increase in intangible assets.

PROBLEM 5-4

a.   The Interpublic Group of Companies
                         Vertical Common-Size Statement
                        Consolidated Statement of Income

| | (In Percentages) | | |
Year Ended December 31	1998	1997	1996
Commissions and Fees	96.9	96.3	96.3
Other income, net	3.1	3.7	3.7
Gross income	100.0	100.0	100.0
Salaries and related expenses	54.6	54.9	54.3
Office and general expenses	29.7	30.9	31.5
Interest expense	1.5	1.7	1.7
Special compensation charges	−	.9	−
Total costs and expenses	85.8	88.4	87.5
Income before provision for income taxes	14.2	11.6	12.5
Provision for income taxes	5.8	5.3	5.3
Income of consolidated companies	8.3	6.2	7.3
Income applicable to minority interests	(.7)	(.7)	(.5)
Equity in net income of unconsolidated affiliates	.2	.2	.4
Net income	7.8	5.8	7.2

Problem 5-4 (continued)

b.   The Interpublic Group of Companies
                        Horizontal Common-Size Statement
                        Consolidated Statement of Income

	(In Percentages)		
Year Ended December 31	1998	1997	1996
Commissions and fees	133.7	116.6%	100.0
Other income, net	113.6	118.4	100.0
Gross income	133.0	116.7	100.0
Salaries and related expenses	133.9	118.1	100.0
Office and general expenses	125.6	114.5	100.0
Interest expense	113.5	111.8	100.0
Special compensation charges	–	N/A	100.0
Total costs and expenses	130.5	118.0	100.0
Income before provision for income taxes	150.5	108.0	100.0
Provision for income taxes	148.0	118.8	100.0
Income of consolidated companies	152.4	00.2	00.0
Income applicable to minority interests	188.6	159.3	100.0
Equity in net income of nonconsolidated	57.6	52.6	100.0
affiliates	144.4	93.4	100.0
Net income			

c. Vertical Common-Size

    Significant decline in total costs and expenses

    Horizontal Common-Size

    Most items increased materially except for equity income,
    which declined.

    Total costs and expenses increased less than the increase in
    gross income. Thus resulted in a material increase in
    profits.

PROBLEM 5-5

Item	Year 1	Year 2	Change Analysis	
			Amount	Percent
1	—	3,000	3,000	—
2	6,000	(4,000)	(10,000)	
3	(7,000)	4,000	11,000	
4	4,000	—	(4,000)	(100%)
5	8,000	10,000	2,000	25%

PROBLEM 5-6

Item	Year 1	Year 2	Change Analysis	
			Amount	Percent
1	4,000	—	(4,000)	100
2	5,000	(3,000)	(8,000)	—
3	(9,000)	2,000	11,000	—
4	7,000	—	(7,000)	100
5	—	15,000	15,000	—

Chapter 6
Liquidity of Short-term Assets;
Related Debt-Paying Ability

QUESTIONS

6- 1. In the very short run, the procedure of making more funds
       available by slowing the rate of payments on accounts payable
       would work and the firm would have more funds to purchase
       inventory, which would in turn enable the firm to generate
       more sales. This procedure would not work very long because
       creditors would demand payment and they may refuse to sell to
       our firm or demand cash upon delivery. In either case, the
       end result would be the opposite of what was intended.

6- 2. When a firm is growing fast, it needs a large amount of
       funds to expand its inventory and receivables. At the
       same time, payroll and payables require funds. Although Jones
       Wholesale Company has maintained an above average current
       ratio for the wholesale industry, it has probably built up
       inventory and receivables, which require funds. The inventory
       and the receivables are probably being carried for longer
       periods of time than the credit terms received on the
       payables.

       Funds may have also been applied from current operations
       towards long-term assets in order to expand capacity.

       Fast-growing firms typically do have a problem with a
       shortage of funds. It is important that they minimize
       this problem in order to avoid a bad credit rating and
       possible bankruptcy.

6- 3. Current assets are assets that are in the form of cash or
       that will be realized in cash or that conserve the use of
       cash within an operating cycle of a business, or one year,
       whichever is the longer period of time.

       The other assets are not expected to be realized in cash in
       the near future and should, therefore, be segregated from
       current assets.

6- 4. The operating cycle is the period of time elapsing between the acquisition of goods and the final cash realization resulting from sales and subsequent collections.

6- 5. Current assets are assets that are in the form of cash or that will be realized in cash or that conserve the use of cash within the operating cycle of a business, or one year, whichever is the longer period of time.

6- 6. The five major categories of items that are found in current assets are the following:
   a. cash
   b. marketable securities
   c. receivables
   d. inventories
   e. prepaids

6- 7. The cash frozen in a bank in Cuba should not be classified as a current asset because it is not readily available to be used in operations.

6- 8. This guaranteed note would not be recorded by A.B. Smith Company; therefore, it would not influence the liquidity ratios. The potential impact on the liquidity of A.B. Smith Company should be considered, because A.B. Smith Company could be called upon to pay the note.

6- 9. This investment would not be classified as a marketable security because there is no intent to sell the securities and use the funds in current operations.

6-10. a. Number of days' sales in receivables
      b. Accounts receivable turnover

6-11. a. Number of days' sales in inventory
      b. Inventory turnover

6-12. A company that uses a natural business year would tend to overstate the liquidity of its receivables. The two computations that are made to indicate the liquidity of receivables are the days' sales in receivables and the accounts receivable turnover. Because the receivables would be at or near their low point at the end of a natural business year, the days' sales in receivables would be low at the end of the year in comparison with usual days' sales in receivables during the year. The accounts receivable turnover would be high, based on the natural business year in relation to the turnover and the receivables figures during the year.

6-13. Since the receivables will be at their peak at the end of the year, the days' sales in receivables will be high and the accounts receivable turnover will be low; thus, the liquidity will be understated when a firm closes its year at or near the peak of its business.

6-14. This distortion can be eliminated by using the average monthly receivables figures in the liquidity computations. The average monthly receivables figure will eliminate the year's high or low in receivables.

6-15. The liquidity of the receivables will be overstated if the sales figure includes both cash sales and credit sales. The exact liquidity indicated by the days' sales in receivables and the accounts receivable turnover will be meaningless but the trend that can be determined from these computations will be meaningful.

6-16. Inventories of a trading concern, whether it is a wholesale or a retail concern, are usually classified in one inventory account called "merchandise inventory." Inventories of a manufacturing concern are normally classified in three inventory accounts. These inventory accounts distinguish between getting ready to produce - raw material inventory; inventory in production, work in process inventory; and inventory completed - finished goods inventory.

6-17. The most realistic valuation of inventory would be the FIFO method because the most recent cost would be in the inventory. The LIFO method would result in the least realistic valuation of inventory. This is the result of having old cost in inventory.

6-18. a. If the company uses a natural business year for its accounting period, the number of days' sales in inventory will tend to be understated. When the average daily cost of goods sold for the year is divided into the ending inventory, the resulting answer will be a lower number of days' sales in inventory than actually exists.

       b. If the company closes the year when the activities are at a peak, the number of days' sales in inventory would tend to be overstated and the liquidity would be understated. When the average daily cost of goods sold for the year is divided into the ending inventory, the resulting answer will be a higher number of days' sales in inventory than actually exists.

c. If the company uses LIFO inventory, the number of days' sales in inventory would tend to be understated during inflation because the inventory would be at low cost figures, while the cost of goods sold would be at higher current cost.

6-19. a. There is no ideal number of days' sales in inventory. The number that a company should have would be guided by company policy and industry averages.

b. In general, a company wants to minimize the days' sales in inventory. Excess inventory is expensive to the company. Some of these costs are storage cost, additional funds required, and financing cost.

c. Days' sales in inventory can be too low, resulting in lost sales, limited production runs, higher transportation costs, etc.

6-20. When the cost of goods sold is not available to compute days' sales in inventory, use net sales. The result will not be a realistic number of days' sales in inventory, but the result will be useful in comparing one period with another for the same firm and in comparing one firm with another firm, also using net sales.

6-21. The distortions from seasonal fluctuations or the use of a natural business year can be eliminated by using monthly inventory figures when computing the average inventory that will then be divided into cost of goods sold.

6-22. When prices are rising the use of LIFO inventory will result in a much higher inventory turnover because of the lower inventory and the higher cost of goods sold. Therefore, the inventory turnover of a firm that uses LIFO should not be compared with the inventury turnover of a firm that does not use LIFO.

6-23. Working capital is defined as current assets less current liabilities.

6-24. Current liabilities are obligations whose liquidation is reasonably expected to require the use of existing current assets or the creation of other current liabilities within a year or an operating cycle, whichever is longer.

6-25. (1) a. Working capital - The excess of current assets over current liabilities.

       b. Current ratio - The ratio of total current assets to total current liabilities.

       c. Acid-test ratio - The ratio of total current assets less inventory to total current liabilities.

       d. Cash ratio - The ratio of total current assets less inventory and receivables to total current liabilities.

   (2) a. Working capital - Working capital based on cost figures will tend to be understated because inventory will be stated at amounts that do not represent current value.

       b. Current ratio - The current ratio will tend to be understated because inventory will be stated at amounts that do not represent current value.

       c. Acid-test ratio - The acid-test ratio will tend to be accurate.

       d. Cash ratio - The cash ratio will tend to be accurate.

   (3) To avoid the understatements in working capital and the current ratio, use the replacement cost of inventory when it is disclosed.

6-26. The current working capital amount should be compared with past working capital amounts to determine if working capital is reasonable. Caution must be exercised because the relative size of the firm may be expanding or contracting. Comparing working capital of one firm with working capital of another firm will usually be meaningless because of the different sizes of the firms.

6-27. The current ratio is considered to be more indicative of the short-term debt-paying ability than the working capital because the current ratio takes into account the relative relation between the size of the current assets and the size of the current liabilities. Working capital only determines the absolute difference between the current assets and the current liabilities.

6-28. The acid-test ratio is considered to be a better guide to short-term liquidity than the current ratio when there are problems with the short-run liquidity of inventory. Some problems with inventory could be in determining a reasonable dollar amount in relation to the quantity on hand (LIFO inventory), the inventory has been pledged, or the inventory is held for a long period of time. The cash ratio would be preferred over the acid-test ratio when there is a problem with the liquidity of receivables. An example would be an entity that has a long collection period for receivables.

6-29. If a firm can reduce its operating cycle, it can benefit from having more funds available for operating or it could reduce the funds that it uses in operations. Since funds cost the firm money, it can increase profits by operating at a more efficient operating cycle. An improved operating cycle will enable the firm to operate with less plant and equipment and still maintain the present level of sales, thereby increasing profits. Or, the firm could expand the level of sales with the improved operating cycle without expanding plant and equipment. This expansion in sales could also mean greater profits. Opportunities to improve the operating cycle will be found in the management of the inventory and the accounts receivable.

6-30. Some industries naturally need a longer operating cycle than others because of the nature of the industry. For example, we could not expect the car manufacturer to have an operating cycle that compares with that of a food store because it takes much longer to manufacture cars and collect the receivables

from the sales than it does for the food store to buy its
inventory and sell it for cash. Thus, comparing the operating
cycles of a car manufacturer and a food store would not be a
fair comparison.

6-31. Because funds to operate the business are costly to the firm,
a firm with a longer operating cycle usually charges a high
mark-up on its inventory cost when selling than does a firm
with a short operating cycle. This enables the firm to
recover the cost for the funds that are used to operate the
business. A food store usually has a very low mark-up, while
a car manufacturer would have a higher mark-up.

Within the same industry, it is difficult to have a different
mark-up from firm to firm, unless different services are
provided or a different quality is supplied, due to
competitive forces in price.

6-32. Profitability is often not of major importance in determining
the short-term debt-paying ability of a firm. One of the
reasons for this is that many revenue items and many expense
items do not directly affect cash flow during the same period.

6-33. The use of the allowance for doubtful accounts approach
results in the bad debt expense being charged to the period of
sale, thus matching this expense in the period of sale. It
also results in the recognition of the impairment of the
asset.

6-34. This is true because the most recent purchases end up in
cost of goods sold on the income statement.

6-35. This type of a current asset would not be a normal recurring
current asset. The firm's liquidity would be overstated in
terms of normal sources.

6-36. Accounts receivable and inventory are often major segments of
current assets. Therefore, they can have a material influence
on the current ratio. Accounts receivable turnover and the
merchandise inventory turnover are ratios that will aid the
analyst in forming an opinion as to the quality of receivables
and inventory. Poor quality in receivables and/or inventory
will increase the current ratio, which indicates better
liquidity than is the case.

6-37. Receivables can have a material influence on the acid-test ratio. Accounts receivable turnover will give some indication as to the quality of receivables. Poor quality in receivables will increase the acid-test ratio, which will result in the acid-test ratio appearing to be more favorable than it actually is.

6-38. FIFO represents the highest inventory balance under inflationary conditions.

6-39. Under inflationary conditions the cash flow under LIFO is greater than the cash flow under the other inventory methods by the difference in the resulting tax between the alternative cost methods.

6-40. No, a low sales to working capital ratio is an indication of an unprofitable use of working capital. It indicates that low amounts of sales are being generated for each dollar of working capital.

Yes, a high ratio is a tentative indication that the firm is undercapitalized. This firm will likely have a high inventory turnover and a low current ratio.

6-41. (1) Unused bank credit lines.

(2) Long-term assets that have the potential to be converted to cash quickly.

(3) Capability to issue debt or stock.

6-42. There are many situations where the liquidity position of the firm may not be as good as that indicated by the liquidity ratios. Some of the situations are the following:

(1) Notes discounted in which the other party has full recourse against the firm.

(2) Guarantee of a bank note for another firm.

(3) Major pending lawsuits against the firm.

(4) A major portion of the inventory is obsolete.

(5) A major portion of the receivables are uncollectible.

6-43.   The sales to working capital ratio gives an indication of
        whether working capital is used unprofitably or is possibly
        overworked.

6-44.   Because the higher costs are reflected in the cost of sales
        (last in, first out), leaving old costs (lower) in inventory.

6-45.   FIFO inventory - reported profit

Reported profit under lifo	$100,000
Increase in ending inventory	10,000
Reported profit under fifo	$110,000
Reported profit under lifo	$100,000
Increase in ending inventory	5,000
Reported profit under average cost	$105,000

        Yes, the inventory costing market
        should be disclosed.

TO THE NET

1. a. Auto controls for regulating residential and commercial environment.

    b. $1,116,000,000.

    c. Inventories are valued at the lower of cost or market. Cost is determined using the weighted average method. Market is based on net realizable value. Payments received from customers relating to the uncompleted portion are deducted from applicable inventories.

    d. Cost is determined using the weighted average method.

    e. Often payments received in advance are considered to be a current liability. When payments in advance relate to specific inventory it is conservative to deduct these payments from the specific inventories.

2. a. Kroger (Standard Industrial Classification - Retail - grocery stores)

    b. Cooper Tire & Rubber Company (Standard Industrial Classification - Tires and inner tubes.

    c. Cooper Tire & Rubber Company would likely have the higher current ratio. The receivables of Cooper Tire would likely be more material than the receivables of Kroger. The receivables of Cooper Tire would likely be of a longer term than the receivables of Kroger.
    The Cooper Tire inventory would consist of materials, work in process, and finished goods. Thus, the inventory of Cooper Tire would likely be of a longer term than the merchandise inventory of Kroger.

PROBLEM 6-1

$$\frac{\text{Current Assets}}{\text{Current Liabilities}} = \text{Current Ratio} \qquad \frac{\text{Current Assets-Inventory}}{\text{Current Liabilities}} = \text{Acid-Test Ratio}$$

$$\frac{\text{Current Assets}}{400,000} = 2.5 \qquad\qquad \frac{\$1,000,000-\text{Inventory}}{\$400,000} = 2.0$$

Current Assets = \$1,000,000   \$1,000,000-Inventory = 800,000
\$1,000,000-\$800,000 = Inventory
\$ 200,000 = Inventory

$$\frac{\text{Cost of Sales}}{\text{Inventory}} = 3$$

Note: In order to work this problem, it must be assumed that the acid-test ratio is computed as follows:

$$\frac{\text{Cost of Sales}}{\$200,000} = 3 \qquad\qquad \frac{\text{Current Assets-Inventory}}{\text{Current Liabilities}}$$

Cost of Sales = \$600,000

PROBLEM 6-2

a.
$$\text{Days' sales in receivables} = \frac{\text{Gross Receivables}}{\text{Net Sales}/365}$$

2000: $\dfrac{\$220,385 + \$11,180}{\$1,180,178/365} = 71.62 \text{ days}$

1999: $\dfrac{\$240,360 + \$12,300}{\$2,200,000/365} = 41.92 \text{ days}$

b. $\text{Accounts receivable turnover} = \dfrac{\text{Net Sales}}{\text{Average Gross Receivables}}$

2000: $\dfrac{\$1,180,178}{(\$240,360 + \$12,300 + \$220,385 + \$11,180)/2} = 4.87 \text{ times per year}$

1999: $\dfrac{\$2,200,000}{(\$230,180 + \$7,180 + \$240,360 + \$12,300)/2} = 8.98 \text{ times per year}$

c. The Hawk Company receivables have been much less liquid in 2000 in comparison with 1999. The days' sales in receivables at the end of the year have increased from 41.92 days in 1999 to 71.62 days in 2000. The accounts receivable turnover declined in 2000 to 4.87 from a turnover of 8.98 in 1999. These figures represent a major deterioration in the liquidation of receivables. The reasons for this deterioration should be determined. Some possible reasons are a major customer not paying its bills, a general deterioration of all receivable accounts, or a change in the Hawk Company credit terms.

PROBLEM 6-3

a. Days' sales in receivables = $\dfrac{\text{Gross Receivables}}{\text{Net Sales}/365}$

December 31, 2000: $\dfrac{\$55,400 + \$3,500}{\$800,000/365}$ = 26.87 days

July 31, 2000: $\dfrac{\$90,150 + \$4,100}{\$790,000/365}$ = 43.55 days

b. Accounts receivable turnover = $\dfrac{\text{Net Sales}}{\text{Average Gross Receivables}}$

December 31, 2000: $\dfrac{\$800,000}{(\$50,000 + \$3,000 + \$55,400 + \$3,500)/2}$

14.30 times per year

July 31, 2000: $\dfrac{\$790,000}{(\$89,000 + \$4,000 + \$90,150 + \$4,100)/2}$

8.44 times per year

c. This company appears to have a seasonal business because of the materially different days' sales in receivables and accounts receivable turnover when computed at the two different dates. The ratios computed will not be meaningful in an absolute sense, but they would be meaningful in a comparative sense when comparing the same dates from year to year. They would not be meaningful when comparing different dates.

PROBLEM 6-4

a. Days' sales in receivables = $\dfrac{\text{Gross Receivables}}{\text{Net Sales}/365}$

    L. Solomon Company days'
    sales in receivables = $\dfrac{\$110,000 + \$8,000}{\$1,800,000/365}$ = 23.93 days

    L. Konrath Company days'
    sales in receivables = $\dfrac{\$60,000 + \$4,000}{\$1,850,000/365}$ = 12.63 days

b.   It appears that the L. Konrath Company manages receivables better than does L. Solomon Company. They have 12.6 days' sales in receivables while the L. Solomon Company has 23.9 days' sales in receivables. Actually, we cannot make a fair comparison between these two companies because the L. Solomon Company is using the calendar year while the L. Konrath Company appears to be using a natural business year. By using a natural business year, the L. Konrath Company has its receivables at a low point at the end of the year. This would make its liquidity overstated at the end of the year.

PROBLEM 6-5

a. $\dfrac{365 \text{ days}}{\text{Accounts receivable turnover in days}}$ = $\dfrac{365}{36}$ = 10.14 times per year

b. $\dfrac{365 \text{ days}}{12.0 \text{ times per year}}$ = 30.42 days

c. $\dfrac{\text{Gross Receivables}}{\text{Net Sales}/365}$ = $\dfrac{\$280,000}{\$2,158,000/365}$ = 47.36 days

d. $\dfrac{\text{Net Sales}}{\text{Average Gross Receivables}}$ = $\dfrac{\$3,500,000}{\$324,000}$ = 10.80 times per year

PROBLEM 6-6

a. $\dfrac{\text{Ending Inventory}}{\text{Cost of Goods Sold}/365}$ = Days' Sales In Inventory

    $\dfrac{\$360,500}{\$2,100,000/365}$ = 62.66 days

b.   No. Since J. Shaffer Company uses LIFO inventory, the ending inventory is computed using costs that are not representative of the current cost. The cost of goods sold is representative of the approximate current cost and, therefore, the average daily cost of goods sold is representative of current cost. When the average daily cost of goods sold is divided into the inventory, the result is an unrealistically low number of days' sales in inventory. Thus, the liquidity is overstated.

c.   The number of days' sales in inventory would be a helpful guide when compared with prior periods. The actual computed number of days' sales in inventory would not be meaningful because of the LIFO inventory.

PROBLEM 6-7

a. $\dfrac{\text{Average Inventory}}{\text{Cost of Goods Sold}/365}$ = Inventory Turnover In Days

   = $\dfrac{\$280,000}{\$1,250,000/365}$ = 81.76 Days

b. $\dfrac{\text{Cost of Goods Sold}}{\text{Average Inventory}}$ = Merchandise Inventory Turnover

   $\dfrac{\$1,250,000}{\$\ 280,000}$ = 4.46 times per year

or

   $\dfrac{365}{\text{Inventory Turnover in days}}$ = Merchandise Inventory Turnover

   $\dfrac{365}{81.8}$ = 4.46 times per year

PROBLEM 6-8

a.   Accounts Receivable Turnover (in days) = $\dfrac{\text{Average Gross Receivable}}{\text{Net Sales}/365}$

   $\dfrac{(\$180,000 + \$160,000)/2}{\$3,150,000/365}$ = 19.70 days

117

b. Inventory Turnover In Days $=$ $\dfrac{\text{Average Inventory}}{\text{Cost of Goods Sold}/365}$

$\dfrac{(\$480,000 + \$390,000)/2}{\$2,250,000/365}$ $=$ $\dfrac{\$435,000}{\$2,250,000/365}$ $= 70.57$ days

c. Operating $=$ Accounts Receivable $+$ Inventory Turnover
   Cycle   Turnover In Days   In Days

   $= 19.70$ days $+ 70.57$ days $= 90.27$ days

PROBLEM 6-9

Days' Sales In $+$ Days Sales In $=$ Estimated days to realize
Receivables   Inventory   cash from ending
                                     inventory

Days' Sales In Receivables $= \dfrac{\text{Gross Receivables}}{\text{Net Sales}/365}$

$\dfrac{\$560,000 + \$30,000}{\$4,350,000/365}$ $=$ $\dfrac{\$590,000}{\$4,350,000/365}$ $= 49.51$ days

Days' Sales $= \dfrac{\text{Ending Inventory}}{\text{Cost of Goods Sold}/365}$ $= \dfrac{\$680,000}{\$3,600,000/365}$ $= 68.94$ days
In Inventory

49.51 Days $+ 68.94$ Days $= 118.45$ days

PROBLEM 6-10

a. Days' Sales In $= \dfrac{\text{Gross Receivables}}{\text{Net Sales}/365}$ $= \dfrac{\$480,000+\$25,000}{\$3,650,000/365}$ $= 50.5$ days
   Receivables

b. Days' Sales In $\dfrac{\text{Ending Inventory}}{\text{Cost of Goods Sold}/365}$ $= \dfrac{\$570,000}{\$2,850,000/365}$
   Inventory Using $=$
   The Cost Figure

   $= 73.00$ days

c. Days' sales in inventory using the replacement cost for the inventory and the cost of goods sold.

   $\dfrac{\text{Ending Inventory}}{\text{Cost of Goods Sold}/365}$ $= \dfrac{\$900,000}{\$3,150,000/365}$ $= 104.29$ days

d. The replacement cost data should be used for inventory and cost
    of goods sold when it is disclosed. Replacement cost places
    inventory and cost of goods sold on a comparable basis. When the
    historical cost figures are used and the company uses LIFO, then
    the cost of goods sold and the inventory are not on a comparable
    basis. This is because the inventory has rather old cost and the
    cost of goods sold has recent cost. For Laura Badora Company,
    the actual days' sales in inventory based on replacement cost are
    over 30 days more than was indicated by using the cost figures.

PROBLEM 6-11

a. Working   = Current   - Current
    Capital   Assets   Liabilities

             = $1,052,820   - $459,842   = $592,978

b. Current Ratio = $\frac{\text{Current Assets}}{\text{Current Liabilities}}$ = $\frac{\$1,052,820}{\$459,842}$ = 2.29

c. Acid-Test Ratio = $\frac{\text{Cash Equivalents \& Net Receivables \& Marketable Securities}}{\text{Current Liabilities}}$

    $\frac{\$33,493 + \$215,147 + \$255,000}{\$459,842}$ = $\frac{\$503,640}{\$459,842}$ = 1.10

d. Cash Ratio = $\frac{\text{Cash Equivalents + Marketable Securities}}{\text{Current Liabilities}}$

    $\frac{\$33,493 + \$215,147}{\$459,842}$ = $\frac{\$248,640}{\$459,842}$ = .54

e. Days' Sales In Receivables = $\frac{\text{Gross Receivables}}{\text{Net Sales/365}}$

    $\frac{\$255,000 + \$6,000}{\$3,050,600/365}$ = $\frac{\$261,000}{\$3,050,600/365}$ = 31.23 days

f. Accounts Receivable Turnover = $\frac{\text{Average Gross Receivables}}{\text{Net Sales/365}}$
         (in days)

    $\frac{(\$255,000+ \$6,000+\$288,000)/2}{\$3,050,600/365}$ = $\frac{\$274,50}{\$3,050,600/365}$ = 32.84 days

g. Days' Sales = ___Ending Inventory___ = ___$523,000___ = 87.36
   In Inventory   Cost of Goods Sold/365 $2,185,100/365   days

h. Inventory Turnover In Days = ___Average Inventory___
                                  Cost of Goods Sold/365

    ($523,000 + $565,000)/2 = ___$544,000___ = 90.87 days
         $2,185,100/365 $2,185,100/365

i. Operating Cycle = Accounts Receivable + Inventory Turnover
                      Turnover In Days   In Days

       123.71 days   = 32.84 days   + 90.87 days

PROBLEM 6-12

	Total Current Assets	Total Current Liabilities	Net Working Capital	Current Ratio
a.	+	0	+	+
b.	+	0	+	+
c.	+	0	+	+
d.	-	-	0	+
e.	-	0	-	-
f.	0	0	0	0
g.	+	0	+	+
h.	0	0	0	0
i.	-	0	-	-
j.	0	-	+	+
k.	0	0	0	0
l.	0	+	-	-
m.	+	+	0	-
n.	0	+	-	-
o.	-	0	-	-

PROBLEM 6-13

    Company E and Company D have the same amount of working
capital. Company D has a current ratio of 2 to 1, while Company E
has a current ratio of 1.29 to 1. Company D is in a better short-
term financial position than Company E because its liabilities are
covered better with a higher current ratio. Working capital is not
very significant because the amount of working capital does not
indicate the relative size of the companies and the amount needed.

PROBLEM 6-14

Company T has twice the working capital of Company R. Both companies have a current ratio of 2 to 1. In general, both companies are in the same relative position because of the same current ratio. The greater amount of working capital in Company T is not very significant because the amount of working capital does not indicate the relative size of the companies and the amount needed.

PROBLEM 6-15

a. (1) Working Capital:

2001: $500,000 - $340,000 = $160,000

2000: $400,000 - $300,000 = $100,000

(2) Current Ratio:

2001: $500,000 / $340,000 = 1.47 to 1

2000: $400,000 / $300,000 = 1.33 to 1

(3) Acid-Test Ratio:

2001: $\frac{\$500,000 - \$250,000}{\$340,000}$ = .74 to 1

2000: $\frac{\$400,000 - \$200,000}{\$300,000}$ = .67 to 1

(4) Accounts Receivable Turnover:

2001: $\frac{\$1,400,000}{(\$110,000 + \$105,000)/2}$ = 13.02 times per year

2000: $\frac{\$1,500,000}{(\$120,000 + \$110,000)/2}$ = 13.04 times per year

(5) Inventory Turnover:

2001: $\frac{\$1,120,000}{(\$200,000 + \$250,000)/2}$ = 4.98 times per year

2000: $\frac{\$1,020,000}{(\$280,000 + \$200,000)/2}$ = 4.25 times per year

(6) Inventory Turnover In Days:

    2001:   365 / 4.98 = 73.29 days

    2000:   365 / 4.25 = 85.88 days

b. The short-term liquidity of the firm has improved between 2000 and 2001. The working capital increased by $60,000, while the current ratio increased from 1.33 to 1.47. The acid-test ratio increased from .67 to .74. Using a rule of thumb of two for the current ratio and one for the acid-test, this firm needs to improve its current liquidity position.

The accounts receivable turnover stayed the same, while the inventory improved from 4.25 to 4.98. The days' sales in inventory improved from 85.88 to 73.29 days.

Much of the improvement in the current position can be attributed to the improved control of the inventory.

PROBLEM 6-16

a. Based on the year-end figures

(1) Accounts Receivable Turnover in Days:

$$\frac{\text{Average Gross Receivables}}{\text{Net Sales} / 365} = \frac{(\$75,000 + \$50,000)/2}{\$4,000,000} = \frac{5.70}{\text{Days}}$$

(2) Accounts Receivable Turnover Per Year:

$$\frac{\text{Net Sales}}{\text{Average Gross Receivables}} = \frac{\$4,000,000}{(\$75,000 + \$50,000)/2} = \frac{64}{\text{times per year}}$$

(3) Inventory Turnover in Days:

$$\frac{\text{Average Inventory}}{\text{Cost of Goods Sold}/365} = \frac{(\$350,000 + \$400,000)/2}{\$1,800,000/365} = \frac{76.04}{\text{days}}$$

(4) Inventory Turnover per Year

$$\frac{\text{Cost of Goods Sold}}{\text{Average Inventory}} = \frac{\$1,800,000}{(\$350,000 + \$400,000)/2} = \frac{4.80 \text{ times}}{\text{per year}}$$

b. Using average figures:

Total monthly Gross Receivables $6,360,000
                                              12
Average $ 530,000

Total monthly Inventory $5,875,000
                                              12
Average $ 489,583

(1) Accounts Receivable Turnover in Days:

$\dfrac{\text{Average Gross Receivables}}{\text{Net Sales}/365}$ = $\dfrac{\$\quad 530,000}{\$4,000,000/365}$ = 48.36 days

(2) Accounts Receivable Turnover Per Year:

$\dfrac{\text{Net Sales}}{\text{Average Gross Receivables}}$ = $\dfrac{\$4,000,000}{\$530,000}$ = 7.55 times per year

(3) Inventory Turnover in Days:

$\dfrac{\text{Average Inventory}}{\text{Cost of Goods Sold}/365}$ = $\dfrac{\$\quad 489,583}{\$1,800,000/365}$ = 99.28 days

(4) Inventory Turnover per Year:

$\dfrac{\text{Cost of Goods Sold}}{\text{Average Inventory}}$ = $\dfrac{\$1,800,000}{\$\quad 489,583}$ = 3.68 times per year

c. Based on the year-end averages, the liquidity of the receivables and inventory are overstated and, therefore, they are unrealistic. The table shows the overstatement of liquidity in comparison with monthly averages.

	Based on Year-End Figures	Based on Monthly Figures
Accounts Receivable Turnover in Days	5.70 days	48.36 days
Accounts Receivable Turnover Per Year	64 times per year	7.55 times per year
Inventory Turnover In Days	76.04 days	99.28 days
Inventory Turnover Per Year	4.80 times per year	3.68 times per year

123

d. Days' Sales In Receivables:

$$\frac{\text{Gross Receivables}}{\text{Net Sales}/365} = \frac{\$\quad 50,000}{\$4,000,000/365} = 4.56 \text{ days}$$

e. Days' Sales In Inventory:

$$\frac{\text{Ending Inventory}}{\text{Cost of Goods sold}/365} = \frac{\$\quad 400,000}{\$1,800,000/365} = 81.11 \text{ days}$$

f. The days' sales in receivables and the days' sales in inventory are understated based on the year-end figures because the receivables and inventory numbers are abnormally low at this time. Therefore, the liquidity of the receivables and the inventory is overstated.

Anne Elizabeth Corporation is using a natural business year and, therefore, at the year-end the receivables and the inventory are below average for the year.

PROBLEM 6-17

a. First-In, First-Out (FIFO):

		Inventory	Cost of Goods Sold
August 1	Purchase 200 @ $7.00	$1,400	
November 1	Purchase 200 @ $7.50	$1,500	
		$2,900	

Remaining cost in cost of goods sold ($10,900-$2,900) $8,000
    b. Last-In, First-Out (LIFO):
        Inventory   Cost of Goods Sold
    c. January 1 Inventory 400 x $5.00 $2000

Remaining cost in cost of goods sold ($10,900-$2,000) $8,900

c. Average Cost (Weighted Average):

                                        Inventory   Cost of Goods Sold

Total cost $10,900 = $6.06
Total Units   1,800

Inventory (400 x $6.06) = $2,424

Remaining cost in cost of goods sold ($10,900-$2,424) $8,476

d. Specific Identification:

	Inventory	Cost of Goods Sold
March 1, Purchase cost $6.00
Inventory 400 x $6.00 .... $2,400

Remaining cost in cost of goods sold ($10,900-$2,400) $8,500

PROBLEM 6-18

a. First-In, First-Out (FIFO):

	Inventory	Cost of Goods Sold

December 10 Purchase
   500 x $5.00 .... $2,500
October 22 Purchase
   100 x $4.90   490
                 $2,990

Remaining cost in cost of goods sold ($20,325-$2,990) $17,335

b. Last-In, First-Out (LIFO):

	Inventory	Cost of Goods Sold

January 1 Beginning inventory
   (600 x $4.00) $2,400

Remaining cost in cost of goods sold ($20,325-$2,400) $17,925

c. Average Cost:
   Total Cost $\dfrac{\$20,325}{4,400} = \$4.619$
   Total Units
   Inventory (600 x $4.62) = $2,772
   Cost of Goods Sold ($20,325-$2,772) = $17,553

d. Specific Identification:

   Inventory (600 x $5.00)   = $ 3,000
   Cost of Goods Sold ($20,325-$3,000) = $17,325

PROBLEM 6-19

a. Sales to Working Capital:

2001		2000		1999	
$\dfrac{\$650,000}{\$270,000}$	= 2.41	$\dfrac{\$600,000}{\$260,000}$	= 2.31	$\dfrac{\$500,000}{\$240,000}$	= 2.08

b. The sales to working capital ratio for J.A. Appliance Company was substantially below the industry average for all three years. This tentatively indicates that working capital is not efficient in relation to the sales. There was some improvement in the ratio each year.

PROBLEM 6-20

a. __3__ A payment of a trade account payable would reduce both current assets and current liabilities. This would have the effect of increasing both the current and quick ratios since total quick assets exceeded total current liabilities both before and after the transactions.

b. __2__ This would increase current assets and current liabilities by the same amount. This would have the effect of decreasing the current ratio because total quick assets exceeded total current liabilities both before and after the transaction.

c. __5__ The collection of a current account receivable would not change the numerator or the denominator in either the current or quick ratios.

d. __4__ A write-off of inventory would decrease the numerator in the current ratio.

e. __2__ The liquidation of a long-term note would reduce the numerator in both the quick ratio and the current ratio, but it would reduce the numerator of the quick ratio proportionately more than the numerator of the current ratio.

PROBLEM 6-21

a. __1__ $\dfrac{\text{Net Sales}}{\text{Average Gross Receivables}} =$

$$\frac{\$1,500,000}{(\$8,0000 + \$72,000 + \$10,000 + \$60,000) / 2} = \begin{array}{c} 20.0 \text{ times} \\ \text{per year} \end{array}$$

b. __2__ December 31 represents a date when the accounts receivable would be low and unrepresentative; thus the accounts receivable turnover computed on December 31 will be overstated.

PROBLEM 6-22

a. __2__

$$\frac{\text{Cash Equivalents} + \text{Marketable Securities} + \text{Net Receivables}}{\text{Current Liabilities}}$$

$$\frac{\$2,100,000 + \$7,200,000 + \$50,500,000}{\$34,000,000} = 1.76$$

b. __1__   The collection of accounts receivable does not change the total numerator or the denominator of the current ratio formula, nor does the collection change total current assets or total current liabilities.

PROBLEM 6-23

a. __3__

$$\frac{\text{Cash Equivalents} + \text{Marketable Securities} + \text{Net Receivables}}{\text{Current Liabilities}}$$

$$\frac{\$8,000 + \$32,000 + \$40,000}{\$60,000 + \$30,000} = \frac{\$80,000}{\$90,000} = .89$$

b. __1__   Net Sales (use only credit sales when available)
Average Gross Receivables (only net receivables available in this problem)

$$\frac{\text{Net Sales}}{\text{Average Gross Receivables}}$$

Note: Use only credit sales when available.

$$\frac{\$600,000}{(\$40,000 + \$110,000) / 2} = \frac{\$600,000}{\$75,000} = 8.00 \text{ times}$$

c. __1__

$$\frac{\text{Cost of Goods Sold}}{\text{Average Inventory}}$$

$$\frac{\$1,260,000}{(\$80,000 + \$140,000) / 2} = \frac{\$1,260,000}{\$110,000} = 11.45 \text{ times}$$

127

d. __4__
$$\frac{\text{Current Assets}}{\text{Current Liabilities}}$$

$$\frac{\$8,000 + \$32,000 + \$40,000 + \$80,000}{\$60,000 + \$30,000} = \frac{\$160,000}{\$90,000} = 1.78 \text{ times}$$

e. __2__ As long as the current ratio is greater than 1 to 1, any payment will increase the current ratio because the current liabilities go down more in proportion than do the current assets.

PROBLEM 6-24

a. __1__ An increase in inventory would increase the current ratio. To the extent that the increase in inventory used current funds available, this would decrease the acid-test.

b. __4__ LIFO would result in a lower inventory figure. This would decrease the current ratio and increase inventory turnover.

c. __3__
$$\frac{\text{Current Assets}}{\text{Current Liabilities}} = \frac{X}{\$600,000} = 3.0$$

X = \$1,800,000

$$\frac{\text{Current Assets - Inventory}}{\text{Current Liabilities}} = \frac{\$1,800,000 - Y}{\$600,000} = 2.5$$

Y = \$300,000

$$\frac{\text{Cost of Sales}}{\text{Inventory}} = \frac{\$500,000}{\$300,000} = 1.67$$

d. __2__ The most logical reason for the current ratio to be high and the quick ratio low is that the firm has a large investment in inventory.

e. __5__ Low default risk, readily marketable, and a short-term to maturity is a proper description of investment instruments used to invest temporarily idle cash balances.

128

f. __1__   A proper management of accounts receivable should achieve a combination of sales volume, bad debt experience, and receivables turnover that maximizes the profits of the corporation.

g. __5__   Any of the four items could be used to cover payroll expenses.

PROBLEM 6-25

Revenue:

10,000 x 4 x $15 =	$ 600,000	
20,000 x 3 x $15 =	900,000	
30,000 x 2 x $15 =	900,000	
40,000 x 1 x $15 =	600,000	$3,000,000

Expenses:
  Cost of goods sold:

120,000 x $11 =	1,320,000	
80,000 x $10 =	800,000	2,120,000
Selling and administrative		270,000
		$2,390,000

Earnings before taxes	610,000
Taxes, 40%	244,000
Net income	$ 366,000

PROBLEM 6-26

a. 1. Days' Sales In Receivables = $\dfrac{\text{Gross Receivables}}{\text{Net Sales}/365}$

2002: $\dfrac{\$131,000 + \$1,000}{\$880,000/365}$ = 54.75 days

2001: $\dfrac{\$128,000 + \$900}{\$910,000/365}$ = 51.70 days

2000: $\dfrac{\$127,000 + \$900}{\$840,000/365}$ = 55.58 days

1999: $\dfrac{\$126,000 + \$800}{\$825,000/365}$ = 56.10 days

1998: $\dfrac{\$125,000 + \$1,200}{\$820,000/365}$ = 56.17 days

2. Accounts Receivable Turnover = $\dfrac{\text{Net Sales}}{\text{Gross Receivables}}$

2002: $\dfrac{\$880,000}{\$131,000 + \$1,000}$ = 6.67 times per year

2001: $\dfrac{\$910,000}{\$128,000 + \$900}$ = 7.06 times per year

2000: $\dfrac{\$840,000}{\$127,000 + \$900}$ = 6.57 times per year

1999: $\dfrac{\$825,000}{\$126,000 + \$800}$ = 6.51 times per year

1998: $\dfrac{\$820,000}{\$125,000 + \$1,200}$ = 6.50 times per year

3. Accounts Receivable Turnover in Days =

$\dfrac{\text{Average Gross Receivables}}{\text{Net Sales/365}}$

2002: $\dfrac{\$131,000 + \$1,000}{\$880,000/365}$ = 54.75 days

2001: $\dfrac{\$128,000 + \$900}{\$910,000/365}$ = 51.70 days

2000: $\dfrac{\$127,000 + \$900}{\$840,000/365}$ = 55.58 days

1999: $\dfrac{\$126,000 + \$800}{\$825,000/365}$ = 56.10 days

1998: $\dfrac{\$125,000 + \$1,200}{\$820,000/365}$ = 56.17 days

4. Days' Sales in Inventory = $\dfrac{\underline{\text{Ending Inventory}}}{\text{Cost of Goods Sold}/365}$

2002: $\dfrac{\$122,000}{\$740,000/365}$ = 60.18 days

2001: $\dfrac{\$124,000}{\$760,000/365}$ = 59.55 days

2000: $\dfrac{\$126,000}{\$704,000/365}$ = 65.33 days

1999: $\dfrac{\$127,000}{\$695,000/365}$ = 66.70 days

1998: $\dfrac{\$125,000}{\$692,000/365}$ = 65.93 days

5. Merchandise Inventory Turnover =

$\dfrac{\underline{\text{Cost of Goods Sold}}}{\text{Average Inventory}}$

2002: $\dfrac{\$740,000}{\$122,000}$ = 6.07 times per year

2001: $\dfrac{\$760,000}{\$124,000}$ = 6.13 times per year

2000: $\dfrac{\$704,000}{\$126,000}$ = 5.59 times per year

1999: $\dfrac{\$695,000}{\$127,000}$ = 5.47 times per year

1998: $\dfrac{\$692,000}{\$125,000}$ = 5.54 times per year

6. Inventory Turnover in Days =

$$\frac{\text{Average Inventory}}{\text{Cost of Goods Sold}/365}$$

2002: $\dfrac{\$122,000}{\$740,000/365}$ = 60.18 days

2001: $\dfrac{\$124,000}{\$760,000/365}$ = 59.55 days

2000: $\dfrac{\$126,000}{\$704,000/365}$ = 65.33 days

1999: $\dfrac{\$127,000}{\$695,000/365}$ = 66.70 days

1998: $\dfrac{\$125,000}{\$692,000/365}$ = 65.93 days

7. Operating Cycle =

Accounts Receivable + Inventory Turnover
Turnover In Days   In Days

2002:   54.75 + 60.18   = 114.93

2001:   51.70 + 59.55   = 111.25

2000:   55.58 + 65.33   = 120.91

1999:   56.10 + 66.70   = 122.80

1998:   56.17 + 65.93   = 122.10

8. Working Capital = Current Assets - Current Liabilities

2002: $305,200 - $109,500 = $195,700

2001: $303,000 - $110,000 = $193,000

2000: $303,000 - $113,500 = $189,500

1999: $301,000 - $114,500 = $186,500

1998: $297,000 - $115,500 = $181,500

9. Current Ratio = $\dfrac{\text{Current Assets}}{\text{Current Liabilities}}$

2002: $\dfrac{\$305,200}{\$109,500}$ = 2.79

2001: $\dfrac{\$303,000}{\$110,000}$ = 2.75

2000: $\dfrac{\$303,000}{\$113,500}$ = 2.67

1999: $\dfrac{\$301,000}{\$114,500}$ = 2.63

1998: $\dfrac{\$297,000}{\$115,500}$ = 2.57

10. Acid – Test Ratio = $\dfrac{\text{Cash Equivalents + Marketable Securities + Net Receivables}}{\text{Current Liabilities}}$

2002: $\dfrac{\$47,200 + \$2,000 + \$131,000}{\$109,500}$ = 1.65

2001: $\dfrac{\$46,000 + \$2,500 + \$128,000}{\$110,000}$ = 1.60

2000: $\dfrac{\$45,000 + \$3,000 + \$127,000}{\$113,500}$ = 1.54

1999: $\dfrac{\$44,000 + \$3,000 + \$126,000}{\$114,500}$ = 1.51

1998: $\dfrac{\$43,000 + \$3,000 + \$125,000}{\$115,500}$ = 1.48

11. Cash Ratio = $\dfrac{\text{Cash Equivalents + Marketable Securities}}{\text{Current Liabilities}}$

2002: $\dfrac{\$47,200 + \$2,000}{\$109,500}$ = .45

2001: $\dfrac{\$46,000 + \$2,500}{\$110,000}$ = .44

2000: $\dfrac{\$45,000 + \$3,000}{\$113,500}$ = .42

1999: $\dfrac{\$44,000 + \$3,000}{\$114,500}$ = .41

1998: $\dfrac{\$43,000 + \$3,000}{\$115,500}$ = .40

12. Sales to Working Capital = $\dfrac{\text{Net Sales}}{\text{Average Working Capital}}$

2002: $\dfrac{\$880,000}{\$195,700}$ = 4.50

2001: $\dfrac{\$910,000}{\$193,000}$ = 4.72

2000: $\dfrac{\$840,000}{\$189,500}$ = 4.43

1999: $\dfrac{\$825,000}{\$186,500}$ = 4.42

1998: $\dfrac{\$820,000}{\$181,500}$ = 4.52

b. 1. Days' Sales in Receivables = $\dfrac{\text{Gross Receivables}}{\text{Net Sales/365}}$

2002:   Same as part a   54.75 days

2001:   Same as part a   51.70 days

```
2000:      Same as part a      55.58 days

1999:      Same as part a      56.10 days

1998:      Same as part a      56.17 days
```

2. Accounts Receivable Turnover = $\dfrac{\text{Net Sales}}{\text{Gross Receivables}}$

```
2002:      Same as part a      6.67 times per year

2001:      Same as part a      7.06 times per year

2000:      Same as part a      6.57 times per year

1999:      Same as part a      6.51 times per year

1998:      Same as part a      6.50 times per year
```

3. Accounts Receivable Turnover In Days =

$$\frac{\text{Average Gross Receivables}}{\text{Net Sales}/365}$$

2002: $\dfrac{(\$131,000 + \$1,000 + \$128,000 + \$900)/2}{\$880,000/365}$ = 54.11 days

2001: $\dfrac{\$128,000 + \$900 + \$127,000 + \$900/2}{\$910,000/365}$ = 51.50 days

2000: $\dfrac{(\$127,000 + \$900 + \$126,000 + \$800)/2}{\$840,000/365}$ = 55.34 days

1999: $\dfrac{(\$126,000 + \$800 + \$125,000 + \$1,200)/2}{\$825,000/365}$ = 55.97 days

1998:   Not sufficient data to compute using average
           gross receivables

4. Days' Sales In Inventory = $\dfrac{\text{Ending Inventory}}{\text{Cost of Goods Sold}/365}$

```
2002:      Same as part a      60.18 days
```

2001:	Same as part a	59.55 days
2000:	Same as part a	65.33 days
1999:	Same as part a	66.70 days
1998:	Same as part a	65.93 days

5. Merchandise Inventory Turnover = $\dfrac{\text{Cost of Goods Sold}}{\text{Average Inventory}}$

2002: $\dfrac{\$740,000}{(\$122,000 + \$124,000)/2}$ = 6.02 times per year

2001: $\dfrac{\$760,000}{(\$124,000 + \$126,000)/2}$ = 6.08 times per year

2000: $\dfrac{\$704,000}{(\$126,000 + \$127,000)/2}$ = 5.57 times per year

1999: $\dfrac{\$695,000}{(\$127,000 + \$125,000)/2}$ = 5.52 times per year

1998: Not sufficient data to compute using average inventory.

6. Inventory Turnover In Days = $\dfrac{\text{Average Inventory}}{\text{Cost of Goods Sold}/365}$

2002: $\dfrac{(\$122,000 + \$124,000)/2}{\$740,000/365}$ = 60.67 days

2001: $\dfrac{(\$124,000 + \$126,000)/2}{\$760,000/365}$ = 60.03 days

2000: $\dfrac{(\$126,000 + \$127,000)/2}{\$704,000/365}$ = 65.59 days

1999: $\dfrac{(\$127,000 + \$125,000)/2}{\$695,000/365}$ = 66.17 days

1998: Not sufficient data to compute using average inventory.

7. Operating Cycle =

$$\frac{\text{Accounts Receivable}}{\text{Turnover In Days}} + \frac{\text{Inventory Turnover}}{\text{In Days}}$$

2002:   54.11 + 60.67   = 114.78

2001:   51.50 + 60.03   = 111.53

2000:   55.34 + 65.59   = 120.93

1999:   55.97 + 66.17   = 122.14

1998:   Not sufficient data to compute.

8. Working Capital = Current Assets - Current Liabilities

2002:   Same as part a   = $195,700

2001:   Same as part a   = $193,000

2000:   Same as part a   = $189,500

1999:   Same as part a   = $186,500

1998:   Same as part a   = $181,500

9. Current Ratio = $\dfrac{\text{Current Assets}}{\text{Current Liabilities}}$

2002:   Same as part a   = 2.79

2001:   Same as part a   = 2.75

2000:   Same as part a   = 2.67

1999:   Same as part a   = 2.63

1998:   Same as part a   = 2.57

10. Acid-Test = Cash Equivalents + Marketable + Net
                                   Securities   Receivables

2002:   Same as part a   = 1.65

2001:   Same as part a   = 1.60

2000:   Same as part a   = 1.54

1999:   Same as part a   = 1.51

1998:   Same as part a   = 1.48

11. Cash Ratio = $\dfrac{\text{Cash Equivalents + Marketable Securities}}{\text{Current Liabilities}}$

2002:   Same as part a   = .45

2001:   Same as part a   = .44

2000:   Same as part a   = .42

1999:   Same as part a   = .41

1998:   Same as part a   = .40

12. Sales to Working Capital = $\dfrac{\text{Net Sales}}{\text{Average Working Capital}}$

2002: $\dfrac{\$880,000}{(\$305,200 - \$109,500 + \$303,000 - \$110,000)/2} = 4.53$

2001: $\dfrac{\$910,000}{(\$303,000 - \$110,000 + \$303,000 - \$113,500)/2} = 4.76$

2000: $\dfrac{\$840,000}{(\$303,000 - \$113,500 + \$301,000 - \$114,500)/2} = 4.47$

1999: $\dfrac{\$825,000}{(\$301,000 - \$114,500 + \$297,000 - \$115,500)/2} = 4.48$

1998: Not sufficient data to compute.

c. Days' Sales in Receivables, Accounts Receivable Turnover, and Accounts Receivable Turnover in Days improved between 1993 and 1996 and slipped somewhat in 1997.

In general, the inventory ratios of Days' Sales in Inventory, Merchandise Inventory Turnover, and Inventory Turnover in Days improved between 1993 and 1996. There was somewhat of a deterioration in these ratios in 1997.

The operating cycle improved substantially between 1993 and 1996 and slipped somewhat in 1997. This is consistent with what we found with the Accounts Receivable Turnover in Days and the Inventory Turnover in Days.

The Working Capital and the Current Ratio improved each year. This indicates that current assets improved in relation to current liabilities. The Acid Test improved each year. The most liquid ratio, Cash Ratio, improved slightly each year.

The Sales to Working Capital was inconsistent with decline years and increase years. It ended with 1997 being approximately the same as 1993.

Seven of the twelve ratios were the same between part a and part b because no average was in the formula. For those with differences, the differences appear to be immaterial between part a and part b. It should be noted that one less year could be computed when an average was required.

CASES

CASE 6-1 LIFO-FIFO

(This case provides an opportunity to compare LIFO and FIFO.)

a. Working Capital = Current Assets - Current Liabilities

    ($154,600,000) = $703,200,000 - $548,600,000

b. The LIFO reserve account is the amount needed to reduce the FIFO cost inventory to a LIFO cost inventory. The balance at the end of 1998 was $10,800,000.

c. Inventory $ 356,200,000
    LIFO Reserve   10,800,000
                        $ 367,000,000

    The inventory amount with the LIFO Reserve added back would be more realistic.

d. (1) Price increases:

        LIFO results in lower income

    (2) Price decreases:

        LIFO results in higher income

    (3) Constant Cost:

        If prices remain constant, then the same profit will result with both LIFO and FIFO.

e. (1) Price Increases:

        (a) Pre-Tax Cash Flows:

            No difference in cash flow

        (b) After-Tax Cash Flows:

            Because of the lower income under LIFO, there will be less tax. This will result in higher cash flow.

(2) Price Decreases:

    (a) Pre-Tax Cash Flows:

        No difference in cash flow

    (b) After-Tax Cash Flows:

        Because of the higher income under LIFO, there will be more tax under LIFO.

(3) Constant cost:

    (a) Pre-Tax Cash Flows:

        No difference in cash flow

    (b) After-Tax Cash Flows:

        There will be no difference in cash flow because the tax will be the same.

f. Using LIFO, the purchase on the last day of the year would be included in cost of goods sold, thus influencing the income statement.

CASE 6-2   RISING PRICES, A TIME TO SWITCH OFF LIFO?

(This case helps demonstrate that the individual investor must read comments from the company in a critical manner. The reasons given for a change in accounting principle may not appear to be the reasons stated when the data are analyzed critically.)

a. Matching current costs against current revenue is usually considered to result in more realistic earnings, just the opposite of the claim of the anonymous corporation.

b. Taxes on past earnings of $6,150,000 will need to be paid if the company switches from LIFO. The corporation will seek permission to pay these taxes over a ten-year period.

Taxes in the future will be higher because of the increased profits resulting from the switch from LIFO.

c. This year's profits will be higher because of the lower cost of goods sold.

d. Future profits will be higher because of the matching of older costs against current revenue.

e. This year's cash flow will be lower to the extent that there are higher taxes paid.

f. Future cash flow will be lower by the amount of the increase in taxes.

g. The profit picture has declined; it appears that the corporation wants to report higher profits. It will be able to achieve higher profits because of the switch from LIFO.

The results will probably not be worth the price of higher taxes and, therefore, reduced cash flow.

CASE 6-3 ONLINE

(This case provides an opportunity to review the liquidity of a rapidly growing company. Notice that this firm does not have inventory.)

a. 1. days' sales in receivables

1998

$$\frac{\$104 + \$19}{\$2,600 / 365} = 17.27 \text{ Days}$$

1997

$$\frac{\$65 + \$6}{\$1,685 / 365} = 15.38 \text{ Days}$$

2. accounts receivable turnover

1998

$$\frac{\$2,600}{\$104 + \$19} = 21.14 \text{ Times}$$

1997

$$\frac{\$1,685}{\$65 + \$6} = 23.73 \text{ Times}$$

3. days' sales in inventory

(no inventory

4. inventory turnover

(no inventory

5. working capital

1998	1997
$930	$ 323
(894)	(553)
$ 36	($230)

6. Current ratio

1998 1997

$$\frac{\$930}{\$894} = 1.04$$

$$\frac{\$323}{\$553} = .58$$

b.

America Online
Vertical Common-Size
Balance Sheet (In Part)

	(In Percentage) June 30*	
	1998	1997
Assets		
Current assets:		
Cash and cash equivalents	28.5	14.9
Trade accounts receivable	4.7	7.8
Other receivables	4.2	3.1
Prepaid expenses and other current assets	4.7	13.0
Total current assets	42.0	38.8
Property and equipment at cost, net	16.4	28.0
Other assets (detail omitted)	41.6	33.3
	100.0	100.0
Liabilities and Stockholders' Equity		
Current liabilities:		
Trade accounts payable	3.9	8.2
Other accrued expenses and liabilities	20.0	35.9
Deferred revenue	10.9	19.9
Accrued personnel costs	2.1	2.4
Deferred network services credit	3.4	–
Total current liabilities	40.4	66.4
Long-term liabilities (detail omitted)	32.6	16.8
Total liabilities	73.0	83.2
Stockholders' equity: (detail omitted)	27.0	16.8
	100.0	100.0

*Rounded

c.   1. Days' sales in receivables

Both years have very low days' sales in receivables.
This is apparently the result of prepaid subscriptions.

The trend was not favorable. This could be misleading
because of the apparent acquisition of one or more
companies using the purchase method to record.

2. Accounts receivable turnover

Similar results as for days' sales in receivables.

Very good turnover.

3. Days' sales in inventory

No inventory

This would be positive as to liquidity.

4. Inventory turnover

No inventory

This would be positive as to liquidity.

5. Working Capital

From a negative $230,000,000 in 1997 to a positive
$36,000,000 in 1998. This was very positive.

6. Current ratio

Since this company does not have inventory and the
receivable ratios are very good an adequate current
ratio would likely be less than 1.00.
      The current ratio substantially improved from .58
to 1.04.

d.   Vertical Common-Size

    Total current assets improved from 38.8% to 42.0%. The
    substantial improvement was in the most liquid asset, cash
    and cash equivalents.
        Total current liabilities improved declining from
    66.4% to 40.4%. Major improvements in trade accounts
    payable, other accrued expenses and liabilities, and
    deferred revenue.

  d. Apparent total liquidity is excellent. From a
     profitability view liquidity can be too good as liquidity
     does not produce good profits.

CASE 6-4   THE OTHER SIDE OF LIFO

The Significance of LIFO Liquidation

(This case provides a forum to discuss the effects of LIFO
liquidation. The basis of this case is an article that appeared
in the Professional Notes section of the Journal of Accountancy,
May 1983, pages 120-121.)

a.   The use of historical cost for inventory can result in
      distorted profits because the costs matched against revenue
      are not based upon the cost to replace the inventory. For a
      going concern, the inventory typically will be replaced.

      LIFO usually does the best job of matching inventory cost
      against revenue. But since LIFO does not provide for
      replacement costs, a distorted profit picture exists even
      when LIFO is used. When the inventory is reduced, the use
      of LIFO can result in a material distortion of profit,
      since old inventory costs become cost of sales.

b.   The steel industry saw the strike as a temporary event.
      Since the industry was using LIFO inventory, a reduction in
      the inventory would trigger old cost to be matched against
      revenue. Assuming the cost of production had increased over
      the years, the old cost would be lower than current
      production costs.

      If inventories would have been reduced, then profits would
      have been high during the strike period, resulting in high
      taxes. When the strike was over, the inventory would have
      to be replaced. The taxes and the replacement of the
      inventory would cause a drain on cash flow.

c. (1) Profits - Profits would be distorted on the high side because of the matching of old cost against the revenue. In some cases, this would be a reduction in a loss to a firm.

    (2) Taxes paid - The distorted profits on the high side would result in higher taxes being paid if the firm is profitable. If the firm has an overall loss, the loss would be reduced, which could reduce a possible tax refund from a loss carryback.

    (3) Cash flow - Cash flow would be reduced because of the effect on taxes explained in (2). Cash flow would also be reduced if the inventory is replenished at a later date.

d. The reduction in inventories brought out old cost against current revenue. This resulted in distorted profits on the high side. Thus, the quality of earnings was low.

e. The case indicates that the major reasons inventory was voluntarily reduced during 1980 and 1981 were as follows:

    (1) "Decreased expected demand associated with a recessionary economy."

        This would mean that the reduced demand was not anticipated to be temporary. In some cases, the demand may never return for the product.

    (2) "High interest rates resulting in high inventory carrying costs. These high rates also present alternative economic opportunities for funds invested in inventories if there is a belief that the inflation rate will decrease in relation to interest rates."

        In general, this statement indicates that the high interest rates made it desirable to turn the inventory into cash so that a high interest rate could be earned on the funds or the firm could avoid paying a high interest rate on needed funds.

    (3) "A sluggish economy that could lead management to minimize losses or improve reported profit."

In general, this statement is indicating that management could prop up earnings by reducing inventories and reporting the resulting high profit.

CASE 6-5   NETWORK SUPREME

(This case provides an opportunity to review the liquidity of a firm that stalled as far as revenue growth. Notice that the firm has immaterial inventory.)

a.   1.   Days' Sales in Receivables

<u>1998</u>

$$\frac{\$246,577 \; + \; \$47,921}{\$1,083,877 \; / \; 365} \; =$$

99.17 Days

<u>1997</u>

$$\frac{\$211,531 \; + \; \$33,053}{\$1,007,311 \; / \; 365} \; =$$

88.63 Days

2.   Accounts Receivable Turnover

<u>1998</u>

$$\frac{\$1,083,887}{\$246,577 \; + \; \$47,921} \; =$$

3.68 Times

<u>1997</u>

$$\frac{\$1,007,311}{\$211,531 \; + \; \$33,053} \; =$$

4.12 Times

3.   Days' Sales in Inventory

$$\frac{\$3,562}{\$238,649 \; / \; 365} \; =$$

5.45 Days

$$\frac{\$10,656}{\$277,446 \; / \; 365} \; =$$

14.02 Days

4.   Inventory Turnover

<u>1998</u>

$$\frac{\$238,649}{\$3,562} \; =$$

67.00 Times

<u>1997</u>

$$\frac{\$277,446}{\$10,656} \; =$$

26.04 Times

5. Working Capital

1998	1997
$1,435,700,000	$1,470,382,000
(414,695,000)	(321,956,000)
$1,021,016,000	$1,148,426,000

6. Current Ratio

1998

$$\frac{\$1,435,700,000}{\$414,695,000} = 3.46$$

1997

$$\frac{\$1,470,382,000}{\$321,956,000} = 4.57$$

7. Acid Test Ratio

1998

$$\frac{\$1,007,167 + \$246,577}{\$414,695} =$$

1997

$$\frac{\$1,033,473 + \$211,531}{\$321,956} =$$

3.02

3.87

b.
Novell
Vertical Common-Size
Balance Sheets

	(In Percentage October 31	
	1998	1997
ASSETS		
Current assets:		
Cash and short-term investments	53.34%	54.09%
Receivables, less allowances	12.82	11.07
Inventories	.19	.56
Prepaid expenses	3.28	3.02
Deferred and refundable income taxes	4.96	7.02
Other current assets	1.03	1.19
Total current assets	74.62	76.96
Property, plant, and equipment, net	18.00	19.57
Long-term investments	5.97	1.00
Other assets	1.42	2.48
Total assets	100.00	100.00
LIABILITIES AND SHAREHOLDERS' EQUITY		
Current liabilities:		
Accounts payable	4.05	4.33
Accrued compensation	2.72	2.69
Accrued marketing liabilities	.85	1.45
Other accrued liabilities	3.23	4.46
Income taxes payable	3.33	–
Deferred revenue	7.37	3.92
Total current liabilities	21.55	16.85
Minority interests	.83	1.22
Shareholders' equity (detail omitted)	77.63	81.93
Total liabilities and shareholder's equity	100.00	100.00

c. 1. Days' Sales in Receivables

There appears to be a major problem with the collection
of receivables and the problem appears to be getting
worse.

2. Accounts Receivable Turnover

There appears to be a major problem with the turnover of
accounts receivable and the problem appears to be
getting worse.

3. Days' Sales in Inventory

    Very few days' sales in inventory and the number of days declined substantially. A substantial decline in inventory.
    Apparently with this being a software network company inventory is not substantial. What appears to be a very positive situation may not be. There apparently is a problem with demand.

4. Inventory Turnover

    Inventory turnover was very good in 1997 and substantially improved in 1998. This appears to be very positive, but there appears to be a problem with demand.

5. Working Capital

    Working capital declined substantially in 1998. This would normally appear to be negative.
    This company appears to have too much in working capital. Working capital is over $1 billion in a company with total assets less than $2 billion.

6. Current Ratio

    The current ratio declined substantially in 1998. This would normally appear to be negative, but this company has more than adequate liquidity.

7. Acid Test Ratio

    The acid test ratio declined substantially in 1998. This would normally appear to be negative, but this company has more than adequate liquidity.

d. Vertical Common-Size

    Over half of the assets are in cash and short-term investments. This is much more liquidity than required for an efficient operation.
    Apparently there is a problem with what to do with the substantial liquidity. Substantial amounts have been used for long-term investments and repurchases of common stock. Neither of these uses grow the company from an operating perspective.

e.   The company has substantial more liquidity than needed for
     an efficient operation. At the same time there appears to
     be a problem with the liquidity of receivables.

CASE 6-6   BOOMING RETAIL

(The data for this case relate to W.T. Grant for the years ended
January 3, 1966 - 1970. This relatively short case provides
insight into why W.T. Grant went bankrupt.)

a.

	Year				
	5	4	3	2	1
Sales	136.2%	131.5%	119.0%	106.4%	100.0%
Net accounts receivable	182.2%	159.8%	135.7%	118.2%	100.0%

b.
$$\frac{\text{Accounts Receivable}}{\text{Turnover}} = \frac{\text{Net Sales}}{\text{Average Gross Receivables}}$$

Year 5: $\dfrac{\$1,254,131}{(\$419,731 + \$368,267) / 2} = \dfrac{\$1,254,131}{\$393,999} = 3.18$ times per year

Year 4: $\dfrac{\$1,210,918}{(\$368,267 + \$312,776) / 2} = \dfrac{\$1,210,918}{\$340,521} = 3.56$ times per year

Year 3: $\dfrac{\$1,096,152}{(\$312,776 + \$272,450) / 2} = \dfrac{\$1,096,152}{\$292,613} = 3.75$ times per year

Year 2: $\dfrac{\$979,458}{(\$272,450 + \$230,427) / 2} = \dfrac{\$979,458}{\$251,438} = 3.90$ times per year

c.   Yes. With installment sales, the period to pay is
     relatively long. Thus, it is important that the firms
     have good credit controls.

d.   It appears that the Grand has a problem with credit
     controls and subsequent collection of the receivables.
     Net accounts receivable has been increasing much faster
     than sales. This could result in substantial write-offs
     of receivables and recognition of losses.

Chapter 7
Long-Term Debt-Paying Ability

QUESTIONS

7- 1. Yes, profitability is important to a firm's long-term debt-paying ability. Although the reported income does not agree with cash available in the short run, eventually the revenue and expense items do result in cash movements. Because there is a close relationship between the reported income and the ability of the entity to meet its long-run obligations, the major emphasis when determining the long-term debt-paying ability is on the profitability of the entity.

7- 2. (1) Income statement.

(2) Balance sheet.

The income statement approach is important because in the long run, there is usually a relationship between the reported income that is the result of accrual accounting and the ability of the firm to meet its long-term obligations. The balance sheet indicates the amount of funds provided by outsiders in relation to those provided by owners of the firm. If a high proportion of the resources have been provided by outsiders, then this indicates that the risks of the business have been shifted to outsiders.

7- 3. A relatively high, stable coverage of interest over the years is desirable. A relatively low, fluctuating coverage of interest over the years is not desirable.

7- 4. No. The auto manufacturing business is known for its cyclical nature. The times interest expense, therefore, would fluctuate materially. We would expect the auto manufacturer to finance a relatively small proportion of its long-term funds from debt.

7- 5. A telephone company has its rate of return and, therefore, profits controlled by public utility commissions. We would expect the times interest earned to be moderate and relatively stable, which should be a relatively favorable times interest earned ratio. This stability allows for carrying a high portion of debt financing.

7- 6. A firm must pay for the interest capitalized; therefore, this interest should be included along with interest expense in order to obtain total interest.

7- 7.   To get a better indication of a firm's ability to cover
        interest payments in the short run, the non-cash charges for
        depreciation, depletion, and amortization can be added back to
        the times interest earned numerator. The resulting income can
        be related to interest earned on a cash basis for a short-run
        indication of the firm's ability to cover interest.

7- 8.   The financial statements are predominately prepared based upon
        historical cost. Seldom is the market value or liquidation
        value disclosed.

7- 9.   No, the determination of the current value of the long-term
        assets is very subjective. The best that can be achieved is a
        reasonable relationship of long-term assets to long-term debt,
        based on historical cost or estimates of current value.

7-10.   The intent of this ratio is to indicate the percentage of the
        assets that were financed by creditors. The ratio should
        indicate a reasonably accurate picture of how the assets were
        financed, but it will not be precise because all of the
        liabilities have been included, while the assets are at book
        value, which may be less than or more than their liquidation
        value.

7-11.   No, the debt ratio would not be as high as the debt/equity
        ratio because the debt ratio relates total liabilities to total
        assets, while the debt/equity ratio relates total liabilities
        to shareholders' equity. The total asset figure is equal to
        both the liabilities and the shareholders' equity.

7-12.   The balance sheet equation has assets = liabilities +
        shareholders' equity. Given any set of figures that agree with
        the basic balance sheet equation, the liabilities are the same,
        whether they are related to assets or shareholders' equity.

        For example, assets ($100,000) = liabilities ($40,000) +
        shareholders' equity ($60,000).

$$\text{Debt Ratio} = \frac{\$\,40,000}{\$100,000} = 40\%$$

$$\text{Debt/Equity Ratio} = \frac{\$40,000}{\$60,000} = 66\,\tfrac{2}{3}\%$$

7-13. Industry averages tend to indicate the degree of debt that is considered to be acceptable for an industry. The industry average does not necessarily indicate the degree of debt that an individual firm should have, but it is the best indication of a reasonable amount outside of the individual firm.

7-14. Operating leases simply require recording rent expense in the income statement accounts. Under a capital lease, the asset and related lease obligations are recorded on the balance sheet of the lessee. The lessee then records depreciation expense and interest expense as would be done if the asset had been acquired with a loan.

7-15. If a firm has not capitalized, its leases, then its debt ratios will be lower than those of a firm that has capitalized leases. Also, its times interest earned will be higher. These two factors overstate the debt position.

7-16. If leases are capitalized, then more interest expense must be covered. This causes a decline in times interest earned.

7-17. Pension claims have the status of tax liens, which gives them senior claim over other creditors.

7-18. When an employee is vested in the pension plan, she/he is eligible to receive some pension benefits at retirement regardless of whether they continue working for the employer. ERISA has had a major impact on reducing the vesting time.

7-19. Under the Employee Retirement Income Security Act, a contributor to a multiemployer pension plan may be liable, upon withdrawal from or upon termination of such plan, for its share of any unfunded liability.

7-20. An operating lease for a relatively long term is a type of long-term financing. Therefore, a part of the lease payment, in reality, is a financing charge called interest. When a portion of operating lease payments is included in fixed charges, it is an effort to recognize the true total interest that the firm is paying.

7-21. The Employee Retirement Income Security Act contains a feature that a company can be liable for its pension plan up to 30% of its net worth. Also, the pension claims have the same status as tax liens, which gives them senior claim over other creditors.

7-22. Short-term funds in total become part of the total sources of outside funds in the long run. Thus, short-term funds should be included in the debt ratio. Another view is that the debt ratio is intended to relate long-term outside sources of funds to total assets, and short-term funds are not a valid part of long-term funds. The approach that includes short-term liabilities is the more conservative.

7-23. The bond payable account would represent a definite commitment that must be paid at some date in the future. This would be considered to be a "firm" liability. The reserve for rebuilding furnaces does not represent a "firm" commitment to pay out funds in the future, and when funds are used for rebuilding furnaces, this will be at the discretion of management. The reserve for rebuilding furnaces could be considered to be a "soft" liability account.

7-24. The specific assets that caused the deferred tax will likely be replaced by similar specific assets in the future and also the firm may expand. The replacement assets are likely to cost more than the original items. This would result in an additional deferred tax. This is the total firm view of deferred taxes and this view indicates that the deferred tax amount may not result in actual cash outlays in the future. In any specific year, there may be a cash outlay because the firm may not have acquired sufficient assets in that year in relation to the assets being expensed.

7-25. This tentatively indicates that this firm has higher risk in terms of paying commitments than it did in prior periods and in relation to competitors and the industry.

7-26. This would indicate an increase in risk as management will more frequently be faced with debt coming due. It also indicates that short-term debt is becoming a more permanent part of the financial structure of the firm.

7-27. This statement would be correct. A footnote will disclose the guaranteed bank loan. The overall potential debt position will not be obvious from the face of the balance sheet.

7-28. True. Significant potential liabilities may be described in the contingency footnote. If a contingency loss meets one, but not both, of the criteria for recording, and as a result is not accrued, disclosure by footnote is made when it is at least reasonably possible that there has been an impairment of assets or that a liability has been incurred.

7-29. Instead of having a potential additional liability from a pension plan, the plan may be overfunded. This may present an opportunity for the company to cancel the pension plan by paying off the pension obligations and transferring the remaining money in the pension plan to the company.

7-30. Most firms must accrue or set a reserve for postretirement benefits other than pensions. Firms can usually spread the catch-up accrual costs over twenty years or take the charge in one lump sum. This choice can represent a major problem when comparing financial results of two or more firms.

7-31 Concentration of credit risk (lack of diversification) is perceived as indicative of greater credit risk. Disclosure in this area allows investors, creditors, and other users to make their own assessments of credit risk related to concentration.

7-32. Off-balance-sheet means that the risk has not been recorded. There is a potential accounting loss from these obligations that is not apparent from the face of the balance sheet.

7-33. The disclosure of the fair value of financial instruments could possibly indicate significant opportunity or additional risk to the company.

a. The Katzenberg suit is not directly addressed.
The footnote relates to the following:

"The company, together with, in some instances, certain of its
directors and officers, is a defendant or co-defendant in
various legal actions involving copyright, breach of contract
and various other claims incident to the conduct of its
businesses. Management does not expect the company to suffer
any material liability by reason of such actions, nor does it
expect that such actions will have a material effect on the
company's liquidity or operating results."

b. In the author's opinion the settlement was material in
dollars and could damage the reputation of Disney.
    Law suits pending are difficult to handle in financial
reporting.

c. In the author's opinion the disclosure is material.
The cruise ship situation is more objective and therefore
easier for accountants to handle.

2. a. Tires and inner tubes.

   b.

	1998	1997	1996
Postretirement benefits cost	$16,121,000	$14,933,000	$13,928,000
Operating revenue (net sales)	$1,876,125,000	$1,813,005,000	$1,619,345,000
Income before income taxes	$198,217,000	$194,792,000	$172,092,000
Benefit obligation	$183,017,000	$153,137,000	----
Plan assets	- 0 -	- 0 -	- 0 -
Net liability recognized	$160,550,000	$153,566,000	----
Discount rate	7.5%	8.0%	----
Expected return on plan assets	----	----	----

c. 1. Expense (cost) in relation to operating revenue

	1998	1997	1996
Expense (cost) (A)	$16,121,000	$14,933,000	$13,928,000
Operating revenue (net sales) (B)	$1,876,125,000	$1,813,005,000	$1,619,345,000
Expense/Operating Revenue (A÷B)	.86%	.82%	.86%

2. Expense (cost) in relation to income before taxes.

	1998	1997	1996
Expense (cost) (A)	$16,121,000	$14,933,000	$13,928,000
Income before income taxes (B)	$198,217,000	$194,792,000	$172,092,000
Expense (cost) in relation to income before taxes (A÷B)	8.13%	7.67%	8.09%

d. 1. Comparison of benefit obligations with the value of plan assets.

	1998	1997
Benefit obligation (A)	$183,017,000	$153,137,000
Value of plan assets (B)	– 0 –	– 0 –
Benefit obligations in excess of value of plan assets [A-B]	$183,017,000	$153,137,000

2. Net balance sheet liability (asset) recognized.

	1998	1997
Net liability recognized	$160,550,000	$153,566,000

3. Assumptions as to discount rate.

1998	1997
7.5%	8.0%

The reduction in rate increased the benefit obligations an the expense.

The reduction in rate increased the benefit obligations and the expense.

4. Assumption as to expected return on plan assets.
A rate was not used for plan assets because there were no plan assets.

e. Postretirement benefits appear to be material. This especially appears to be the case when relating expense (cost) in relation to income before taxes.

f. "The Company has reserved the right to modify or terminate such benefits at any time, subject to applicable terms and conditions contained in union agreements for non-salary participants. In recent years benefit changes have been implemented throughout the Company."

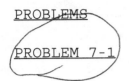

PROBLEM 7-1

$$\text{Times Interest Earned} = \frac{\text{Recurring Earnings, Excluding Interest Expense, Tax Expense, Equity Earnings, and Minority Earnings}}{\text{Interest Expense, Including Capitalized Interest}}$$

Earnings before interest and tax:

Net sales	$1,079,143
Cost of sales	(792,755)
Selling and administration	(264,566)
	$ 21,822

a.   Times Interest Earned = $\dfrac{\$21,822}{\$4,311}$ = 5.06 times per year

b.   Cash basis times interest earned:

$$\frac{\$21,822 + \$40,000}{\$4,311} = \frac{\$61,822}{\$4,311} = 14.34 \text{ times per year}$$

PROBLEM 7-2

$$\text{a. Times Interest Earned} = \frac{\text{Recurring Earnings Excluding Interest Expense, Tax Expense, Equity Earnings, and Minority Earnings}}{\text{Interest Expense, Including Capitalized Interest}}$$

Income before income taxes	$675
Plus interest	60
Adjusted income	$735
Interest expense	$ 60

$$\text{Times Interest Earned} = \frac{\$735}{\$60} = 12.25 \text{ times per year}$$

$$b. \quad \text{Fixed Charge Coverage} = \frac{\text{Recurring Earnings, Excluding Interest Expense, Tax Expense, Equity Earnings, and Minority Earnings + Interest Portion of Rentals}}{\text{Interest Expense, Including Capitalized Interest + Interest Portion Of Rentals}}$$

```
Adjusted income from (part a)          $735
1/3 of operating lease payments
   (1/3 x $150)                          50
Adjusted income, including rentals     $785


Interest expense                       $ 60
1/3 of operating lease payments          50
                                       $110
```

```
Fixed Charge Coverage = $785 = 7.14 times per year
                        $110
```

PROBLEM 7-3

$$a. \quad \text{Times Interest Earned} = \frac{\text{Recurring Earnings, Excluding Interest Expense, Tax Expense, Equity Earning, and Minority Earnings}}{\text{Interest Expense, Including Capitalized Interest}}$$

```
Income before income taxes and
   extraordinary charges               $36
Plus interest                           16
(1) Adjusted income                     52
(2) Interest expense                   $16
```

Times Interest Earned: (1) divided by (2) = 3.25 times per year

Recurring Earnings, Excluding Interest
Expense, Tax Expense, Equity Earnings,
and Minority Earnings + Interest Portion

b. Fixed Charge Coverage = Of Rentals

Interest Expense, Including Capitalized
Interest + Interest Portion Of Rentals

Adjusted income (part a) $ 52
1/3 of operating lease payments
   (1/3 x $60)   20
(1) Adjusted income, including rentals $72

Interest expense $16
1/3 of operating lease payments   20
(2) Adjusted interest expense $36

Fixed charge coverage: (1) divided by (2) = 2.00 times per year

PROBLEM 7-4

a. Debt Ratio = $\dfrac{\text{Total Liabilities}}{\text{Total Assets}} = \dfrac{\$174{,}979}{\$424{,}201} = 41.2\%$

b. Debt/Equity Ratio = $\dfrac{\text{Total Liabilities}}{\text{Stockholders' Equity}} = \dfrac{\$174{,}979}{\$249{,}222} = 70.2\%$

c. Ratio of Total Debt to Tangible Net Worth =

$\dfrac{\text{Total Liabilities}}{\text{Tangible Net Worth}} = \dfrac{\$174{,}979}{\$249{,}222 - \$2{,}324} = \dfrac{\$174{,}979}{\$246{,}898} = 70.9\%$

d. Kaufman Company has financed over 41% of its assets by the use of funds from outside creditors. The Debt/Equity Ratio and the Debt to Tangible Net Worth Ratio are over 70%. Whether these ratios are reasonable depends upon the stability of earnings.

PROBLEM 7-5

Transaction	Times Interest Earned	Debt Ratio	Debt/ Equity	Total Debt/ Tangible Net Worth
a. Purchase of buildings financed by mortgage	-	+	+	+
b. Purchase inventory on short-term loan	-	+	+	+
c. Declaration and payment of cash dividend	0	+	+	+
d. Declaration and payment of stock dividend	0	0	0	0
e. Firm increases profits by cutting cost of sales	+	-	-	-
f. Appropriation of retained earnings	0	0	0	0
g. Sale of common stock	0	-	-	-
h. Repayment of long-term bank loan	+	-	-	-
i. Conversion of bonds to common stock	+	-	-	-
j. Sale of inventory at greater than cost	+	-	-	-

PROBLEM 7-6

a. Times Interest Earned:

Times interest earned relates earnings before interest expense, tax, minority earnings, and equity income to interest expense. The higher this ratio, the better the interest coverage. The times interest earned has improved materially in strengthening the long-term debt position. Considering that the debt ratio and the debt to tangible net worth have remained fairly constant, the probable reason for the improvement is an increase in profits.

The times interest earned only indicates the interest coverage. It is limited in that it does not consider other possible fixed charges, and it does not indicate the proportion of the firms resources that have come from debt.

Debt Ratio:

The debt ratio relates the total liabilities to the total assets.

The lower this ratio, the lower the proportion of assets that have been financed by creditors.

For Arodex Company, this ratio has been steady for the past three years. This ratio indicates that about 40% of the total assets have been financed by creditors. For most firms, a 40% debt ratio would be considered to be reasonable.

The debt ratio is limited in that it relates liabilities to the book value of total assets. Many assets would have a value greater than book value. This tends to overstate the debt ratio and, therefore, usually results in a conservative ratio. The debt ratio does not consider immediate profitability and, therefore, can be misleading as to the firm's ability to handle long-term debt.

Debt to Tangible Net Worth:

The debt to tangible net worth relates total liabilities to shareholders' equity less intangible assets. The lower this ratio, the lower the proportion of tangible assets that has been financed by creditors.

Arodex Company has had a stable ratio of approximately 81% for the past three years. This indicates that creditors have financed 81% as much as the shareholders after eliminating intangibles from the shareholders contribution--for most firms, this would be considered to be reasonable. The debt to tangible net worth ratio is more conservative than the debt ratio because of the elimination of intangible items. It is also conservative for the same reason that the debt ratio was conservative, in that book value is used for the assets and many assets have a value greater than book value. The debt to tangible net worth ratio also does not consider immediate profitability and, therefore, can be misleading as to the firm's ability to handle long-term debt.

Collective inferences one may draw from the ratios of Arodex, Company:

Overall it appears that Arodex Company has a reasonable and improving long-term debt position. The debt ratio and the debt to tangible net worth ratios indicate that the proportion of debt appears to be reasonable. The times interest earned appears to be reasonable and improving.

The stability of earnings and comparison with industry ratios will be important in reaching a conclusion on the long-term debt position of Arodex Company.

b. Ratios are based on past data. The future is what is important, and uncertainties of the future cannot be accurately determined by ratios based upon past data.

Ratios provide only one aspect of a firm's long-term debt-paying ability. Other information, such as information about management and products, is also important.

A comparison of this firm's ratios with ratios of other firms in the same industry would be helpful in order to decide if the ratios are reasonable.

PROBLEM 7-7

a. 1. Times Interest
      Earned
$$= \frac{\text{Recurring Earnings, Excluding Interest Expense, Tax Expense, Equity Earnings, and Minority Earnings}}{\text{Interest Expense, Including Capitalized Interest}}$$

$$\frac{\$162,000}{\$20,000} = 8.1 \text{ times per year}$$

2. Debt Ratio $= \dfrac{\text{Total Liabilities}}{\text{Total Assets}}$

$$\frac{\$193,000}{\$600,000} = 32.2\%$$

3. Debt/Equity Ratio $= \dfrac{\text{Total Liabilities}}{\text{Stockholders' Equity}}$

$$\frac{\$193,000}{\$407,000} = 47.4\%$$

4. Debt to Tangible Net Worth Ratio $= \dfrac{\text{Total Liabilities}}{\text{Tangible Net Worth}}$

$$\frac{\$193,000}{\$407,000 - \$20,000} = 49.9\%$$

b. New asset structure for all plans:

                    Assets
        Current assets $226,000
        Property, plant, and
            equipment   554,000
        Intangibles   20,000
        Total assets $800,000

Liabilities and Equity

Plan A

Current Liabilities	$ 93,000	$200,000,000/100 =
Long-term debt	100,000	2,000,000 shares
Preferred stock	250,000	
Common equity	357,000	No change in net income
	$800,000	

Plan B

Current liabilities	$ 93,000	$200,000,000/10 =
Long-term debt	100,000	20,000,000 shares
Preferred stock	50,000	
Common stock	120,000	
Premium on common stock	300,000	
Retained earnings	137,000	No change in net income
	$800,000	

Plan C

Current liabilities	$ 93,000	Operating Income	$162,000
Long-term debt	300,000	Interest expense	52,000*
Preferred stock	50,000		110,000
Common equity	357,000	Taxes (40%)	44,000
	$800,000	Net Income	$ 66,000

* $20,000 + 16% ($200,000) = $52,000

1.

$$\text{Times Interest Earned} = \frac{\text{Recurring Earnings, Excluding Interest Expense, Tax Expense, Equity Earnings, and Minority Earnings}}{\text{Interest Expense, Including Capitalized Interest}}$$

Plan A	Plan B	Plan C

$$\frac{\$162,000}{\$20,000} = 8.1 \text{ times}$$ $$\frac{\$162,000}{\$20,000} = 8.1 \text{ times}$$ $$\frac{\$162,000}{\$52,000} = 3.1 \text{ times}$$

2. $\text{Debt Ratio} = \dfrac{\text{Total Liabilities}}{\text{Total Assets}}$

Plan A	Plan B	Plan C

$$\frac{\$193,000}{\$800,000} = 24.1\%$$ $$\frac{\$193,000}{\$800,000} = 24.1\%$$ $$\frac{\$393,000}{\$800,000} = 49.1\%$$

3. $\text{Debt/Equity Ratio} = \dfrac{\text{Total Liabilities}}{\text{Stockholders' Equity}}$

Plan A	Plan B	Plan C

$$\frac{\$193,000}{\$607,000} = 31.8\%$$ $$\frac{\$193,000}{\$607,000} = 31.8\%$$ $$\frac{\$393,000}{\$407,000} = 96.6\%$$

4. $\text{Debt to Tangible Net Worth} = \dfrac{\text{Total Liabilities}}{\text{Tangible Net Worth}}$

Plan A	Plan B	Plan C

$$\frac{\$193,000}{\$607000 - \$20,000} = 32.9\%$$ $$\frac{\$193,000}{\$607,000 - \$20,000} = 32.9\%$$ $$\frac{\$393,000}{\$407,000 - \$20,000} = 101.6\%$$

c. Preferred Stock Alternative:

Advantages:
1. Lesser drop in earnings per share than under the common stock alternative.

2. Not the absolute reduction in earnings that accompanied the debt alternative.

3. There would be an improvement in the Debt Ratio, Debt/Equity Ratio, and Total Debt to Tangible Net Worth Ratio.

4. Does not have the reduced times interest earned that accompanied alternative of issuing long-term debt.

Disadvantages:
1. An increase in the fixed preferred dividend charge that the firm must pay before any dividends can be paid to common stockholders.

Common Stock Alternative:

Advantages:
1. No increase in fixed obligations.

2. There would be an improvement in the Debt Ratio, Debt/Equity Ratio, and the Total Debt to Tangible Net Worth Ratio.

3. Not the absolute reduction in earnings that accompanied the debt alternative.

4. Does not have the reduced times interest earned that accompanied alternative of issuing long-term debt.

Disadvantages:
1. Maximum dilution in earnings per share of the three alternatives.

Long-Term Bonds Alternative:

Advantages:
1. Higher earnings per share than with common stock.

Disadvantages:
1. Material decline in Times Interest Earned.

2. A material increase in the Debt Ratio, Debt/Equity Ratio, and Total Debt to Tangible Net Worth Ratio.

3. Absolute reduction in earnings.

4. Increase in the interest fixed charge that must be paid.

d. The 10% preferred stock increased the preferred dividends which are not tax deductible; therefore, the cost of these funds is the 10% amount. The 16% bonds are tax deductible and, therefore, the after-tax cost is 9.6% (16% x (1-.40).

Note to Instructor: You may want to take this opportunity to point out to the students that the alternative that should be selected is greatly influenced by the change in earnings and the specific debt structure. The conclusions in this problem would not necessarily be true with changed assumptions.

PROBLEM 7-8

a. Times Interest Earned = $\dfrac{\text{Expense, Tax Expense, Equity Earnings, and Minority Earnings}}{\text{Interest Expense Including Capitalized Interest}}$

Earnings from continuing operations before income taxes and equity earnings	(1)	$ 74,780,000
(1) Add back interest expense	(2)	37,646,000
(2) Adjusted earnings		$112,426,000

Times interest earned: [(2) divided by (1)] 2.99 times per year

b.

Earnings from continuing operations	$ 65,135,000
Plus:	
(1) Interest	37,646,000
Income taxes	37,394,000
(2) Adjusted earnings	$140,175,000

Times interest earned: [(2) divided by (1)] 3.72 times per year

c. Removing equity earnings gives a more conservative times interest earned ratio. The equity income is usually substantially more than the cash dividend received from the related investments. Therefore, the firm cannot depend on this income to cover interest payments.

PROBLEM 7-9

a. 1. Times Interest Earned = $\dfrac{\text{Recurring Earnings, Excluding Interest Expense, Tax Expense, Equity Earnings, and Minority Earnings}}{\text{Interest Expense, Including Capitalized Interest}}$

$$\frac{\$95,000}{\$10,000} = 9.5 \text{ Times} \qquad \frac{\$170,000}{\$33,000} = 5.3 \text{ Times}$$

2. Debt Ratio = $\dfrac{\text{Total Liabilities}}{\text{Shareholders' Equity}} = \dfrac{\$160,000}{\$356,000} = 44.9 \qquad \dfrac{\$575,000}{\$985,000} = 58.4\%$

3. Debt/Equity = $\dfrac{\text{Total Liabilities}}{\text{Shareholders' Equity}} = \dfrac{\$160,000}{\$196,000} = 81.6\% \qquad \dfrac{\$575,000}{\$410,000} = 140.2\%$

4. Debt to Tangible Net Worth =

$$\frac{\text{Total Liabilities}}{\text{Shareholders' Equity} - \text{Intangibles}} = \frac{\$160,000}{\$196,000 - \$11,000} = 86.5\%$$

$$\frac{\$575,000}{\$410,000 - \$20,000} = 147.4\%$$

b. No, Barker Company has a times interest earned of 5.3 times while the industry average is 7.2 times. This indicates that Barker Company has less than average coverage of its interest. Also, Barker Company has a much higher than average debt/equity, and debt to tangible net worth ratio.

c. Allen Company has a better times interest earned, debt ratio, debt/equity, and debt to tangible net worth.

PROBLEM 7-10

a. 1. Times Interest Earned =

2001: $\dfrac{\$280,000 - \$156,000}{\$17,000}$ = 7.29 times per year

2000: $\dfrac{\$302,000 - \$157,000}{\$16,000}$ = 9.06 times per year

1999: $\dfrac{\$286,000 - \$154,000}{\$15,000}$ = 8.80 times per year

1998: $$\frac{\$270,000 - \$150,000}{\$14,500} = 8.28 \text{ times per year}$$

1997: $$\frac{\$248,000 - \$147,000}{\$23,000} = 4.39 \text{ times per year}$$

2. Fixed Charge Coverage = $\dfrac{\text{Recurring Earnings, Excluding Interest, Tax Expense, Equity Earnings, and Minority Earnings + \underline{Interest Portion of Rentals}}}{\text{Interest Expense, Including Capitalized Interest + Interest Portion of Rentals}}$

2001: $$\frac{\$280,000 - \$156,000 + \$10,000}{\$17,000 + \$10,000} = 4.96 \text{ times per year}$$

2000: $$\frac{\$302,000 - \$157,000 + \$9,000}{\$16,000 + \$9,000} = 6.16 \text{ times per year}$$

1999: $$\frac{\$286,000 - \$154,000 + \$9,500}{\$15,000 + \$9,500} = 5.78 \text{ times per year}$$

1998: $$\frac{\$270,000 - \$150,000 + \$10,000}{\$14,500 + \$10,000} = 5.31 \text{ times per year}$$

1997: $$\frac{\$248,000 - \$147,000 + \$9,000}{\$23,000 + \$9,000} = 3.44 \text{ times per year}$$

3. Debt Ratio = $\dfrac{\text{Total Liabilities}}{\text{Total Assets}}$

2001: $$\frac{\$88,000 + \$170,000}{\$560,000} = 46.07\%$$

2000: $$\frac{\$89,500 + \$168,000}{\$554,000} = 46.48\%$$

1999: $$\frac{\$90,500 + \$165,000}{\$553,800} = 46.14\%$$

1998: $$\frac{\$90,000 + \$164,000}{\$548,500} = 46.31\%$$

1997: $$\frac{\$91,500 + \$262,000}{\$537,000} = 65.83\%$$

4. Debt/Equity = <u>Total Liabilities</u>

Shareholders' Equity

2001:	<u>$88,000 + $170,000</u> $302,000	= 85.43%
2000:	<u>$89,500 + $168,000</u> $296,500	= 86.85%
1999:	<u>$90,500 + $165,000</u> $298,300	= 85.65%
1998:	<u>$90,000 + $164,000</u> $294,500	= 86.25%
1997:	<u>$91,500 + $262,000</u> $183,500	= 192.64%

5. Debt to Tangible Net Worth = <u>Total Liabilities</u>
Shareholders' Equity -
Intangible Assets

2001:	<u>$88,000 + $170,000</u> $302,000 - $20,000	= 91.49%
2000:	<u>$89,500 + $168,000</u> $296,500 - $18,000	= 92.46%
1999:	<u>$90,500 + $165,000</u> $298,300 - $17,000	= 90.83%
1998:	<u>$90,000 + $164,000</u> $294,500 - $16,000	= 91.20%
1997:	<u>$91,500 + $262,000</u> $183,500 - $15,000	= 209.79%

b. Both the times interest earned and the fixed charge coverage are good. The times interest earned is substantially better than the fixed charge coverage because of the operating leases. Both of these ratios materially declined in 1996.

The debt ratio, debt/equity, and debt to tangible net worth materially improved between 1997 and 1998. During the period 1998-2001, these ratios were relatively steady and appeared to be good. The debt to tangible net worth ratio is not as good as the debt/equity ratio because of the influence of intangibles.

CASES

CASE 7-1 EXPENSING INTEREST NOW AND LATER

(This case provides an opportunity to review capitalized interest.)

a.

	1998	1997	1996
Income statement interest expense	$110,000,000	$120,000,000	$125,000,000
Capitalized interest	71,000,000	40,000,000	55,000,000
Total interest	$181,000,000	$160,000,000	$180,000,000

b. $110,000,000 (1998); $120,000,000 (1997); $125,000,000 (1996)

c. $71,000,000 (1998); $40,000,000 (1997); $55,000,000 (1996)

d. It is capitalized in fixed assets and becomes part of the depreciation expense when the fixed asset is depreciated.

e. In the period when interest is capitalized, income is increased. Income is later decreased when the asset is depreciated.

CASE 7-2 CONSIDERATION OF LEASES

(This case provides the opportunity to review the influence of operating and capital leases.)

a.1. Times Interest Earned

$$\frac{\$119,299 - \$93,438 - \$19,358}{\$555 + \$229} = \frac{\$6,503}{\$784} = 8.29 \text{ Times}$$

2. Fixed Charge Coverage

$$\frac{\$119,299 - \$93,438 - \$19,358 + 1/3 (\$596)}{\$555 + \$229 + 1/3 (\$596)} =$$

$$\frac{\$6,503 + \$198.7}{\$555 + \$229 + \$198.7} = \frac{\$6,701.7}{\$982.7} = 6.82 \text{ Times}$$

3. Debt Ratio

$$\frac{\$26,881}{\$45,384} = 59.23\%$$

4. Debt/Equity

$$\frac{\$26,881}{\$18,503} = 145.28\%$$

b. Debt ratio considering operating leases

$$\frac{\$26,881 + 2/3 \; (\$4,424)}{\$45,384 + 2/3 \; (\$4,424)} = \frac{\$29,830.32}{\$48,333.32} = 61.72\%$$

c. Debt ratio without operating leases 59.23%.
   Debt ratio considering operating leases 61.72%.
   The influence of operating leases on the debt ratio was less than 5%. Many would consider this to be immaterial.

d. The amounts would be the same at the time of the initial entry. Subsequent to the initial entry the asset is depreciated, while the liability is reduced as payments are made.

CASE 7-3   LOCKOUT

(This case provides an opportunity to review an interesting commitments and contingencies footnote of the Boston Celtics.)

The footnote must be subjectively incorporated into the analysis. This is part of the art of analysis.

To quote from the footnote:

> "Although the ultimate outcome of this matter cannot be determined at this time, any loss of games as a result of the absence of a collective bargaining agreement or the continuation of the lockout will have a material advance effect on the partnership's financial condition and its results of operations."

In the long run the lockout may be positive as aggregate salaries may be reduced .

CASE 7-4   DETERMINE THE LIABILITY

(This case provides an opportunity to review a multi-employer pension plan. Consider assigning the related case "Play It Safe". The related case indicates that pensions outside of the multi-employer plans were overfunded.)

a.

	1998	1997	1996
Contributions (A)	$119 million	$130 million	$112 million
Sales (B)	$24,484,200,000	$22,483,800,000	$17,269,000,000
Contributions/Sales (A÷B)	.49%	.58%	.65%

Contributions appear to be immaterial in relation to sales, but it should be noted that Safeway is in an industry that has relatively low profit margins.

b. The total liability cannot be determined. To quote from the case:

"Specific benefit levels are not negotiated with or known by the employer-contributors."

"Safeway participates in a number of these pension plans, and the potential obligation as a participant in these plans may be significant."

"The information required to determine the total amount of this contingent obligation, as well as the total amount of accumulated benefits and net assets of such plans, is not readily available."

CASE 7-5 PLAY IT SAFE

(This case provides an opportunity to review a pension footnote. In this case the fair value of plan assets is materially more than the benefit obligation. Consider assigning the related case "Determine the Liability". The related case indicates that significant pensions were under multi-employer plans.)

a.

	1998	1997	1996
Pension expense (A)	Net pension income	Net pension income	$800,000
Operating revenue (B)			$17,269,000,000
Pension expense/ Operating revenue (A÷B)			.005%

There was a net pension income of $18,300,000 in 1998 and $4,100,000 in 1997. The expense in 1996 was nominal in relation to operating revenue.

b.

	1998	1997	1996
Pension expense (A)	Net pension income	Net pension income	$800,000
Income before income taxes (B)			$767,600,000
Pension expense/ Income before income taxes (A÷B)			.10%

There was a net pension income of $18,300,000 in 1998 and $4,100,000 in 1997. The expense in 1996 was nominal in relation to income before income taxes.

c. Benefit obligation $1,165,700,000
   Fair value of plan assets $1,766,100,000
   Overfunded $ 600,400,000

There is significant overfunding. The overfunding has resulted in net pension income in 1997 and 1998.

d. <u>Discount rate used to determine the projected benefit obligation</u>.

	1998	1997	1996
Combined weighted average rate	6.5%	6.8%	7.4%

The discount rate was slightly low in relation to the Accounting Trends & Techniques rates cited in the chapter. A lower discount rate results in a higher benefit obligation.
    The lowering of the discount rate results in a higher benefit obligation.

Expected return on plan assets

	1998	1997	1996
United States Plans	9.0%	9.0%	9.0%
Canadian Plans	8.0%	8.0%	8.0%

The United States rate is a frequently used rate according to the Accounting Trends & Techniques cited in the chapter. The Canadian rate is a little lower than the United States. The lower rate appears reasonable.

Note that there was no change in the rate between 1996 and 1978.

Rate of compensation increase

	1998	1997	1996
United States Plans	5.0%	5.0%	5.5%
Canadian Plans	4.5%	4.5%	5.5%

The rates used were reasonable in relation to the rates cited in Accounting Trends & Techniques, as cited in the chapter.

A decrease in the rate of compensation projected would decrease the projected benefit obligation.

CASE 7-6 RETIREMENT PLANS REVISITED

(This case provides an opportunity to review the influence of pension plans.)

a. Defined contribution

b. 1. Pension expense to operating revenue.

1996	1995	1994
$3,200,000	$3,500,000	$3,700,000
$1,031,548,000	$992,106,000	$869,975,000
.31%	.35%	.43%

2. <u>Pension expense to income before income taxes</u>.

	1996	1995	1994
Pension expense (A)	$3,200,000	$3,500,000	$3,700,000
Income before			
income taxes (B)	$50,925,000	$59,663,000	$69,870,000
[A÷B]	6.28%	5.87%	5.30%

Opinion: The pension costs do not appear to be material in relation to operating revenue. Pension costs would possibly be considered to be material in relation to income before income taxes.

c. "The company has a retirement plan which covers most regular employees and provides for annual contributions at the discretion of the board of directors."

The board appears to be exercising its discretion, since pension expense has declined in 1995 and 1996.

CASE 7-7 FAIR VALUE OF FINANCIAL INSTRUMENTS

(This case provides an opportunity to review fair value of financial instruments.)

	1995 Carrying Amount	Fair Value
	$ in thousands	
<u>Assets</u>	$545,197	$549,588
Fair value in excess		
of carrying value		$4,391
<u>Liabilities</u>	$59,757	$60,929
Fair value in excess of		
carrying value		$1,172
<u>Off-balance-sheet</u>		
<u>financial instruments</u>	-0-	(577)

The difference between carrying amount and fair value of financial instruments is immaterial in relation to total assets and earnings before taxes.

Chapter 8
Profitability

<u>QUESTIONS</u>

8- 1.   Profits can be compared to the sales from which they are the residual. They can be compared to the assets that generate sales. Or, they can be viewed as return to the owner. Each measure looks at profits differently. The trends might move in different directions, depending on the base.

8- 2.   Extraordinary items are by nature nonrecurring. They should be segregated in order to concentrate on profit that will be expected again the next period. Recurring earnings should be used in trend analysis of profitability.

8- 3.   Expenses as a percent of sales must have increased if profits as a percent of sales declined.

8- 4.   Profit margin in jewelry is usually much higher than in groceries. Groceries generate total profits based on volume of sales rather than high markup.

8- 5.   A drop in profits or a rise in the asset base could cause a decline in the ratio. For example, higher cost of sales could cause a decline; or, a substantial investment in fixed assets that are not yet fully utilized could cause a decline.

8- 6.   DuPont analysis relates return on assets to turnover and margin. It allows for further analysis of return on assets by this breakdown.

8- 7.   Operating income is sales minus cost of sales and operating expenses. It does not include nonoperating items, such as other income, interest, and taxes. Operating assets are basically current assets plus plant, property, and equipment. They do not include investments, intangibles, and other assets.

        Removing nonoperating items from the DuPont analysis gives a clearer picture of productive operations.

8- 8.   Equity earnings are the owner's proportionate share of the nonconsolidated subsidiary income. Cash is generated only to the extent that dividends are declared and paid. Equity earnings distort the profitability picture because they don't provide funds if not matched by dividends.

8- 9.   Return on assets is a function of net profit margin and
        total asset turnover. Return on assets could decline,
        given an increase in net profit margin, if the total asset
        turnover declined sufficiently.

8-10.   Return on investment measures return to all long-term
        suppliers of funds. It includes net income plus
        tax-adjusted interest in the numerator and all long-term
        funds in the denominator. Return on total equity is just
        return to shareholders.

        Return on common equity is return only to common
        shareholders. Net income is reduced by preferred dividends
        in the numerator, and only common equity is in the
        denominator.

8-11.   Return on investment is a profitability measure comparing
        income to capital utilized by the firm. Some measures are
        return on assets, return on equity, or income available to
        all capital sources, divided by capital. The given ratio
        is preferred, since it measures the profit available to
        all long-term sources of capital against that capital. The
        interest is multiplied by the tax adjustment factor to put
        interest on an after-tax basis.

8-12.   This cannot be determined based only upon the absolute
        measures. It is necessary to compare these dollar figures
        to a base, such as investment or sales. Also, it is
        necessary to know if nonrecurring items are part of the
        firm's income picture.

8-13.   Interim reports are less reliable because they are not
        audited, but they can be very meaningful in indicating
        trends before the end of the year.

8-14.   An objective of this opinion is timeliness rather than
        completeness. Full statements would take too long and
        involve too much cost to produce.

8-15.   Comprehensive income includes net changes in (a) foreign
        currency translation adjustments, (b) unrealized holding
        gains and losses on available-for-sale marketable
        securities, and (c) changes to stockholders equity
        resulting from additional minimum pension liability
        adjustment.

TO THE NET

1. This problem calls for a general review of a site to better your understanding of financials.

2. a.   Retail - grocery stores

   b.

	1998	1997	1996
	(In millions)		
Recurring earnings	$806.7	$621.5	$460.6

   c.

	1998	1997	1996
	(In millions)		
Net income	$806.7	$557.4	$460.6

   d. Recurring earnings
      Recurring earnings will provide a better base to project the future.

PROBLEMS

PROBLEM 8-1

$$\text{Net Profit Margin} = \frac{\text{Net Income Before Minority Share Of Earnings And Nonrecurring Items}}{\text{Net Sales}}$$

	2001	2000
	$\dfrac{\$52,500}{\$1,050,000}$	$\dfrac{\$40,000}{\$1,000,000}$
	5.00%	4.00%

$$\text{Return On Assets} = \frac{\text{Net Income Before Minority Share Of Earnings And Nonrecurring Items}}{\text{Average Total Assets}}$$

	2001	2000
	$\dfrac{\$52,500}{\$230,000}$	$\dfrac{\$40,000}{\$200,000}$
	22.83%	20.00%

$$\frac{\text{Total Asset}}{\text{Turnover}} = \frac{\text{Net Sales}}{\text{Average Total Assets}}$$

	2001	2000
	$\dfrac{\$1,050,000}{\$230,000}$	$\dfrac{\$1,000,000}{\$200,000}$
	4.57 times per year	5.00 times per year

$$= \text{Return on Common Equity} \frac{\text{Net Income Before Nonrecurring Items Minus Preferred Dividends}}{\text{Average Common Equity}}$$

	2001	2000
	$\dfrac{\$52,500}{\$170,000}$	$\dfrac{\$40,000}{\$160,000}$
	30.88%	25.00%

Ahl Enterprise has had a substantial rise in profit to sales. This is somewhat tempered by a reduction in asset turnover. Given a slight rise in common equity, there is a substantial rise in return on common equity.

PROBLEM 8-2

		2001	2000
a.	Sales	100.0%	100.0%
	Cost of goods sold	60.7	60.8
	Gross profit	39.3	39.2
	Selling expense	14.6	20.0
	General expense	10.0	8.3
	Operating income	14.7	10.9
	Income tax	5.9	4.2
	Net income	8.8%	6.7%

b. Starr Canning has had a sharp decrease in selling expense coupled with only a modest rise in general expenses giving an overall rise in the net profit margin.

PROBLEM 8-3

Earnings before interest and tax	$245,000
Interest (750,000 x 6%)	45,000
Earnings before tax	$200,000
Tax	80,000
Net income	$120,000
Preferred dividends	15,000
Income available to common	$105,000

a. $\text{Return on Assets} = \dfrac{\text{Net Income Before Minority Share of Earnings and Nonrecurring Items}}{\text{Average Total Assets}} = \dfrac{\$120,000}{\$3,000,000} = 4.00\%$

b. $\text{Return on Total Equity} = \dfrac{\text{Net Income Before Nonrecurring Items - Dividends on Redeemable Preferred Stock}}{\text{Average Total Equity}} = \dfrac{\$120,000}{\$3,000,000} = 4.00\%$

c. $\dfrac{\text{Return on}}{\text{Common Equity}} = \dfrac{\text{Net Income Before Nonrecurring Items - Preferred Dividends}}{\text{Average Common Equity}}$

$$\dfrac{\$200,000 - \$80,000 - \$15,000}{\$1,500,000} = 7.00\%$$

d. $\text{Times Interest Earned} = \dfrac{\text{Recurring Earnings, Excluding Interest Expense, Tax Expense, Equity Earnings, and Minority Earnings}}{\text{Interest Expense, Including Capitalized Interest}} = \dfrac{\$245,000}{\$45,000}$

$$= 5.44 \text{ times}$$
$$\text{per year}$$

PROBLEM 8-4

	Vent Molded Plastics	Plastics Industry
Sales	101.0%	100.3%
Sales returns	1.0	.3
Cost of goods sold	72.1	67.1
Selling expense	9.4	10.1
General expense	7.0	7.9
Other income	.4	.4
Other expense	1.5	1.3
Income tax	4.8	5.5
Net income	5.6%	8.5%

Sales returns are higher than the industry's. Cost of sales is much higher, offset some by lower operating expenses. Other expense (perhaps interest) is somewhat higher. Lower taxes are perhaps caused by lower income. Overall profit is less, primarily due to cost of sales.

PROBLEM 8-5

a. $\dfrac{\$1,589,150}{\$1,294,966} = 122.72\%$

2001 sales were 122.72% of those in 2000.

b. $\dfrac{\$138,204}{\$137,110} = 100.80\%$

2001 net earnings were 100.80% of those in 2000.

c. 1.

$$\text{Net Profit Margin} = \frac{\text{Net Profit Before Minority Share Of Earnings And Nonrecurring Items}}{\text{Net Sales}}$$

2001

$$\frac{\$149,260}{\$1,589,150} = 9.39\%$$

2000

$$\frac{\$149,760}{\$1,294,966} = 11.56\%$$

2.

$$\text{Return on Assets} = \frac{\text{Net Income Before Minority Share Of Earnings And Nonrecurring Items}}{\text{Average Total Assets}}$$

2001

$$\frac{\$149,260}{\$1,437,636} = 10.38\%$$

2000

$$\frac{\$149,760}{\$1,182,110} = 12.67\%$$

3. Total Asset Turnover = $\dfrac{\text{Net Sales}}{\text{Average Total Assets}}$

2001	2000
$\dfrac{\$1,589,150}{\$1,437,636}$	$\dfrac{\$1,294,966}{\$1,182,110}$
1.11 times per year	1.10 times per year

4. DuPont Analysis:

	Return On Assets		Net Profit Margin		Total Asset Turnover
2001	10.42*	=	9.39%	x	1.11
2000	12.72*	=	11.50%	x	1.10

*Rounding causes the difference from the 10.38% and 12.67% computed in part 2.

	2001	2000
5. Operating income		
Net sales	$1,589,150	$1,294,966
Less: Cost of products sold	651,390	466,250
Research and development expenses	135,314	113,100
General and selling	526,680	446,110
Operating income	$ 275,766	$ 269,506

Operating Income Margin = $\dfrac{\text{Operating Income}}{\text{Net Sales}}$

2001	2000
$\dfrac{\$275,766}{\$1,589,150}$	$\dfrac{\$269,506}{\$1,294,966}$
= 17.35%	= 20.81%

6. Return on Operating Assets = $\dfrac{\text{Operating Income}}{\text{Average Operating Assets}}$

2001	2000
$\dfrac{\$275,766}{\$1,411,686}$	$\dfrac{\$269,506}{\$1,159,666}$
= 19.53%	= 23.24%

7. Operating Asset Turnover = $\dfrac{\text{Net Sales}}{\text{Average Operating Assets}}$

2001	2000
$\dfrac{\$1,589,150}{\$1,411,686}$	$\dfrac{\$1,294,966}{\$1,159,666}$
= 1.13 times per year	= 1.12 times per year

8. DuPont Analysis With Operating Ratios

	Return On Operating Assets		Operating Income Margin		Operating Asset Turnover
2001	19.61%*	=	17.35%	x	1.13
2000	23.31%*	=	20.81%	x	1.12

*Rounding causes the difference from the 19.53% and 23.24% computed in part 6.

9. Return On Investment

	2001	2000
Net earnings before minority share	$149,260	$149,760
Interest expense	18,768	11,522
Earnings before tax	263,762	271,500
Provision for income tax	114,502	121,740
Tax rate	43.4%	44.8%
1 - tax rate	56.6%	55.2%
(interest expense) x (1 - tax rate)	10,623	6,360
Net earnings before minority share + (interest expense) x (1 - tax rate)	159,883	156,120
Long-term debt + equity	1,019,420	933,232
Return On Investment	15.7%	16.7%

10. Return On Common Equity = $\dfrac{\text{Net Sales}}{\text{Average Operating Assets}}$

2001	2000
$\dfrac{\$138,204}{\$810,292}$	$\dfrac{\$137,110}{\$720,530}$
= 17.06%	= 19.03%

d. Profits in relation to sales, assets, and equity have all declined. Turnover has remained stable. Overall, although absolute profits have increased in 2001, compared with 2000, the profitability ratios show a decline.

PROBLEM 8-6

a.   1. Net Profit Margin = $\dfrac{\text{Net Income Before Minority Share Of Earnings And Nonrecurring Items}}{\text{Net sales}}$

2001	2000	1999
$\dfrac{\$\ \ \ 97,051}{\$1,600,000}$	$\dfrac{\$\ \ \ 51,419}{\$1,300,000}$	$\dfrac{\$\ \ \ 45,101}{\$1,200,000}$
= 6.07%	= 3.96%	= 3.76%

2. Return on Assets = $\dfrac{\text{Net Income Before Minority Share Of Earnings And Nonrecurring Items}}{\text{Average total assets}}$

2001	2000	1999
$\dfrac{\$\ \ \ 97,051}{\$1,440,600}$	$\dfrac{\$\ \ \ 51,419}{\$1,220,000}$	$\dfrac{\$\ \ \ 45,101}{\$1,180,000}$
= 6.74%	= 4.21%	= 3.82%

3. Total Asset Turnover = $\dfrac{\text{Net Sales}}{\text{Average Total Assets}}$

2001	2000	1999
$\dfrac{\$1,600,000}{\$1,440,600}$	$\dfrac{\$1,300,000}{\$1,220,000}$	$\dfrac{\$1,200,000}{\$1,180,000}$
= 1.11 times per year	= 1.07 times per year	= 1.02 times per year

4. DuPont Analysis

Return On Assets	=	Net Profit Margin	x	Total Asset Turnover
2001: 6.74%	=	6.07%	x	1.11 times
2000: 4.24%	=	3.96%*	x	1.07 times
1999: 3.84%	=	3.76%*	x	1.02 times

*Rounding difference from the 4.21% and 3.82% computed in 2.

5. Operating Income Margin $= \dfrac{\text{Operating Income}}{\text{Net Sales}}$

	2001	2000	1999
(2) Net sales	$1,600,000	$1,300,000	$1,200,000
Less:			
Material and manufacturing costs of products sold	740,000	624,000	576,000
Research and development	90,000	78,000	71,400
General and selling	600,000	500,500	465,000
	1,430,000	1,202,500	1,112,400
(1) Operating income	170,000	97,500	87,600
(1) dividend by (20	10.63%	7.50%	7.30%

6. Return On Operating Assets $= \dfrac{\text{Operating Income}}{\text{Average Operating Assets}}$

	2001	2000	1999
Operating Income	$ 170,000	$ 97,500	$ 87,600
Average Operating Assets	$1,390,200	$1,160,000	$1,090,000

7. Operating Asset Turnover $= \dfrac{\text{Net Sales}}{\text{Average Operating Assets}}$

	2001	2000	1999
Net Sales	$1,600,000	$1,300,000	$1,200,000
Average Operating Assets	$1,390,200	$1,160,000	$1,090,000

8. DuPont Analysis with operating ratios

Return On Operating Assets	=	Operating Income Margin	x	Operating Asset Turnover
2001 12.22%*	=	10.63%	x	1.15
2000 8.40%*	=	7.50%	x	1.12
1999 8.03%	=	7.30%	x	1.10

*Rounding difference from the 12.23%, 8.41%, and 8.04% computed in 6.

9. Return On Investment = $\dfrac{\begin{array}{c}\text{Net Income Before Minority Share Of}\\ \text{Earnings And Nonrecurring Items +}\\ \text{[(Interest Expense) x (1-Tax Rate)]}\end{array}}{\text{Average (Long-Term Liabilities + Equity)}}$

Estimated tax rate:

	2001	2000	1999
(1) Provision for income taxes	$ 62,049	$ 35,731	$ 32,659
(2) Earnings before income taxes and minority equity	$159,100	$ 87,150	$ 77,760
(1) divided by (2)	39.00%	41.00%	42.00%
1 - tax rate	61.00%	59.00%	58.00%
(3) Interest expense x (1-tax rate)			
$19,000 x 61.00%	11,590		
$18,200 x 59.00%		10,738	
$17,040 x 58.00%			9,883
(4) Earnings before minority equity	97,051	51,419	45,101
(3) plus (4) (A)	108,641	62,157	54,984
(5) Total long-term debt	211,100	212,800	214,000
(6) Total stockholders' equity	811,200	790,100	770,000
(5) plus (6) (B)	1,022,300	1,002,900	984,000
(A) divided by (B)	10.63%	6.20%	5.59%

10. Return on Total Equity = $\dfrac{\begin{array}{c}\text{Net Income Before Nonrecurring Items -}\\ \text{Dividends on Redeemable Preferred Stock}\end{array}}{\text{Average Total Equity}}$

	2001	2000	1999
Net income, etc.	$ 86,851	$ 42,919	$ 37,001
Average total equity	$811,200	$790,100	$770,000

b. All ratios computed indicate a significant improvement in profitability.

PROBLEM 8-7

a. 1. Net Profit Margin = $\dfrac{\begin{array}{c}\text{Net Income Before Minority Share Of}\\ \text{Earnings And Nonrecurring Items}\end{array}}{\text{Net Sales}}$

2001	2000	1999
$171,115	$163,497	$143,990
$1,002,100	$980,500	$900,000
= 17.08%	= 16.67%	= 16.00%

2. Return on Assets = $\dfrac{\text{Net Income Before Minority Share Of Earnings And Nonrecurring Items}}{\text{Average Total Assets}}$

2001	2000	1999
$\dfrac{\$171,115}{\$839,000}$	$\dfrac{\$163,497}{\$770,000}$	$\dfrac{\$143,990}{\$765,000}$
= 20.40%	= 21.23%	= 18.82%

3. Total Asset Turnover = $\dfrac{\text{Net Sales}}{\text{Average Total Assets}}$

2001	2000	1999
$\dfrac{\$1,002,100}{\$\ \ \ 839,000}$	$\dfrac{\$980,500}{\$770,000}$	$\dfrac{\$900,000}{\$765,000}$
= 1.19 times per year	= 1.27 times per year	= 1.18 times per year

4. DuPont Analysis

Return On Assets	=	Net Profit Margin	x Total Asset Turnover
2001: 20.33%*	=	17.08%	x 1.19 times per year
2000: 21.17%*	=	16.67%	x 1.27 times per year
1999: 18.88%*	=	16.00%	x 1.18 times per year

*Rounding difference from the 20.40%, 21.23%, and 18.82% computed in 2.

5. Return on Investment = $\dfrac{\text{Net Income Before Minority Share Of Earnings And Nonrecurring Items} + [(\text{Interest Expense}) \times (1-\text{Tax Rate})]}{\text{Average (Long-Term Liabilities + Equity}}$

Estimated tax rate:

	2001	2000	1999
(1) Provision for income taxes	$116,473	$113,616	$105,560
(2) Earnings before income taxes	$287,588	$277,113	$249,550
tax rate [(1) divided by (2)]	40.50%	41.00%	42.30%
1 - tax rate	59.50%	59.00%	57.70%

(3) Interest expense x (1-tax rate)

	2001	2000	1999
$14,620 x 59.50%	8,699		
$12,100 x 59.00%		7,139	
$11,250 x 57.70%			6,491

	2001	2000	1999
(4) Net earnings	171,115	163,497	143,990
(3) plus (4) (A)	179,814	170,636	150,481

```
(5) Average long-term debt        120,000   112,000   101,000
(6) Average shareholders' equity  406,000   369,500   342,000
    (5) plus (6)        (B)       526,000   481,500   443,000

    (A) divided by (B)             34.19%    35.44%    33.97%
```

$$6. \quad \text{Return on Equity} = \frac{\text{Net Income Before Nonrecurring Items} - \text{Dividends On Redeemable Preferred Stock}}{\text{Average Total Equity}}$$

	2001	2000	1999
Net earnings	$171,115	$163,497	$143,990
Average total equity	$406,000	$369,500	$342,000
	= 42.15%	= 44.25%	= 42.10%

$$7. \quad \text{Sales To Fixed Assets} = \frac{\text{Net Sales}}{\text{Average Net Fixed Assets}}$$

	2001	2000	1999
	$1,002,100	$980,500	$900,000
	$ 302,500	$281,000	$173,000
	= 3.31	= 3.49	= 5.20

b. The ratios computed indicate a very profitable firm. Most
    ratios indicate a very slight reduction in profitability in
    2000.
    Sales to fixed assets has declined materially, but this is
    the only ratio for which the trend appears to be negative.

PROBLEM 8-8

$$\text{a.} \quad 1. \quad \text{Net Profit Margin} = \frac{\text{Net Income Before Minority Share Of Earnings And Nonrecurring Items}}{\text{Net Sales}}$$

	2001	2000	1999
	$20,070-$8,028	$16,660-$6,830	$15,380-$6,229
	$297,580	$256,360	$242,150
	= 4.05%	= 3.83%	= 3.78%

2. Return on Assets = $\dfrac{\text{Net Income Before Minority Share Of Earnings And Nonrecurring Items}}{\text{Average Total Assets}}$

2001	2000	1999
$\dfrac{\$20,070-\$8,028}{\$145,760}$	$\dfrac{\$16,660-\$6,830}{\$137,000}$	$\dfrac{\$15,380-\$6,229}{\$136,000}$
= 8.26%	= 7.18%	= 6.73%

3. Total Asset Turnover = $\dfrac{\text{Net Sales}}{\text{Average Total Assets}}$

2001	2000	1999
$\dfrac{\$297,580}{\$145,760}$	$\dfrac{\$256,360}{\$137,000}$	$\dfrac{\$242,150}{\$136,000}$
= 2.04 times per year	= 1.87 times per year	= 1.78 times per year

4. DuPont Analysis

Return on Assets = Net Profit Margin x Total Asset Turnover

2001	8.26%	=	4.05%	x	2.04 times
2000	7.16%*	=	3.83%	x	1.87 times
1999	6.73%	=	3.78%	x	1.78 times

*Rounding difference from the 7.18% computed in 2.

5. Operating Income Margin = $\dfrac{\text{Operating Income}}{\text{Net Sales}}$

2001	2000	1999
$\dfrac{\$26,380}{\$297,580}$	$\dfrac{\$22,860}{\$256,360}$	$\dfrac{\$20,180}{\$242,150}$
= 8.86%	= 8.92%	= 8.33%

6. Return on Operating Assets = $\dfrac{\text{Operating Income}}{\text{Average Operating Assets}}$

2001	2000	1999
$\dfrac{\$26,380}{\$89,800+\$45,850}$	$\dfrac{\$22,860}{\$84,500+\$40,300}$	$\dfrac{\$20,180}{\$83,100+\$39,800}$
= 19.45%	= 18.32%	= 16.42%

7. Operating Asset Turnover = $\dfrac{\text{Net Sales}}{\text{Average Operating Assets}}$

2001	2000	1999
$\dfrac{\$297,580}{\$89,800+\$45,850}$	$\dfrac{\$256,360}{\$84,500+\$40,300}$	$\dfrac{\$242,150}{\$83,100+\$39,800}$
= 2.19 times per year	= 2.05 times per year	= 1.97 times per year

8. DuPont Analysis with Operating Ratios

Return On Operating Assets	=	Operating Income Margin	x	Operating Asset Turnover
2001: 19.40%*	=	8.86%	x	2.19 times
2000: 18.29%*	=	8.92%	x	2.05 times
1999: 16.41%*	=	8.33%	x	1.97 times

*Rounding difference from the 19.45%, 18.32%, and 16.42% computed in 6.

9. Gross Profit Margin = $\dfrac{\text{Gross Profit}}{\text{Net Sales}}$

2001	2000	1999
$\dfrac{\$91,580}{\$297,580}$	$\dfrac{\$80,060}{\$256,360}$	$\dfrac{\$76,180}{\$242,150}$
= 30.77%	= 31.23%	= 31.46%

b. Net profit margin and total asset turnover both improved. This resulted in a substantial improvement to return on assets.

Operating income margin declined slightly in 2000 after a substantial improvement in 1999. Operating asset turnover improved each year. The result of the improvement in operating income margin and operating asset turnover was a substantial improvement in return on operating assets.

Gross profit margin declined slightly each year.

Overall profitability improved substantially over the three-year period.

PROBLEM 8-9

a.
1. Return On Assets = $\dfrac{\text{Net Income Before Minority Share Of Earnings And Nonrecurring Items}}{\text{Average Total Assets}}$

	2001	2000	1999
(A)	$ 2,100,000	$ 1,950,000	$ 1,700,000
	$ 2,600,000	$ 2,300,000	$ 2,200,000
	7,000,000	6,200,000	5,800,000
	100,000	100,000	100,000
	10,000,000	9,000,000	8,300,000
(B)	$19,700,000	$17,600,000	$16,400,000
(A) divided by (B)	10.66%	11.08%	10.37%

2. Return On Investment = $\dfrac{\text{Net Income Before Minority Share Of Earnings And Nonrecurring Items} + [(\text{Interest Expense}) \times (1-\text{Tax Rate})]}{\text{Average (Long-Term Liabilities + Equity)}}$

Estimated tax rate:

	2001	2000	1999
(1) Provision for income taxes	$ 1,500,000	$ 1,450,000	$1,050,000
(2) Income before tax	3,600,000	3,400,000	2,750,000
tax rate = (1) divided by (2)	41.67%	42.65%	38.18%
1 - tax rate	58.33%	57.35%	61.82%

(3) Interest expense x (1-tax rate)			
$800,000 x 58.33%	$ 466,640		
$600,000 x 57.35%		$ 344,100	
$550,000 x 61.82%			$ 340,010
(4) Net income	$ 2,100,000	$ 1,950,000	$1,700,000
(3) plus (4) (A)	$ 2,566,640	$ 2,294,100	$2,040,010
Long-term debt	$ 7,000,000	$ 6,200,000	$5,800,000
Preferred stock	100,000	100,000	100,000
Common equity	10,000,000	9,000,000	8,300,000
(B)	$17,100,000	$15,300,000	$14,200,000
(A) divided by (B)	15.01%	14.99%	14.37%

3. Return On Total Equity = $\dfrac{\text{Net Income Before Nonrecurring Items Dividends On Redeemable Preferred Stock}}{\text{Average Total Equity}}$

2001	2000	1999
$\dfrac{\$2,100,000}{\$100,000+\$10,000,000}$	$\dfrac{\$1,950,000}{\$100,000+\$9,000,000}$	$\dfrac{\$1,700,000}{\$100,000+\$8,300,000}$
$= 20.79\%$	$= 21.43\%$	$= 20.24\%$

4. Return On Common Equity = $\dfrac{\text{Net Income Before Nonrecurring Items - Preferred Dividends}}{\text{Average Common Equity}}$

2001	2000	1999
$\dfrac{\$2,100,000-\$14,000}{\$10,000,000}$	$\dfrac{\$1,950,000-\$14,000}{\$9,000,000}$	$\dfrac{\$1,700,000-\$14,000}{\$8,300,000}$
$= 20.86\%$	$= 21.51\%$	$= 20.31\%$

b. Return on assets improved in 2000 and then declined in 2001. Return on investment improved each year. Return on total equity improved and then declined. Return on common equity improved and then declined.

In general, profitability has improved in 2000 over 1999 but was down slightly in 2001.

c. The use of long-term debt and preferred stock both benefited profitability.

Return on common equity is slightly more than return on total equity, indicating a benefit from preferred stock.

Return on total equity is substantially higher than return on investment, indicating a benefit from long-term debt.

PROBLEM 8-10

a.
Sales	$120,000
Gross profit (40%)	48,000
Cost of goods sold (60%)	72,000

Beginning inventory	$ 10,000
+ purchases	100,000
Total available	110,000
- Ending inventory	?
Cost of goods sold	$ 72,000

Ending inventory (110,000 - 72,000) = $38,000

b. If gross profit were 50%, the analysis would be as follows:

Sales	$120,000
Gross profit (50%)	60,000
Cost of goods sold (50%)	60,000

Beginning inventory	$ 10,000
Purchases	100,000
Total available	$110,000
- Ending inventory	50,000
Cost of goods sold	$ 60,000

If gross profit were higher, the loss would be higher.

PROBLEM 8-11

		Net Profit	Retained Earnings	Total Stockholders' Equity
a.	A stock dividend is declared and paid.	0	-	0
b.	Merchandise is purchased on credit.	0	0	0
c.	Marketable securities are sold above cost.	+	+	+
d.	Accounts receivable are collected.	0	0	0
e.	A cash dividend is declared and paid.	0	-	-
f.	Treasury stock is purchased and recorded at cost.	0	0	-

g.	Treasury stock is sold above cost.	0	0	+
h.	Common stock is sold.	0	0	+
i.	A fixed asset is sold for less than book value.	–	–	–
j.	Bonds are converted into common stock.	0	0	+

PROBLEM 8-12

a. 1. Net Profit Margin = $\dfrac{\text{Net Income Before Minority Share of Earnings and Nonrecurring Items}}{\text{Net Sales}}$

2001: $\dfrac{\$\ 72,700}{\$980,000}$ = 7.42%

2000: $\dfrac{\$\ 64,900}{\$960,000}$ = 6.76%

1999: $\dfrac{\$\ 57,800}{\$940,000}$ = 6.15%

1998: $\dfrac{\$\ 51,200}{\$900,000}$ = 5.69%

1997: $\dfrac{\$\ 44,900}{\$880,000}$ = 5.10%

2. Total Asset Turnover = $\dfrac{\text{Net Sales}}{\text{Average Total Assets}}$

Average Balance Sheet Figures

2001: $\dfrac{\$980,000}{(\$859,000 + \$861,000)/2}$ = 1.14 times per year

2000: $\dfrac{\$960,000}{(\$861,000 + \$870,000)/2}$ = 1.11 times per year

1999: $\dfrac{\$940,000}{(\$870,000 + \$867,000)/2}$ = 1.08 times per year

1998: $\dfrac{\$900,000}{(\$867,000 + \$863,000)/2}$ = 1.04 times per year

1997: Cannot compute average assets.

Year-End Balance Sheet Figures

2001: $\dfrac{\$980,000}{\$859,000}$ = 1.14 times per year

2000: $\dfrac{\$960,000}{\$861,000}$ = 1.11 times per year

1999: $\dfrac{\$940,000}{\$870,000}$ = 1.08 times per year

1998: $\dfrac{\$900,000}{\$867,000}$ = 1.04 times per year

1997: $\dfrac{\$880,000}{\$863,000}$ = 1.02 times per year

3. Return on Assets = $\dfrac{\text{Net Income Before Minority Share of Earnings and Nonrecurring Items}}{\text{Average Total Assets}}$

Average Balance Sheet Figures

2001: $\dfrac{\$72,700}{(\$859,000 + \$861,000)/2}$ = 8.45%

2000: $\dfrac{\$64,900}{(\$861,000 + \$870,000)/2}$ = 7.50%

1999: $\dfrac{\$57,800}{(\$870,000 + \$867,000)/2}$ = 6.66%

1998: $\dfrac{\$51,200}{(\$867,000 + \$863,000)/2}$ = 5.92%

1997:   Cannot compute average assets.

Year-End Balance Sheet Figures

2001: $\dfrac{\$72,700}{\$859,000}$ = 8.46%

2000: $\dfrac{\$64,900}{\$861,000}$ = 7.54%

1999: $\dfrac{\$57,800}{\$870,000}$ = 6.64%

1998: $\dfrac{\$51,200}{\$867,000}$ = 5.91%

1997: $\dfrac{\$44,900}{\$863,000}$ = 5.20%

4. DuPont Return On Assets = Net Profit Margin x
                              Total Asset Turnover

Average Balance Sheet Figures

2001:   7.42% x 1.14 Times = 8.46%

2000:   6.76% x 1.11 Times = 7.50%

1999:   6.15% x 1.08 Times = 6.64%

1998:   5.69% x 1.04 Times = 5.92%

1997:   Cannot compute average assets.

Year-End Balance Sheet Figures
2001:   7.42% x 1.14 times = 8.46%
2000:   6.76% x 1.11 times = 7.50%
1999:   6.15% x 1.08 times = 6.64%
1998   5.69% x 1.04 times = 5.92%
1997:   5.10% x 1.02 times = 5.20%

5. Operating Income Margin = $\dfrac{\text{Operating Income}}{\text{Net Sales}}$

2001: $\dfrac{\$355,000 - \$240,000}{\$980,000}$ = 11.73%

2000: $\dfrac{\$344,000 - \$239,000}{\$960,000}$ = 10.94%

1999: $\dfrac{\$333,000 - \$238,000}{\$940,000}$ = 10.11%

1998: $\dfrac{\$320,000 - \$239,000}{\$900,000}$ = 9.00%

1997: $\dfrac{\$314,000 - \$235,000}{\$880,000}$ = 8.98%

6. Operating Asset Turnover = $\dfrac{\text{Net Sales}}{\text{Average Operating Assets}}$

Average Balance Sheet Figures

2001: $\dfrac{\$980,000}{(\$859,000 - \$80,000 + \$861,000 - \$85,000)/2}$ = 1.26 times per year

2000: $\dfrac{\$960,000}{(\$861,000 - \$85,000 + \$870,000 - \$90,000)/2}$ = 1.23 times per year

199

1999: $$\frac{\$940,000}{(\$870,000 - \$90,000 + \$867,000 - \$95,000)/2} = 1.21 \text{ times per year}$$

1998: $$\frac{\$900,000}{(\$867,000 - \$95,000 + \$863,000 - \$100,000)/2} = 1.17 \text{ times per year}$$

1997: Average Assets Cannot Be Computed.

Year-End Balance Sheet Figures

2001: $$\frac{\$980,000}{\$859,000 - \$80,000} = 1.26 \text{ times per year}$$

2000: $$\frac{\$960,000}{\$861,000 - \$85,000} = 1.24 \text{ times per year}$$

1999: $$\frac{\$940,000}{\$870,000 - \$90,000} = 1.21 \text{ times per year}$$

1998: $$\frac{\$900,000}{\$867,000 - \$95,000} = 1.17 \text{ times per year}$$

1997: $$\frac{\$880,000}{\$863,000 - \$100,000} = 1.15 \text{ times per year}$$

7. Return on Operating Assets = $\dfrac{\text{Operating Income}}{\text{Average Operating Assets}}$

Average Balance Sheet Figures

2001: $$\frac{\$355,000 - \$240,000}{(\$859,000 - \$80,000 + \$861,000 - \$85,000)/2} = 14.79\%$$

2000: $$\frac{\$344,000 - \$239,000}{(\$861,000 - \$85,000 + \$870,000 - \$90,000)/2} = 13.50\%$$

1999: $$\frac{\$333,000 - \$238,000}{(\$870,000 - \$90,000 + \$867,000 - \$95,000)/2} = 12.24\%$$

1998: $$\frac{\$320,000 - \$239,000}{(\$867,000 - \$95,000 + \$863,000 - \$100,000)/2} = 10.55\%$$

1997: Average assets cannot be computed.

Year-End Balance Sheet Figures

2001: $$\frac{\$355,000 - \$240,000}{\$859,000 - \$80,000} = 14.76\%$$

2000: $$\frac{\$344,000 - \$239,000}{\$861,000 - \$85,000} = 13.53\%$$

1999: $$\frac{\$333,000 - \$238,000}{\$870,000 - \$90,000} = 12.18\%$$

1998: $\dfrac{\$320,000 - \$239,000}{\$867,000 - \$95,000}$ = 10.49%

1997: $\dfrac{\$314,000 - \$235,000}{\$863,000 - \$100,000}$ = 10.35%

8. DuPont Return on Operating Assets =

   Operating Income Margin x Operating Asset Turnover

Average Balance Sheet Figures

2001: 11.73% x 1.26 = 14.78%

2000: 10.94% x 1.23 = 13.46%

1999: 10.11% x 1.21 = 12.23%

1998: 9.00% x 1.17 = 10.53%

1997: Average Assets Cannot Be Computed.

Year-End Balance Sheet Figures

2001: 11.73% x 1.26 = 14.78%

2000: 10.94% x 1.24 = 13.57%

1999: 10.11% x 1.21 = 12.23%

1998: 9.00% x 1.17 = 10.53%

1997: 8.98% x 1.15 = 10.33%

9. Sales To Fixed Assets = $\dfrac{\text{Net Sales}}{\text{Average Net Fixed Assets}}$

2001: $\dfrac{\$980,000}{(\$500,000 + \$491,000)/2}$ = 1.98

2000: $\dfrac{\$960,000}{(\$491,000 + \$485,000)/2}$ = 1.97

1999: $\dfrac{\$940,000}{(\$485,000 + \$479,000)/2}$ = 1.95

1998: $\dfrac{\$900,000}{(\$479,000 + \$470,000)/2}$ = 1.90

1997: Average Net Fixed Assets Cannot Be Computed.

<u>Year-End Balance Sheet Figures</u>

2001: $\dfrac{\$980,000}{\$500,000}$ = 1.96

2000: $\dfrac{\$960,000}{\$491,000}$ = 1.96

1999: $\dfrac{\$940,000}{\$485,000}$ = 1.94

1998: $\dfrac{\$900,000}{\$479,000}$ = 1.88

1997: $\dfrac{\$880,000}{\$470,000}$ = 1.87

10. Return on Investment = $\dfrac{\text{Net Income Before Minority Share of Earnings and Nonrecurring Items + [Interest Expense) x (1-Tax Rate)]}}{\text{Average (Long-Term Liabilities + Equity)}}$

<u>Average Balance Sheet Figures</u>

2001: $\dfrac{\$72,700 + \$6,500\,(1 - .33)}{(\$859,000 - \$194,000 + \$861,000 - \$195,500)/2}$ = 11.58%

2000: $\dfrac{\$64,900 + \$6,700\,(1 - .34)}{(\$861,000 - \$195,500 + \$870,000 - \$195,500)/2}$ = 10.35%

1999: $\dfrac{\$57,800 + \$8,000\,(1 - .34)}{(\$870,000 - \$195,500 + \$867,000 - \$195,000)/2}$ = 9.37%

1998: $\dfrac{\$51,200 + \$8,100\,(1 - .30)}{(\$867,000 - \$195,000 + \$863,000 - \$196,500)/2}$ = 8.50%

1997: Average (Long-term liabilities + Equity) cannot be computed.

<u>Year-End Balance Sheet Figures</u>

2001: $\dfrac{\$72,700 + \$6,500\,(1 - .33)}{\$859,000 - \$194,000}$ = 11.59%

2000: $\dfrac{\$64,900 + \$6,700\,(1 - .34)}{\$861,000 - \$195,500}$ = 10.42%

1999: $\dfrac{\$57,800 + \$8,000\,(1 - .34)}{\$870,000 - \$195,500}$ = 9.35%

1998: $\dfrac{\$51{,}200 + \$8{,}100\ (1 - .30)}{\$867{,}000 - \$195{,}000} = 8.46\%$

1997: $\dfrac{\$44{,}900 + \$11{,}000\ (1 - .34)}{\$863{,}000 - \$196{,}500} = 7.83\%$

11. Return on Total Equity = $\dfrac{\text{Net Income Before Nonrecurring Items} - \text{Dividends on Redeemable Preferred Stock}}{\text{Average Total Equity}}$

Average Balance Sheet Figures

2001: $\dfrac{\$72{,}700 - \$6{,}400}{(\$520{,}000 + \$518{,}000)/2} = 12.77\%$

2000: $\dfrac{\$64{,}900 - \$6{,}400}{(\$518{,}000 + \$515{,}000)/2} = 11.33\%$

1999: $\dfrac{\$57{,}800 - \$6{,}400}{(\$515{,}000 + \$510{,}000)/2} = 10.03\%$

1998: $\dfrac{\$51{,}200 - \$6{,}400}{(\$510{,}000 + \$559{,}000)/2} = 8.38\%$

1997: Average total equity cannot be computed.

Year-End Balance Sheet Figures

2001: $\dfrac{\$72{,}700 - \$6{,}400}{\$520{,}000} = 12.75\%$

2000: $\dfrac{\$64{,}900 - \$6{,}400}{\$518{,}000} = 11.29\%$

1999: $\dfrac{\$57{,}800 - \$6{,}400}{\$515{,}000} = 9.98\%$

1998: $\dfrac{\$51{,}200 - \$6{,}400}{\$510{,}000} = 8.78\%$

1997: $\dfrac{\$44{,}900}{\$559{,}000} = 8.03\%$

12. Return on Common Equity = $\dfrac{\text{Net Income Before Nonrecurring Items} - \text{Preferred Dividends}}{\text{Average Common Equity}}$

203

Average Balance Sheet Figures

2001: $$\frac{\$72,700 - \$6,400 - \$6,300}{(\$520,000 - \$70,000 + \$518,000 - \$70,000)/2} = 13.36\%$$

2000: $$\frac{\$64,900 - \$6,400 - \$6,300}{(\$518,000 - \$70,000 + \$515,000 - \$70,000)/2} = 11.69\%$$

1999: $$\frac{\$57,800 - \$6,400 - \$6,300}{(\$515,000 - \$70,000 + \$510,000 - \$70,000)/2} = 10.19\%$$

1998: $$\frac{\$51,200 - \$6,400 - \$6,300}{(\$510,000 - \$70,000 + \$559,000 - \$120,000)/2} = 8.76\%$$

1997: Average Common Equity Cannot Be Computed.

Year-End Balance Sheet Figures

2001: $$\frac{\$72,700 - \$6,400 - \$6,300}{\$520,000 - \$70,000} = 13.33\%$$

2000: $$\frac{\$64,900 - \$6,400 - \$6,300}{\$518,000 - \$70,000} = 11.65\%$$

1999: $$\frac{\$57,800 - \$6,400 - \$6,300}{\$515,000 - \$70,000} = 10.13\%$$

1998: $$\frac{\$51,200 - \$6,400 - \$6,300}{\$510,000 - \$70,000} = 8.75\%$$

1997: $$\frac{\$44,900 - \$10,800}{\$559,000 - \$120,000} = 7.77\%$$

13. Gross Profit Margin = $\dfrac{\text{Gross Profit}}{\text{Net Sales}}$

2001: $\dfrac{\$355,000}{\$980,000} = 36.22\%$

2000: $\dfrac{\$344,000}{\$960,000} = 35.83\%$

1999: $\dfrac{\$333,000}{\$940,000} = 35.43\%$

1998: $\dfrac{\$320,000}{\$900,000} = 35.56\%$

1997: $\dfrac{\$314,000}{\$880,000} = 35.68\%$

b. In general, the profitability appears to be very good and the trend is positive.

There was not a significant difference in results between using average balance sheet figures and year-end figures. The year-end figure allowed for an additional year of computation. The additional year was not a very profitable year in relation to subsequent years.

CASES

CASE 8-1 JOHNNY'S SELF-SERVICE STATION

Profitability Planning

(This case is effective in illustrating the entity concept, return on investment, cash flow, and the subjective nature of decision making.)

a. Indicated return on investment:

Average profit for 2001 and 2000:	2001:	$20,630
	2000:	17,925
		$38,555
	Average	$19,277

Depreciation as computed on the prior cost base	$ 1,000
Depreciation as computed on the purchase cost	(2,000)
Adjusted profit	18,277
Tax, 50% rate	9,139
Net income	$ 9,138

$$\text{Return On Investment} = \frac{\$9,138}{\$70,000} = 13.05\%$$

b. Indicated return on investment if help were hired to operate the station:

Adjusted profit in part (a)	$18,277
Less cost of hired help	10,000
New adjusted profit	8,277
Tax, 50% rate	4,139
Net income	$ 4,138

$$\text{Return On Investment} = \frac{\$4,138}{\$70,000} = 5.91\%$$

c. In part a, there is no salary expense. In part b, the salary expense for hired help of $10,000 is deducted. This lowers the taxable income and taxes, giving a net effect of $5,000. The rate of return in part (a) must be higher to compensate for the opportunity cost of the salary to the owner.

The difference between the rates of return is misleading in terms of judging the investment. The records only reflect the actual cost, while disregarding opportunity cost and personnel time not compensated. All costs need to be considered when judging the investment.

d. Indicated cash flow:

	2002
Receipts:	
Revenue	$185,060
Outlays:	
Cost of goods sold	160,180
Added inventory	10,000
Real estate and property taxes	1,100
Repairs and maintenance	1,470
Other expenses	680
Total outlays	173,430
Net cash flow, excluding tax expense	11,630
Less taxes (a)	9,815
Net cash flow	$ 1,815
(a) Cash flow prior to taxes	$ 11,630
Add inventory	10,000
Deduct depreciation	(2,000)
Profit	19,630
Taxes	$ 9,815

e. Many other considerations can be discussed. Some of these include:

1. Future tax rate.

2. Psychic value of owning the business.

3. Can Mr. Dearden adequately serve as manager?

4. Will he be able to maintain or increase the business that was enjoyed by Mr. Szabo?

5. Will there be appreciation in the value of the property?

6. Other investment alternatives.

f. This is a subjective question. Either a yes or no answer is acceptable. This question should be discussed in relation to the above questions.

CASE 8-2   THE TALE OF THE SEGMENTS

(Analysis of geographic and supplemental product information.)

a. 1.   Net Sales - Horizontal Common-Size

	1998	1997	1996
North America	102.19	104.27	100.00%
Europe	97.08	97.28	100.00%
Asia-Pacific	87.03	95.08	100.00%
Latin America	125.33	111.75	100.00%
Consolidated	101.28	102.30	100.00%

2. Operating Profit - Horizontal Common Size

	1998	1997	1996
North America	109.09	116.07	100.00%
Europe	69.29	100.23	100.00%
Asia-Pacific	78.79	83.36	100.00%
Latin America	113.80	118.68	100.00%
Consolidated (excludes corporate and other)	98.00	110.68	100.00%

3. Total Assets - Horizontal Common-Size

	1998	1997	1996
North America	94.44	97.87	100.00%
Europe	106.53	92.05	100.00%
Asia-Pacific	73.11	68.90	100.00%
Latin America	133.37	126.54	100.00%
Consolidated	98.10	95.22	100.00%

b. Supplemental geographic information - horizontal common-size.

1. Net Sales - Horizontal Common-Size

	1998	1997	1996
United States	103.33	105.05	100.00%
Great Britain	110.36	106.71	100.00%
Other foreign countries	95.21	96.47	100.00%
Consolidated	101.28	102.30	100.00%

2. Long-Lived Assets - Horizontal Common-Size

	1998	1997	1996
United States	95.59	99.25	100.00%
Great Britain	119.39	97.67	100.00%
Other foreign countries	101.99	93.94	100.00%
Consolidated	101.15	97.05	100.00%

c. Supplemental product information provided for revenues from external customers.

1. Horizontal Common-Size

	1998	1997	1996
Ready-to-eat cereal Net sales	94.98	98.05	100.00%
Convenience foods net sales	132.12	123.08	100.00%
Consolidated	101.28	102.30	100.00%

2. Vertical Common-Size

	1998	1997	1996
Ready-to-eat cereal Net sales	77.87	79.59	83.03
Convenience foods net sales	22.13	20.41	16.97
Consolidated	100.00%	100.00%	100.00%

d. a. 1. Net Sales - Horizontal Common-Size
                Consolidated sales increased an immaterial
                amount. Asia-Pacific decreased materially
                while Latin America increased materially.

        2. Operating Profit - Horizontal Common-Size
                Consolidated operating profit decreased
                slightly. Europe and Asia-Pacific decreased
                materially. North America and Latin America
                increased materially.

        3. Total Assets - Horizontal Common-Size
                Consolidated total assets decreased slightly.
                Material decrease in Asia-Pacific, while a
                material increase in Latin America.

    b. Supplemental Geographic Information - Horizontal
        Common-Size

        1. Net Sales - Horizontal Common-Size
                Consolidated net sales increased slightly. Great
                Britain had a material increase.

        2. Long-lived Assets - Horizontal Common-Size
                Consolidated long-lived assets increased slightly.
                Great Britain had a material increase in long-
                lived assets.

    c. Supplemental product information provided by revenues
        from external customers.

        1. Horizontal Common-Size
                Consolidated increased slightly. There was a
                material increase in convenience foods net sales.

        2. Vertical Common-Size
                Ready-to-eat cereal net sales decreased
                materially. Convenience foods net sales increased
                materially.

CASE 8-3 INSIGHTS ON GEOGRAPHIC AREA

(Analysis of geographic area and major customer.)

a. 1. Net Sales - Horizontal Common-Size

	1998	1997	1996
United States	116.60	116.91	100.00%
Europe and Canada	85.94	89.63	100.00%
Asia and Latin America	89.04	89.12	100.00%
Consolidated Total	105.44	106.59	100.00%

2. Long-Lived Assets - Horizontal Common-Size

	1998	1997	1996
United States	223.57	99.26	100.00%
Europe and Canada	96.16	71.79	100.00%
Asia and Latin America	112.92	95.19	100.00%
Consolidated Total	164.29	92.60	100.00%

b. 1. Analysis of Net Sales - Major Customer-Horizontal Common-Size

	1998	1997	1996
Toys R Us	70.15	82.68	100.00%
Wal-Mart	142.26	132.96	100.00%
Consolidated Total	105.41	106.60	100.00%

2. Analysis of receivables - Major Customer - Horizontal Common-Size

	1998	1997	1996
Toys R Us	80.49	140.92	100.00%
Wal-Mart	322.35	197.57	100.00%

3. Analysis of Net Sales - Major Customer - Vertical Common-
   Size

	1998
Toys R Us	15.25
Wal-Mart	16.54
Consolidated Total	100.00

c. Comment on possible significant insights from the analysis in part (a) through (b).

   a. 1. Total net sales increased an immaterial amount. The only increase was in the United States. The increase in the United States occurred in 1997.

   2. Material increase in long-lived assets consolidated total. This increase took place in 1998. Substantially all of the increase was in the United States in 1998.

b. 1. Net sales decreased substantially to Toys R Us. Net sales increased substantially to Wal-Mart. Consolidated sales increased an immaterial amount.

   2. Receivables from Toys R Us increased in relation to net sales to Toys R Us. Receivables from Wal-Mart increased materially more than the increase in net sales to Wal-Mart. This would impact on the profitability of sales to Wal-Mart.

   2. Net sales to Toys R Us and to Wal-Mart were substantially the same in 1998. Our previous analysis indicated that net sales to Toys R Us have declined materially while the net sales to Wal-Mart have increased materially.

CASE 8-4   TIDE, PAMPERS, and ETC.

(This case presents the opportunity to compute profitability ratios for The Procter & Gamble Company.)

   a. 1. Net Profit Margin =

1998	1997
$\dfrac{\$3,780}{\$37,154} = 10.17\%$	$\dfrac{\$3,415}{\$35,764} = 9.55\%$

2. Total Asset Turnover

1998	1997
$\dfrac{\$37,154}{\$30,966} = 1.20$ Times	$\dfrac{\$35,764}{\$27,544} = 1.30$ Times

3. Return on Assets

1998	1997
$\dfrac{\$3,780}{\$30,966} = 12.21\%$	$\dfrac{\$3,415}{\$27,544} = 12.40\%$

4. Operating Income Margin

1998	1997
$\dfrac{\$6,055}{\$37,154} = 16.30\%$	$\dfrac{\$5,488}{\$35,764} = 15.35\%$

5. Return on Operating Assets

1998	1997
$\dfrac{\$6,055}{\$30,966 - \$7,011 - \$1,198} = 26.61\%$	$\dfrac{\$5,488}{\$27,544 - \$3949 - \$1,43}$

*Exclusion of other non-current assets is open to judgement. The content of this account is not clear.

6. Sales to Fixed Assets

1998	1997
$\dfrac{\$37,154}{\$12,180} = 3.05$ Times Per Year	$\dfrac{\$35,764}{\$11,376} = 3.14$ Times Per Year

7. Return on Investment

1998	1997
$\dfrac{\$3,780 + (\$548 \text{x} (1 - 33.78\%)}{\$3,765 + \$428 + \$3,287 + \$12,236} = 19.0$	$\dfrac{\$3,415 + (\$457 \text{x} (1 - 34.94\%)}{\$4,143 + \$559 + \$2,998 + \$12,046} = 18.80$

213

8. Return on Total Equity

1998

$$\frac{\$3,780}{\$12,236} = 30.89\%$$

1997

$$\frac{\$3,415}{\$12,046} = 28.35\%$$

9. Return on Common Equity

1998

$$\frac{\$3,780}{\$12,236 - \$1,821} = 35.30\%$$

1997

$$\frac{\$3,415 - \$104}{\$12,046 - \$1,859} = 32.50\%$$

10. Gross Profit Margin

1998

$$\frac{\$37,154 - \$21,064}{\$37,154} = 43.31\%$$

1997

$$\frac{\$35,764 - \$20,510}{\$35,764} = 42.65\%$$

b. More profitability measures improved than those that declined. In general very good improvement.

Profitability measures that improved:

Net Profit Margin (material improvement)
Operating Income Margin
Return on Operating Asset
Return on Investment
Return on Total Equity
Return on Common Equity (probably considered material)
Gross Profit Margin

Profitability measures that declined:

Total Asset Turnover
Return on Assets
Sales to Fixed Assets

CASE 8-5   VEHICLES AND HOUSING

(This case presents the opportunity to compute profitability ratios for Coachmen Industries, Inc.)

a. 1. Net Profit Margin

1998

$$\frac{\$33,062,608}{\$756,029,526} = 4.37\%$$

1997

$$\frac{\$24,762,624}{\$661,591,185} = 3.74\%$$

214

2. Total Asset Turnover

1998

$$\frac{\$756,029,526}{\$268,476,286} = 2.82 \text{ Times Per Year}$$

1997

$$\frac{\$661,591,185}{\$259,062,026} = 2.55 \text{ Times Per Year}$$

3. Return On Assets

1998

$$\frac{\$33,062,608}{\$268,476,286} = 12.31\%$$

1997

$$\frac{\$24,762,624}{\$259,062,026} = 9.56\%$$

4. Operating Income Margin

1998

$$\frac{\$45,927,853}{\$756,029,526} = 6.07\%$$

1997

$$\frac{\$35,260,319}{\$661,591,185} = 5.33\%$$

5. Return on Operating Assets

1998

$$\frac{\$45,927,853}{\$268,476,286 - \$19,992,877} = 18.48\%$$

1997

$$\frac{\$35,260,319}{\$259,062,026 - \$22,521,932} = 14.91\%$$

6. Sales to Fixed Assets

1998

$$\frac{\$756,029,526}{\$63,072,124} = 11.99 \text{ Times Per Year}$$

1997

$$\frac{\$661,591,185}{\$46,601,627} = 14.20 \text{ Times Per Year}$$

7. Return On Investment

1998

$$\frac{\$33,062,608 + [(1,738,608) \times (1 - 34.26)]}{\$10,191,476 + \$7,108,956 + \$205,457,660} = 15.36\%$$

1997

$$\frac{\$24,762,624 + [(\$2,544,021) \times (1 - 36.22)]}{\$12,591,144 + \$6,658,872 + \$190,135,792} = 12.60\%$$

8. Return on Total Equity

<u>1998</u>   <u>1997</u>

9. Gross Profit Margin

<u>1998</u>   <u>1997</u>

$$\frac{\$109,910,818}{\$756,029,526} = 14.54\%$$ $$\frac{\$92,755,013}{\$661,591,185} = 14.02\%$$

b. More profitability measures improved than those that declined. In general, a very good improvement.

Profitability measures that improved:

Net Profit Margin (would be considered to be material)
Total Asset Turnover (would be considered to be material)
Return On Assets (would be considered to be material)
Operating Income Margin (would be considered to be material)
Return on Operating Assets (would be considered to be material)
Return on Investment (would be considered to be material)
Gross Profit Margin

Profitability measures that declined:

Sales to Fixed Assets (would be considered to be material. This decline is misleading because of the substantial increase in fixed assets)

Chapter 9
For the Investor

<u>QUESTIONS</u>

9- 1. Earnings per share is the amount of income earned on a share of common stock during an accounting period.

9- 2. The Financial Accounting Standards Board suspended the reporting of earnings per share for nonpublic companies.

9- 3. Keller & Fink is a partnership. Earnings per share is a concept that only applies to corporate income statements.

9- 4. Earnings per share is a concept that only applies to common stock. The earnings per common share computation only uses earnings available to common stockholders. To arrive at the income that applies to common stock, preferred dividends are subtracted from net income in the numerator of the ratio.

9- 5. Since earnings pertain to an entire year, they should be related to the common shares outstanding during the year. The year-end common shares outstanding may not be representative of the shares outstanding during the year.

9- 6. Less preferred dividends will be subtracted from net income in the numerator of the earnings per share computation. This will increase earnings per share. In practice, whether earnings per share <u>will be increased or decreased</u> depends on the after-tax earnings that the firm would have from the funds used to retire the preferred stock in relation to the dividend decrease.

9- 7. Stock dividends and stock splits do not provide the firm with more funds; they only change the number of outstanding shares. Earnings per share should be related to the outstanding common stock after the stock dividend or stock split.

9- 8. Many firms try to maintain a stable percentage because they have a policy on the percentage of earnings that they want retained for internal growth.

9- 9. Financial leverage is the use of financing with a fixed charge. Financial leverage will magnify changes in earnings available to the common shareholder. Its use is advantageous when a firm obtains a greater return on the resources obtained than the rate of interest expense. Its use is disadvantageous when a firm obtains a lower return on the resources obtained than the rate of interest expense.

9-10. If the interest rate rises, the degree of financial leverage will rise. For example, suppose the firm has the following pattern of earnings with $1,000,000 in long-term debt:

Earnings before interest and tax $1,000,000
Interest ($1,000,000 at 8%)   80,000
Earnings before tax $ 920,000

Degree of Financial Leverage = $\dfrac{\text{Income before interest and tax}}{\text{Earnings before tax}}$

$$= \dfrac{\$1,000,000}{\$920,000}$$

$$= 1.09$$

If the rate of interest rises to 12%, then the degree of financial leverage will be as follows:

Earnings before interest and tax $1,000,000
Interest ($1,000,000 at 12%)   120,000
Earnings before tax $ 880,000

Degree of financial leverage = $\dfrac{\$1,000,000}{880,000}$

$$= 1.14$$

The degree of financial leverage has risen.

9-11. Investors attach a higher price to securities that they feel have higher potential. This gives a higher price/earnings ratio.

9-12.   A relatively new firm often has a low dividend payout ratio
        because it needs funds to establish itself (i.e., increase
        inventory, increase accounts receivable, etc.).
        A firm with a substantial growth record and/or substantial
        growth prospects needs funds for expansion. They utilize them
        in this manner rather than paying them out to the owners.

9-13.   A low dividend yield may indicate that the firm is retaining
        its earnings for growth. The investor might expect to get
        his/her returns in the form of market price appreciation.

9-14.   Book value is based on a mixture of valuation basis, such as
        historical costs. Current value accounting should make book
        value closer to market.

9-15.   Stock options are a form of potential dilution of earnings.

9-16.   A relatively small number of stock appreciation rights can
        prove to be a material drain on future earnings and cash of a
        company because stock appreciation rights are tied to the
        future market price of the stock.

9-17.   If the stock price decreases in relation to the prior year,
        then the estimate of total compensation expense related to the
        stock appreciation rights will decrease. The decrease in the
        estimate of total compensation expense will be added to income
        for the current year.

TO THE NET

1. a.

	1998	1997
1. Total assets	$6,700,071,000	$6,301,341
2. Total liabilities	$7,087,903,000	$7,086,189,000
3. Total shareowners' deficit	$387,832,000	$784,848,000
4. Cash dividends per common share	0	0

b.

	1998	1997
1. Price/Earnings	$\frac{\$60.50}{\$2.01} = 29.80$	$\frac{\$36.75}{\$1.69} = 21.75$
2. Dividend Yield	$\frac{\$0}{\$60.50} = 0$	$\frac{\$0}{\$36.75} = 0$

c. The market appears to be projecting future earnings. Much of the traditional analysis cannot effectively be used in this case.

This is an industry with relatively low profit margins and substantial competition. Yet the market appears to be projecting a very good financial future.

2. a. Beverages

b.

Income Per Share-Basic	1998	1997	1996
Continuing Operations	$1.35	$.98	$.60
Discontinued operations	-	.42	.13
Net income	$1.35	$1.40	$.73

Income Per Share-Assuming Dilution	1998	1997	1996
Continuing Operations	$1.31	$.95	$.59
Discontinued operations	-	.41	.13
Net income	$1.31	$1.36	$.72

c.

	1998	1997	1996
Continuing operations - assuming dilution	$1.31	$.95	$.59

Continuing operations should be used because it represents the best base for projecting the future. Diluted earnings should be used because this would be conservative.

PROBLEMS

PROBLEM 9-1

Degree of Financial Leverage +

$$\frac{\text{Earnings Before Interest, Tax, Minority Share of Earnings, Equity Income and Nonrecurring Items}}{\text{Earnings Before Tax, Minority Share of Earnings, Equity Income, and Nonrecurring Items}}$$

$$\frac{\$975,000 + \$70,000}{\$973,000} = \frac{\$1,045,000}{\$975,000} = 1.07$$

PROBLEM 9-2

a.
$$\frac{\text{Degree of}}{\text{Financial Leverage}} = \frac{\text{Earnings Before Interest, Tax Minority Share of Earnings, Equity Income and Nonrecurring Items}}{\text{Earnings Before Tax, Minority Share of Earnings, Equity Income, and Nonrecurring Items}}$$

$$= \frac{\$1,000,000}{\$800,000}$$

$$= 1.25$$

b.
Prior earnings before interest and tax	$1,000,000
10% increase	100,000
Adjusted income before interest and tax	$1,100,000
Interest	200,000
Income before tax	$ 900,000
Tax (50% rate)	450,000
Net income	$ 450,000

Earnings will increase by 12.5% to $450,000
($400,000 x 112.5% = $450,000)

c.
$800,000
200,000
600,000
300,000
$300,000

This is a decline in profit of 25%, with a decline in earnings before interest and tax of 20%.

PROBLEM 9-3

a. 1. $\dfrac{\text{Percentage of}}{\text{Earnings Retained}} = \dfrac{\text{Net income - All dividends}}{\text{Net Income}}$

		2000	1999	1998
Net income (A)		$31,200,000	$30,600,000	$29,800,000
Less:				
Common dividends		21,700,000	19,500,000	18,360,000
Preferred dividends		910,000	910,000	910,000
	(B)	$22,610,000	$20,410,000	$19,270,000
(A) Less (B) = (C)		8,590,000	10,190,000	10,530,000
(C) Divided by (A)		27.53%	33.30%	35.34%

2. Price/Earnings Ratio = $\dfrac{\text{Market Price Per Share}}{\text{Fully Diluted Earnings Per Share}}$

2000	1999	1998
$12.80	$14.00	$16.30
$ 1.12	$ 1.20	$ 1.27
= 11.43	= 11.67	= 12.83

3. Dividend Payout = $\dfrac{\text{Dividends Per Common Share}}{\text{Fully Diluted Earnings Per Share}}$

2000	1999	1998
$ .90	$ .85	$ .82
$1.12	$1.20	$1.27
= 80.36%	= 70.83%	= 64.57%

4. Dividend Yield = $\dfrac{\text{Dividends Per Common Share}}{\text{Market Price Per Common Share}}$

2000	1999	1998
$ .90	$ .85	$ .82
$12.80	$14.00	$16.30
= 7.03%	= 6.07%	= 5.03%

5. Book Value Per Share = $\dfrac{\text{Total Stockholders' Equity -} \text{Preferred Stock Equity}}{\text{Number of Common Shares Outstanding}}$

	2000	1999	1998
Total assets	$1,280,100,000)	$1,267,200,000	$1,260,400,000
Less:			
Liabilities	(800,400,000)	(808,500,000)	(799,200,000)
Stockholders' Equity	479,700,000	458,700,000	461,200,000
Less:			
Nonredeemable preferred			
stock	(15,300,000)	(15,300,000)	(15,300,000)
(A) Common stock equity	$464,400,000	$443,400,000	$445,900,000
(B) Shares outstanding			
end of year	24,280,000	23,100,000	22,500,000
(A) divided by (B)	$19.13	$19.19	$19.82

b. The percentage of earnings retained is decreasing. The related ratio, dividend payout, is also increasing.

The price/earnings ratio has been relatively stable. The dividend yield has increased and is relatively high. The market price per share is substantially below the book value. It appears that this stock is being purchased for the relatively high dividend and not for growth potential.

PROBLEM 9-4

a. 1. Percentage of Earnings Retained = $\dfrac{\text{Net Income - All Dividends}}{\text{Net Income}}$

	2000	1999	1998
Net income (B)	$ 9,100,000	$13,300,000	$16,500,000
Less:			
Cash dividends	(6,080,000)	(5,900,000)	(6,050,000)
(A)	$ 3,020,000	$ 7,400,000	$10,450,000
(A) divided by (B)	33.19%	55.64%	63.33%

2. Price/Earnings Ratio = $\dfrac{\text{Market Price Per Share}}{\text{Fully Diluted Earnings Per Share}}$

	2000	1999	1998
	$41.25	$35.00	$29.00
	$ 2.30	$ 3.40	$ 4.54
	= 17.93	= 10.29	= 6.39

3. Dividend Payout = $\dfrac{\text{Dividends Per Common Share}}{\text{Fully Diluted Earnings Per Share}}$

2000	1999	1998
$\dfrac{\$1.90}{\$2.30}$	$\dfrac{\$1.90}{\$3.40}$	$\dfrac{\$1.90}{\$4.54}$
= 82.61%	= 55.88%	= 41.85%

4. Dividend Yield = $\dfrac{\text{Dividends Per Common Share}}{\text{Market Price Per Common Share}}$

2000	1999	1998
$\dfrac{\$\ 1.90}{\$41.25}$	$\dfrac{\$\ 1.90}{\$35.00}$	$\dfrac{\$\ 1.90}{\$29.00}$
= 4.61%	= 5.43%	= 6.55%

5. Book Value Per Share = $\dfrac{\text{Market Price Value}}{\text{Ratio of Market Price to Book Value}}$

2000	1999	1998
$\dfrac{\$41.25}{120.5\ \%}$	$\dfrac{\$35.00}{108.0\ \%}$	$\dfrac{\$29.00}{105.0\ \%}$
= $34.23	= $32.41	= $27.62

b. The percentage of earnings retained materially declined. The related ratio, dividend payout, materially increased.

The price earnings ratio materially increased, which is difficult to explain, considering the decline in earnings and the other ratios computed.

The dividend yield has declined each year, while the book value per share increased each year.

The increase in market price and the increase in price earnings ratio appears to be explained by the increase in order backlog at year-end and the increase in net contracts awarded.

PROBLEM 9-5

Simple Earnings Per Share = $\dfrac{\text{Net Income - Preferred Dividends}}{\text{Weighted Average Number of Common Shares Outstanding}}$

Year 1	Year 2
$\dfrac{\$40,000 - \$22,500}{38,000}$	$\dfrac{\$42,000 - \$27,500}{38,500}$
$.46	$.38

The decline in earnings per share is caused mainly by the issuance of preferred stock and partially by a rise in the common shares.

PROBLEM 9-6

January 1, shares outstanding	50,000 shares
July 1, two-for-one stock split	2
Adjusted shares outstanding for the year (A)	100,000
October 1 stock issue	10,000 shares
Proportion of year that the new shares were outstanding	.25
Weighted average for the new shares on an annual basis (B)	2,500
Denominator of the earnings per share computation for the current year (A) + (B)	102,500

PROBLEM 9-7

Revision of 1999 earnings per share:

1999 reported earnings per share	$2.00
July 1, 2000 stock split	x .5
Adjusted 1999 earnings per share	$1.00
December 31, 2000 stock split	x .5
Adjusted 1999 earnings per share	$ .50

Comparative Earnings Per Share

	2000	1999
Earnings Per Share	$1.50	$ .50

PROBLEM 9-8

		Numerator	Denominator
a.	Net income	$ 35,000	
	Preferred dividends	(3,000)	
	January 1, 2000 shares of common stock outstanding		20,000
	July 1, 2000 common stock issue, 1,000 shares x 1/2		500
		$ 32,000	20,500
	Earnings per share	$1.56	
b.	From part (a)	$ 32,000	20,500 shares
	Less extraordinary gain	5,000	
		$ 27,000	20,500
	Reccurring earnings per share	$1.32	

PROBLEM 9-9

		Numerator	Denominator
a.	Net income	$200,000	
	Preferred dividends	(10,000)	
	Common shares outstanding on January 1		20,000 shares
	Common stock issue on July 1, 5,000 shares		2,500 (5,000 x ½)
	Weighted average		22,500
	Two-for-one stock split on December 31		2
		$190,000	45,000 shares
	Earnings per share	$190,000/45,000 shares = $4.22	

b.

	Current Year	Prior Year
Earnings per share reported for the prior year		$8.00
Two-for-one stock split on December 31 of the current year ($8.00 x .5) = $4.00		$4.00
Earnings per share computed in part (a) for the current year	$4.22	

PROBLEM 9-10

a. 1. Percentage of Earnings Retained =

$$\frac{\text{Net Income - All Dividends}}{\text{Net Income}}$$

	2000	1999
Cash dividends	$.80 x 25,380,000	$.76 x 25,316,000
	$20,304,000	$19,240,160
Preferred dividends	4,567,000	930,000
Total dividends	24,871,000	20,170,160
Net income (B)	32,094,000	31,049,000
Net income - dividends (A)	7,223,000	10,878,840
Percentage of earnings retained (A)/(B)	22.51%	35.04%

2. Price/Earnings Ratio = $\dfrac{\text{Market Price}}{\text{Fully Diluted Earnings Per Share}}$

	2000	1999
	$12.94	$15.19
	$ 1.08	$ 1.14
	11.98	13.32

3. Dividend Payout = $\dfrac{\text{Dividends Per Share}}{\text{Fully Diluted Earnings Per Share}}$

	2000	1999
	$ .80	$ .76
	$ 1.08	$ 1.14
	74.07%	66.67%

4. Dividend Yield = $\dfrac{\text{Dividends Per Share}}{\text{Market Price Per Share}}$

	2000	1999
	$ .80	$ .76
	$12.94	$15.19
	6.18%	5.00%

5. Book Value Per Share = $\dfrac{\text{Common Equity}}{\text{Shares Outstanding}}$

Total assets	$1,264,086,000	
$1,173,924,000		
Less: total liabilities	(823,758,000)	(742,499,000)
Less: non-redeemable		
preferred stock	(16,600,000)	(16,600,000)
Common equity (A)	$ 423,728,000	$ 414,825,000
Shares out-		
standing (B)	25,380,000	25,316,000
Book value per share (A)/(B)	$16.70	$16.39

b. Having the percentage of earnings retained decline provides mixed feelings. It implies that more is going to shareholders, but at the same time, earnings retained for growth have diminished. The rise in the dividend payout ratio supports this position.

The price/earnings ratio has declined as a result of the drop in price. This decline indicates lower shareholder expectations but might also indicate a good time to buy.

Dividend yield is up, caused by the rise in dividends and more so by the drop in price.

Book value per share is up. However, book value is above market, which shows that the investors do not view the assets as worth their book value. This is not a good sign.

Overall the signals are mixed. There is not enough information to determine if this is a good security.

PROBLEM 9-11

a. The major advantage of receiving stock appreciation rights instead of stock options is that the executive does not have to make a big cash outlay at the date of exercise, but rather receives a payment for the share appreciation. This helps the executive's cash flow.

b. The related credit is to a liability under the stock appreciation plan that would probably be classified as long-term, since exercise cannot occur until 1998.

c. In 2003, the company must pay off the liability related to the appreciation in cash. For this problem, it is $30,000. In doing financial statement analysis, this future cash flow, if

material, must be considered. As in this case, the full
impact may not be apparent until the last year, if the market
price rises sharply.

PROBLEM 9-12

a. __3__ Common shareholders' equity divided by the number of
common shares outstanding gives book value per share.

b. __2__ Book value per share =

Total Stockholders' Equity -
Preferred Stock (At Liquidation)
Number Of Common Shares Outstanding

$\dfrac{\$1,000,000 + \$1,500,000 + \$500,000 - \$1,100,000}{150,000 \text{ shares}} = \$12.67$

PROBLEM 9-13

a. 1. Degree of Financial Leverage = $\dfrac{\text{Earnings Before Interest, Tax, Minority Share of Earnings, Equity Income, and Nonrecurring Items}}{\text{Earnings Before Tax, Minority Share of Earnings, Equity Income, and Nonrecurring Items}}$

2000: $\dfrac{\$110,500 + \$9,500}{\$110,500}$ = 1.09

1999: $\dfrac{\$107,700 + \$6,600}{\$107,700}$ = 1.06

1998: $\dfrac{\$100,450 + \$6,800}{\$100,450}$ = 1.07

1997: $\dfrac{\$124,100 + \$6,900}{\$124,100}$ = 1.06

1996: $\dfrac{\$119,000 + \$7,000}{\$119,000}$ = 1.06

2. Earnings Per Common Share

   2000:   Continuing operations $2.67*
             Extraordinary gain   .69
                                      $3.36

             *Should be used in primary analysis.

   1999: $2.57

   1998: $2.36

   1997: $3.23

   1996: $2.81

3. Price/Earnings Ratio = $\dfrac{\text{Market Price Per Share}}{\text{Earnings Per Share}}$

   2000: $\dfrac{\$24.00}{\$\ 2.67}$ = 8.99

   1999: $\dfrac{\$22.00}{\$\ 2.57}$ = 8.56

   1998: $\dfrac{\$21.00}{\$\ 2.36}$ = 8.90

   1997: $\dfrac{\$37.00}{\$\ 3.23}$ = 11.46

   1996: $\dfrac{\$29.00}{\$\ 2.81}$ = 10.32

4. Percentage Of = $\dfrac{\text{Net Income - All Dividends}}{\text{Net Income}}$
   Earnings Retained

   2000: $\dfrac{\$97,500 - \$3,920 - \$91,640}{\$97,500}$ = 1.99%

   1999: $\dfrac{\$74,400 - \$6,100 - \$66,410}{\$74,400}$ = 2.54%

   1998: $\dfrac{\$68,350 - \$6,400 - \$60,900}{\$68,350}$ = 1.54%

1997: $$\frac{\$93,700 - \$6,600 - \$84,970}{\$93,700} = 2.27\%$$

1996: $$\frac{\$81,600 - \$6,000 - \$81,200}{\$81,600} = (6.86\%)$$

5. Dividend Payout = $$\frac{\text{Dividends Per Common Share}}{\text{Fully Diluted Earnings Per Share}}$$

2000: $$\frac{\$3.16}{\$2.67} = 118.35\%$$

1999: $$\frac{\$2.29}{\$2.57} = 89.11\%$$

1998: $$\frac{\$2.10}{\$2.36} = 88.98\%$$

1997: $$\frac{\$2.93}{\$3.23} = 90.71\%$$

1996: $$\frac{\$2.80}{\$2.81} = 99.64\%$$

6. Dividend Yield = $$\frac{\text{Dividends Per Common Share}}{\text{Market Price Per Common Share}}$$

2000: $$\frac{\$\ 3.16}{\$24.00} = 13.17\%$$

1999: $$\frac{\$\ 2.29}{\$22.00} = 10.41\%$$

1998: $$\frac{\$\ 2.10}{\$21.00} = 10.00\%$$

1997: $$\frac{\$\ 2.93}{\$37.00} = 7.92\%$$

1996: $$\frac{\$\ 2.80}{\$29.00} = 9.66\%$$

7. Book Value Per Share = $$\frac{\text{Total Stockholders' Equity - Preferred Stock Equity}}{\text{Number of Common Shares Outstanding}}$$

2000: $$\frac{\$489,000 - \$49,000}{29,000} = \$15.17$$

1999: $$\frac{\$514,000 - \$76,000}{29,000} = \$15.10$$

1998: $$\frac{\$516,000 - \$80,000}{29,000} = \$15.03$$

1997: $$\frac{\$517,000 - \$82,000}{29,000} = \$15.00$$

1996: $$\frac{\$508,000 - \$75,000}{29,000} = \$14.93$$

8. Materiality Of Options = $\dfrac{\text{Stock Options Outstanding}}{\text{Number of Shares of}}$
Common Stock Outstanding

1996-2000: $$\frac{1,000,000}{29,000,000} = 3.45\%$$

b. This firm has a very low degree of financial leverage. Earnings from continuing operations and the price/earnings ratio have been relatively stable.

Practically all of the earnings have been paid out in dividends; thus, book value per share has only increased slightly.

The dividend yield is very high. The market price has declined substantially.

Options outstanding appear to be immaterial.

In general, the investor analysis is positive if the investor wants high dividends. Growth prospects do not appear to be good.

CASES

CASE 9-1 STOCK SPLIT

(This case provides the opportunity to review a stock split.)

a. The March 1, 1994 stock split must be handled on a retroactive basis.

   1993 annual report

   Number of shares used in per share
     calculations - fully
     diluted: 40,520,000

   Adjusted for March 1, 1994 5-for-2
     stock split

         40,520,000 x 5/2 = 101,300,000

b. The March 1, 1994 stock split must be handled on a retroactive basis.

   1998 annual report

   Earnings per share - fully
     diluted: $2.57 x 2/5 = $1.028 or $1.03

c. Stock splits are intended to lower stock prices from high levels. It is hoped that after a stock split, the stock will be more actively traded. Also, with the stock split, it is hoped that there will not be a full adjustment of market price for the split.

d. The book value per share will decrease because of the stock split. (There will now be more shares outstanding.)

e. The company's par value of $0.10 per share remained unchanged. As a result, $6.1 million was transferred from additional paid-in capital to common stock.

CASE 9-2 WHY THE CHANGE?

(This case provides the opportunity to review the influence of a stock split.)

a. 1. 13,512,317
   2. 14,011,893
   3. 14,011,893 (weighted average)
   4. The outstanding shares decreased between 1997 and 1998 because the treasury shares increased.

b. diluted.
   Using diluted results in a more conservative computation.

c. 1. Yes.
   Nothing is indicated in the case that would have changed the reported net income.

   2. No.
   The reported diluted net income per share would have been much higher. The number was adjusted for the 1998 annual report to take into account the 3 for 1 split.

d. 1. <u>1998</u>   <u>1997</u>

$$\frac{\$141,670,000}{13,512,317} = \$10.48 \qquad \frac{\$158,180,000}{14,681,154} = \$10.77$$

   2. Considering the earnings per share and the cash dividends per share would have increased the book value. The book value decreased because substantial treasury shares were purchased at a market price above book value.

e.

	1998	1997	1996
Dividends per share (a)	$.60	$.53	$.46
Diluted net income per share (b)	$1.48	$1.54	$1.28
Dividend payout (a ÷ b)	40.54%	34.42%	35.94%

CASE 9-3 STOCK SPLIT REVISITED

(This case provides an opportunity to view the effect of a stock split and several other interesting aspects, such as earnings per share.)

a. The two-for-one stock split for the period ended January 27, 1995, is handled on a retroactive basis.

b. 1. Sold and paid for   40,221,000
   2. Treasury stock   5,395,000
   3. Sold and paid for   40,221,000
      Less treasury shares   (5,395,000)
                                                  34,826,000

c. 1. 0
   2. $3,592,000
   3. $3,589,000

d. 1. $27,979,000
   2. $ 2,861,000
   3. $20,972,000

e. 1. Dividends   -0-
      Purchase of treasury stock $27,979,000
                       Total $27,979,000

   2. Dividends $3,592,000
      Purchase of treasury stock   2,861,000
                       Total $6,453,000

   3. Dividends $ 3,589,000
      Purchase of treasury stock   20,972,000
                       Total $24,561,000

   Note: It may be interesting to students that many firms have reduced or eliminated cash dividends.

f. Net income per share is computed by dividing net income by the weighted average number of common shares outstanding during each period. After the two-for-one split, the weighted average common shares outstanding were 35.2 million for fiscal year 1995.

g. $0.01 par value (Note 2)

CASE 9-4 STOCK OPTION PLANS

(This case provides the opportunity to review the materiality of employee stock options on two separate companies, in two widely different industries.)

a. 1.

	1998	1997	1996
Reported net income	$126,967,000	$122,411,000	$107,884,000
Pro forma net income	125,142,000	121,603,000	107,363,000
Difference	$1,825,000	$ 808,000	$ 521,000

2.

	1998	1997	1996
Earnings per share reported	$1.64	$1.55	$1.30
Pro forma earnings per share	1.61	1.54	1.29
Difference	.03	.01	.01

3. Viewing items on % usually gives a better perspective on materiality than whole numbers.

	1998	1997	1996
Reported net income difference in %	1.44%	.66%	.48%
Earnings per share difference in %	1.83%	.65%	.77%

It appears that employee stock options compensation was not material, but it increased substantially in 1998.

b. 1.

	1998	1997	1996
Reported net income	$395,000,000	$1,452,000,000	$1,206,000,000
Pro forma net income	350,000,000	1,429,000,000	1,189,000,000
Difference	$45,000,000	$23,000,000	$17,000,000

2.

	1998	1997	1996
Earnings per share diluted reported	$.52	$2.02	$1.66
Pro forma earnings per share	.45	1.99	1.64
Difference	.07	.03	.02

3. Viewing items in % usually gives a better perspective on materiality than whole numbers.

	1998	1997	1996
Reported net income difference in %	11.39%	1.58%	1.41%
Earnings per share difference in %	13.46%	1.49%	1.20%

It appears that employee stock options compensation was material in 1998, but immaterial in 1997 and 1996.

c. Xerox
   Hi tech companies tend to use employee stock options more than basic low tech companies.

CASE 9-5   VIEW THIS INVESTMENT

(This case provides an opportunity to compute most of the ratios introduced in this chapter, using Tyco International Company.)

a. 1. Degree of Financial Leverage

	1995	1994
	$\dfrac{\$384,878 + \$63,385}{\$384,878}$	$\dfrac{\$328,190 + \$62,431}{\$328,190}$
	$\dfrac{\$448,263}{\$384,878}$	$\dfrac{\$390,621}{\$328,190}$
	116.47%	119.02%

2. Price/Earnings Ratio

	1995	1994
	$\dfrac{\$54.00}{\$2.87}$	$\dfrac{\$45\ 7/8}{\$2.56}$
	18.82	17.92

3. Percentage of Earnings Retained

	1995	1994
	$\dfrac{\$216,593 - \$24,335}{\$216,593}$	$\dfrac{\$189,191 - \$18,510}{\$189,191}$
	$\dfrac{\$192,258}{\$216,593}$	$\dfrac{\$170,691}{\$189,191}$
	88.76%	90.22%

4. Dividend Yield

	1995	1994
	$\dfrac{.40¢}{\$54.00}$	$\dfrac{\$.40¢}{\$45\,7/8}$
	.74%	.87%

5. Book Value Per Share

2000	1999
$\dfrac{\$1,634,681,000}{76,365,001}$	$\dfrac{\$1,367,026,000}{71,084,293}$
$21.41	$19.23

b. For a better use of these ratios, comparison should be made
   with competitors and the industry.

   The degree of financial leverage would likely be considered
   moderate. It is particularly important to consider the
   price/earnings ratio in relation to competitors and the
   industry. It is also important to consider the price/earnings
   ratio in terms of the growth in earnings that is projected.
   The percentage of earnings retained is high, while the
   dividend yield is low. The book value is increasing because
   of the earnings and the low percentage of earnings retained.

Chapter 10
Statement of Cash Flows

0- 1. The basic justification for a statement cash flows is that the balance sheet and the income statement do not adequately indicate changes in cash.

The balance sheet indicates the position of the firm at a particular point of time. Some idea of how the changes in cash occurred can be obtained by comparing consecutive balance sheets, but only a limited amount of information can be obtained this way.

The income statement shows the income or loss for a period of time, but it does not indicate cash generated by operations. Neither the balance sheet nor the income statement summarize the cash flows related to investing or financing activities. Neither presents such items as sale of stock, retirement of bonds, purchase of machinery, or sale of a subsidiary.

Thus, there is a need to summarize the cash flows in another statement.

0- 2. 1.   Cash flows from operating activities
       2.   Cash flows from investing activities
       3.   Cash flows from financing activities

0- 3. The cash inflows (outflows) will be determined by analyzing all balance sheet accounts other than the cash and cash equivalent accounts. The cash inflows will be generated from the following accounts:

1.   Decreases in assets
2.   Increases in liabilities
3.   Increases in stockholders' equity

The cash outflows will be generated from the following accounts.

1.   Increases in assets
2.   Decreases in liabilities
3.   Decreases in stockholders' equity

0- 4. This statement is <u>not</u> correct. The land account may contain an explanation of a source and use of cash.

10- 5. 1.   Visual method
       2.   T-account method
       3.   Worksheet method

10- 6. For the direct approach, the revenue and expense accounts on the income statement are presented on a cash basis. For this purpose, the accrual basis income statement is adjusted to a cash basis. For the indirect approach, start with net income and add back or deduct adjustments necessary to change the income on an accrual basis to income on a cash basis after eliminating gains or losses that relate to investing or financing activities.

10- 7. Items have been included in income that did not provide cash and items have been deducted from income that did not use cash. Net income must be converted to a cash from operations figure for the statement of cash flows.

10- 8. Cash and short-term highly liquid investments. This would include cash on hand, cash on deposit, and investments in short-term highly liquid investments.

10- 9. The purpose of the statement of cash flows is to provide information on why the cash position of the company changed during the period.

10-10. These transactions represent significant investing and/or financing activities and one purpose of the statement of cash flows is to present investing and financing activities.

10-11. No. The write-off of uncollectible accounts against allowance for doubtful accounts would reduce accounts receivable and the allowance for doubtful accounts. It would relate to operations and be a noncash item. The net receivables amount would not change.

10-12. Discarding a fully depreciated asset with no salvage value will not result in cash flow.

10-13. This may be the result of non-cash charges for depreciation, amortization, and depletion. Also, receivables or inventory may have decreased or accounts payable may have increased.

10-14. An increase in accounts payable would be considered to be an increase in cash from operations.

10-15. Investments in receivables, inventories, fixed assets, and the paying off of debt are examples of situations where cash will be used but will not reduce profits.

10-16. Depreciation is not a source of funds. Depreciation has been deducted on the income statement in arriving at income. Since depreciation is a non-fund charge to the income statement, it is added back to income to compute cash from operations.

10-17. The decrease in accounts receivable would increase cash from operations.

10-18. This is an example of noncash investing and financing. As such, it should be disclosed on a schedule that accompanies the statement of cash flows.

10-19. Cash flow per share is not as good an indicator of profitability as earnings per share. In the short-run, cash flow per share is a better indicator of liquidity and ability to pay dividends.

10-20. Since cash flow from operating activities is substantially greater than the cash paid out for dividends, it appears that the company can maintain and possibly increase dividend payments in the future, depending also on its investing and financing goals.

TO THE NET

1. a. Aircraft

   b. The direct method is used for operating activities. This presents individual inflows and outflows from operating activities. The alternative presentation (indirect method) does not present individual inflows and outflows from operati activities.

2. a. Electronic computers

   b.

	January 29, 1999	February 1, 1998
	(In Millions)	
Accounts receivable, net	$2,094	$1,486
Inventories	$273	$233
Accounts payable	$2,397	$1,643

   c.

	January 29, 1999	February 1, 1998
Accounts receivable, net	140.9%	100.0%
Inventories	117.2%	100.0%
Accounts payable	145.9%	100.0%

   d.

	Fiscal Year Ended (In Millions)	
	January 29, 1999	February 1, 1998
Net revenue	$18,243	$12,327
Net income	$1,460	$944
Net cash provided by operating activities	$2,436	$1,592

e.

| | Fiscal Year Ended | |
	January 29, 1999	February 1, 1998
Net revenue	148.0%	100.0%
Net income	154.7%	100.0%
Net cash provided by operating activities	153.8%	100.0%

f. Impressive that the increase in inventories was less than the increase in accounts receivable and accounts payable.

Impressive increase in net revenue, net income, and net cash provided by operating activities. The increase in net cash provided by operating activities was particularly impressive.

PROBLEMS

PROBLEM 10-1

| | Cash Flows Classification | | | Effect on Cash | | |
Data	Operating Activity	Investing Activity	Financing Activity	Increase	Decrease	Non-cash Transaction
a. Net Loss	X				X	
b. Increase in inventory	X				X	
c. Decrease in receivables	X			X		
d. Increase in prepaid insurance					X	
e. Issuance of common stock			X	X		
f. Acquisition of land using notes payable						X
g. Purchase of land using cash		X			X	
h. Paid cash dividend			X		X	
i. Payment of income taxes	X				X	
j. Retirement of bonds using cash			X		X	
k. Sale of equipment for cash		X		X		

PROBLEM 10-2

Data	Cash Flows Classification			Effect on Cash		
	Operating Activity	Investing Activity	Financing Activity	Increase	Decrease	Non-cash Trans-action
a. Net income	X			X		
b. Paid cash dividend			X		X	
c. Increase in receivables	X				X	
d. Retirement of debt, paying cash			X		X	
e. Purchase of treasury stock			X		X	
f. Purchase of equipment		X			X	
g. Sale of equipment		X		X		
h. Decrease in inventory	X			X		
i. Acquisition of land using common stock						X
j. Retired bonds using common stock						X
k. Decrease in accounts payable	X				X	

a.

BBB Company
Statement of Cash Flows
For the Year Ended December 31, 2002

Cash flows from operating activities:

Net income		$ 500
Noncash expenses, revenues, losses, and		
gains included in income:		
Depreciation	$2,800	
Gain on sale of land	(800)	
Decrease in accounts receivable	400	
Decrease in inventory	500	
Increase in accounts payable	800	
Increase in wages payable	50	
Decrease in taxes payable	(1,000)	2,750
Net cash flow from operating activities		3,250
Cash flows from investing activities:		
Land was sold for		1,800
Equipment was purchased for		(3,500)
Net cash used for investing activities		(1,700)
Cash flows from financing activities:		
Dividends declared and paid		(4,350)
Common stock was sold for		3,800
Net cash used for financing activities		(550)
Net increase in cash and marketable securities		$ 1,000

b. Net cash flow from operating activities was substantially more than t
net income. Cash dividends were greater than the net cash flow from
operating activities.

The cash from issuing the common stock was sufficient to cover the ne
cash used for investing activities, increase the cash and marketable
securities accounts, and partially cover the large cash dividend.

The fact that a long-term source of funds (common stock) was used to
cover part of the cash dividends is a negative observation. The larg
cash dividend in relation to net cash flow from operating activities
would also be considered a negative situation.

PROBLEM 10-4

Frish Company

a.   **Schedule of Change From Accrual To**
                        Cash Basis Income Statement

Accrual Basis		Adjustments	Add(Subtract)	Cash Basis
Net sales	$640,000	Increase in accounts receivable	($27,000)	$613,000
Less expenses:				
Cost of goods sold	360,000	Increase in accounts payable	(15,000)	
		Increase in inventories	35,000	
		Depreciation expense	(15,000)	365,000
Selling and administrative expense	43,000	Decrease in prepaid expenses	(1,000)	
		Increase in accrued liabilities	(3,000)	
		Depreciation expense	(5,000)	34,000
Other expense	2,000	Amortization of goodwill	(3,000)	
		Amortization of bond premium	1,000	-0-
Income before income taxes	235,000			214,000
Income tax	92,000	Decrease in income taxes payable	10,000	102,000
Net income	$143,000			$112,000

b. (1) Direct Approach

Receipts from customers	$613,000
Payments to suppliers	(365,000)
Selling and administrative expenses	(34,000)
Income taxes paid	(102,000)
Cash flows from operating activities	$112,000

(2) <u>Indirect Approach</u>

Net income	$143,000
Add (deduct) items not affecting cash	
Depreciation	20,000
Amortization of goodwill	3,000
Amortization of bond premium	(1,000)
Increase in accounts receivable	(27,000)
Increase in accounts payable	15,000
Increase in inventories	(35,000)
Decrease in prepaid expenses	1,000
Increase in accrued liabilities	3,000
Decrease in income taxes payable	(10,000)
Cash flow from operating activities	$112,000

PROBLEM 10-5

a. The income statement and other selected data for the Boyer Company is shown below.

Boyer Company
Schedule of Change From Accrual To
Cash Basis Income Statement

Accrual Basis		Adjustments	Add (Subtract)	Cash Basis
Sales	$19,000	Increase in receivables	(400)	$18,600
Less operating expenses: Depreciation	2,300	Depreciation expense	(2,300)	-0-
		Increase in inventories	800	
Other operating expenses	12,000	Increase in accounts payable	(500)	12,300
Operating income	4,700			6,300
Loss on sale of land	1,500	Loss on sale of land	(1,500)	-0-
Income before tax expense	3,200			6,300
Tax expense	1,000	Decrease in income taxes payable	400	1,400
Net income	$2,200			$4,900

b. (1) Direct Approach

Receipts from customers	$18,600
Payments to suppliers	(12,300)
Income taxes paid	(1,400)
Cash flow from operating activities	$ 4,900

(2) Indirect Approach

Net income		$ 2,200
Add (deduct) items not affecting cash:		
Depreciation	$2,300	
Increase in receivables	(400)	
Increase in inventories	(800)	
Increase in accounts payable	500	
Loss on sale of land	1,500	
Decrease in income taxes payable	(400)	2,700
Cash flow from operating activities		$ 4,900

PROBLEM 10-6

a.

Sampson Company
Statement of Cash Flows
For the Year Ended December 31, 2002

Net cash flow from operating activities:

Net income		$19,000
Noncash expenses, revenues, losses, and gains included in income:		
Depreciation expense	$10,000	
Increase in net receivables	(7,000)	
Increase in inventory	(13,000)	
Increase in accounts payable	5,000	
Decrease in accrued liabilities	(17,000)	
Net cash outflow from operating activities		(3,000)
Cash flows from investing activities:		
Plant assets increase		(15,000)
Cash flows from financing activities:		
Mortgage payable increase	$11,000	
Common stock increase	6,000	
Dividends paid	(21,000)	
Net cash flows from financing activities		$(4,000)
Net decrease in cash		$(22,000)

b.

Sampson Company
Statement of Cash Flows
For the Year Ended December 31, 2002

Cash flow from customers	$138,000	
($145,000 - $7,000)		
Cash payments to suppliers	(123,000)	
($108,000 - $10,000 + $13,000 - $5,000 +		
$17,000)		
Cash outflow for other expenses	(6,000)	
Tax payments	(12,000)	
Net cash outflow from operating activities		($ 3,000)
Cash flows from investing activities:		
Plant assets increase		(15,000)
Cash flows from financing activities:		
Mortgage payable increase	$11,000	
Common stock increase	6,000	
Dividends paid	(21,000)	
Net cash outflow from financing activities		(4,000)
Net decrease in cash		$(22,000)

c. All major segments of cash flows were negative. Net cash outflow fro
operating activities was negative by $3,000, and yet dividends were
paid in the amount of $21,000. Also, the company had a negative cash
flow from investing activities. These negative cash flows were
partially made up for by issuing a mortgage payable ($11,000) and
common stock ($6,000).

PROBLEM 10-7

a. Comment
The usual guideline for the current ratio is two to one. Arrowbell
Company had a 1.14 to 1 ratio in 2001 and a .85 to 1 ratio in 2002.
The usual guideline for the acid-test ratio is one to one. Arrowbell
Company had a .68 to 1 ratio in 2001 and a .49 to 1 ratio in 2002.

The cash ratio dropped from .19 in 2001 to .12 in 2002. The working
capital in 2001 was $197,958, and in 2002 it had declined to a negati
$319,988.

The short-term debt position appears to be very poor.

Computation of Ratios

Current Ratio = <u>Current Assets</u>
Current Liabilities

<u>2002</u>   <u>2001</u>

<u>$1,755,303</u> = .85   <u>$1,599,193</u> = 1.14
$2,075,291 $1,401,235

                Cash Equivalents & Net Receivables &
Acid-Test Ratio = <u>   Marketable Securities</u>
                    Current Liabilities
        <u>2002</u>

        <u>$250,480 + $760,950</u> = .49
            $2,075,291

        <u>2001</u>

        <u>$260,155 + $690,550</u> = .68
            $1,401,235

Cash Ratio = <u>Cash Equivalents & Marketable Securities</u>
                Current Liabilities

        <u>2002</u>   <u>2001</u>

        <u>$250,480   </u> = .12   <u>$260,155   </u> = .19
        $2,075,291 $1,401,235

Operating Cash Flow/Current   <u>   Operating Cash Flow</u>
Maturities of Long-Term Debt=Current Maturities of Long-Term
and Current Notes Payable   Debt and Current Notes Payable

            <u>2002</u>   <u>2001</u>

        <u>$429,491</u> = 46.93%   <u>$177,658</u> = 32.29%
        $915,180 $550,155

b. Suppliers will be concerned that Arrowbell Company will not
    be able to pay its creditors and, if payment is made, it will be later
    than the credit terms. The short-term creditors are financing the
    expansion program.

c. The debt ratio has increased in 2002 to .61 from .58 in 2001. The
    debt/equity ratio has increased in 2002 to 1.55 from 1.36 in 2001. (A
    similar increase in the debt to tangible net worth as the increase in
    the debt/equity ratio.) There was an improvement in the operating cas
    flow/total debt, but this ratio remains very low.

    This indicates that a substantial amount of funds are coming from
    creditors. In general the dependance on creditors worsened in 2002.

    Not enough information is available to compute the times interest
    earned, but we can estimate this to be between 2 and 3, based on the
    earnings and the debt. We would like to see the times interest earned
    to be higher than this amount.
    The review of the Statement of Cash Flows indicates that long-term
    creditors are going to be concerned by the use of debt to expand
    property, plant, and equipment. They also are going to be concerned b
    the payment of a dividend while the working capital is in poor
    condition.

$$\text{Debt Ratio} = \frac{\text{Total Debt}}{\text{Total Assets}}$$

<u>2002</u>

$$\frac{\$2,625,291}{\$4,316,598} = .61$$

<u>2001</u>

$$\frac{\$2,176,894}{\$3,776,711} = .58$$

$$\text{Debt/Equity} = \frac{\text{Total Debt}}{\text{Stockholders' Equity}}$$

<u>2002</u>

$$\frac{\$2,625,291}{\$1,691,307} = 1.55$$

<u>2001</u>

$$\frac{\$2,176,894}{\$1,599,817} = 1.36$$

Debt to Tangible Net Worth =

$$\frac{\text{Total Liabilities}}{\text{Shareholders' Equity - Intangible Assets}}$$

<u>2002</u>   <u>2001</u>

$$\frac{\$2,625,291}{\$1,691,307 - 0} = 155.22\%$$ $$\frac{\$2,176,894}{\$1,599,817 - 0} = 136.07\%$$

$$\text{Operating Cash Flow/Total Debt} = \frac{\text{Operating Cash Flow}}{\text{Total Debt}}$$

<u>2002</u>   <u>2001</u>

$$\frac{\$429,491}{\$2,625,291} = 16.36\%$$ $$\frac{\$177,658}{\$2,176,894} = 8.16\%$$

- A banker would be especially concerned about the short-term debt situation. This could lead to bankruptcy, even though the firm is profitable. A banker would be particularly concerned why management had used short-term credit to finance long-term expansion.

- Management should consider the following or a combination of the following:

1. Discontinue the expansion program at this time and get the short-term debt situation in order. Tighten control of accounts receivable and inventory, along with using funds from operations to reduce short-term debt.

2. Issue additional stock to improve the short-term liquidity problem and the long-term debt situation. Because of the poor record on profitability and the way that management has financed past expansion, additional stock will probably not be well-accepted in the market place at this time.

PROBLEM 10-8

a. Bernett Company had a decrease in cash of $23,000, although net cash
    flow from operating activities was $21,000. Net cash provided by
    financing activities was $116,000, while net cash used by investing
    activities was $160,000. The cash flows from operations and financing
    activities were not sufficient to cover the very significant net cash
    used by investing activities.

b. 1. Current ratio:
        Current assets:
        Cash $ 5,000
        Accounts receivable   92,000
        Inventory   130,000
        Prepaid expense   4,000
            Total current assets $231,000   (A)

        Current liabilities:
        Accounts payable $ 49,000
        Income taxes payable   5,000
        Accrued liabilities   6,000
        Current bonds payable   10,000
            Total current liabilities $ 70,000   (B)

        (A) $231,000 = 3.30
        (B) $ 70,000

    2. Acid-test ratio:
        Cash $ 5,000
        Accounts receivable   92,000
                                                 $ 97,000   (A)

            Total current liabilities   70,000   (B)

        (A) $97,000 = 1.39
        (B) $70,000

    3. Operating cash flow/current maturities of long-term debt and
        current notes payable:

        Operating cash flow (from part (a)) $ 21,000   (A)
        Current maturities of long-term
          debt and current notes payable $ 10,000   (B)

        (A) $21,000 = 2.10
        (B) $10,000

4. Cash ratio:

Cash	$ 5,000	(A)
Total current liabilities	$ 70,000	(B)

(A) $ 5,000 = 7.14%
(B) $70,000

c. 1. Times interest earned:

Income before taxes	$ 99,000	
Plus interest expense	11,000	
	$110,000	(A)
Interest expense	$ 11,000	(B)

(A) $110,000 = 10 times per year
(B) $ 11,000

2. Debt ratio:

Total liabilities:		
Accounts payable	$ 49,000	
Income taxes payable	5,000	
Accrued liabilities	6,000	
Bonds payable	175,000	
Total liabilities	$235,000	(A)
Total assets	$411,000	(B)

$\dfrac{A) \$235,000}{B) \$411,000} = 57.18\%$

3. Operating cash flow/total debt:

Operating cash flow (from part (a))	$ 21,000	(A)
Total debt (from part (d.2.))	$235,000	(B)

(A) $ 21,000 = 8.94%
(B) $235,000

d. 1. Return on assets:

    Net income $ 69,000 (A)
    Average assets
    [($219,000 + $411,000) divided by 2] $315,000 (B)

    (A) $ 69,000 = 21.90%
    (B) $315,000

2. Return on common equity:

    Net income $ 69,000 (A)
    Average common equity
    [($96,000 + $50,000 + $106,000 + $70,000)
       divided by 2] $161,000 (B)

    (A) $ 69,000 = 42.86%
    (B) $161,000

e. Operating cash flow/cash dividends:

    Operating cash flow (from part (a)) $ 21,000 (A)
    Cash dividends $ 49,000 (B)
    (A) $21,000 = .43
    (B) $49,000

f. In general, the liquidity ratios look very good except for the cash ratio. The cash ratio is approximately 7%.

g. Overall, the debt position appears to be good. Times interest earned is very good, and the debt ratio and cash flow/total debt are good.

h. The profitability appears to be extremely good. Both the return on assets and return on common equity are very high.

i. Operating cash flow/cash dividends indicates that operating cash flow was less than half the cash dividends.

j. Alternatives appear to be as follows:

1. Reduce the rate of expansion or possibly stop expansion at this time. This would reduce the need to increase receivables and inventory in the future and provide cash to pay accounts payable.

2. Issue additional long-term debt.

3. Issue additional common stock.

Possibly a combination of these alternatives should be considered. This company is very profitable, has a good debt position, and in general a good liquidity position, except for the most immediate ability to pay its bills. This needs to be corrected or there is the possibility of bankruptcy. The growth rate of this company is very high. Immediate cash is needed to fund the growth.

PROBLEM 10-9

a. Zaro had substantially more net cash flow from operating activities than it had net income. Major reasons for this were depreciation, decrease in accounts receivable, and decrease in inventory.

The substantial cash flows from operating activities were used for investing activities and financing activities. Cash was particularly used for the financing activity of paying dividends.

b. 1. Current Ratio:

Current assets:		
Cash	$ 30,000	
Accounts receivable, net	75,000	
Inventory	90,000	
Prepaid expenses	3,000	
	$198,000	(A)
Current liabilities:		
Accounts payable	$ 25,500	
Income taxes payable	2,500	
Accrued liabilities	5,000	
Current portion of bonds payable	20,000	
	$ 53,000	(B)

(A) $198,000 = 3.74
(B) $ 53,000

2. Acid-Test Ratio:

Cash	$ 30,000	
Accounts receivable, net	75,000	
	105,000	(A)
Current liabilities	$ 53,000	(B)

(A) $105,000 = 1.98
(B) $ 53,000

3. Operating cash flow/current maturities of long-term debt: and current notes payable:

Operating cash flow $ 51,000 (A)
Current maturities of long-term
  debt and current notes payable $ 20,000   (B)

(A) $51,000 = 2.55
(B) $20,000

4. Cash Ratio:

Cash $ 30,000 (A)
Current liabilities $ 53,000 (B)
(A) $30,000 = .57
(B) $53,000

c. 1. Times Interest Earned:

Income before taxes $ 34,000
Plus interest expense   8,000 (B)
                             $ 42,000 (A)

(A) $42,000 = 5.25 times per year
(B) $ 8,000

2. Debt Ratio:

Total liabilities:
  Accounts payable $ 25,500
  Income taxes payable   2,500
  Accrued liabilities   5,000
  Bonds payable   90,000
                            $123,000 (A)

Total assets $253,000 (B)

(A) $123,000 = 48.62%
(B) $253,000

d. 1. Return on assets:

$$\frac{\$20,000}{\$253,000 + \$274,000 \div 2} = \frac{\$20,000}{\$263,500} = 7.59\%$$

2.   Return on Common Equity:

$$\frac{\$20,000}{(\$85,000 + \$54,000 + \$85,000 + \$45,000) \div 2}$$

$$\frac{\$20,000}{\$134,500} = 14.87\%$$

e.   All liquidity ratios are very good.

f.   The debt position is good.

g.   Profitability is good.

h.   Substantial cash flow came from operating activities. A relatively
     small amount of funds were used for investing activities and paying
     down bonds. This left substantial cash available.

PROBLEM 10-10

a.

The Ladies Store
Statement of Cash Flows
For the Year Ended December 31, 2002

Cash flows from operating activities:		
Cash receipts from customers	$150,000	
Cash receipts from interest	5,000	
Cash payments for merchandise	(110,000)	
Cash payments for interest	(2,000)	
Cash payments for income taxes	(15,000)	
Net cash flow from operating activities		$ 28,000
Cash flows from investing activities:		
Cash outflow for purchase of truck	(20,000)	
Cash outflow for purchase of investment	(80,000)	
Cash outflow for purchase of equipment	(45,000)	
Net outflow for investing activities		(145,000)
Cash flows from financing activities:		
Cash inflow from sale of bonds	100,000	
Cash inflow from issuance of note payable	40,000	
Cash inflow from financing activities		140,000
Net increase in cash		$ 23,000

b.   The major inflow of cash was from financing activities. The major
     outflow of cash was for investing activities.

261

PROBLEM 10-11

a.	1	e.	4
b.	5	f.	3
c.	5	g.	3
d.	5	h.	5

PROBLEM 10-12

a.

Szabo Company
Statement of Cash Flows
Years Ended December 31, 2002, 2001, 2000

	Total	2002	2001	2000
Increase (Decrease in Cash)				
Cash flows from operating activities				
Cash received from customers	$508,381	$173,233	$176,446	$158,702
Cash paid to suppliers & employees	(451,801)	(150,668)	(157,073)	(144,060)
Interest received	326	132	105	89
Interest paid	(1,357)	(191)	(389)	(777)
Income taxes paid	(12,225)	(6,626)	(4,754)	(845)
Net cash provided from operations	43,324	15,880	14,335	13,109
Cash flow from investing activities:				
Capital expenditures	(21,156)	(8,988)	(5,387)	(6,781)
Proceeds from property, plant &				
equipment disposals	1,452	1,215	114	123
Net cash used in financing activities	(19,704)	(7,773)	(5,273)	(6,658)
Cash flows from financing activities:				
Net increase (decrease) in short-term debt	12,300	- -	5,100	7,200
Increase in long-term debt	13,000	4,100	3,700	5,200
Dividends paid	(22,250)	(6,050)	(8,200)	(8,000)
Purchase of company stock	(11,412)	(8,233)	(3,109)	(70)
Net cash used in financing activities	(8,362)	(10,183)	(2,509)	4,330
Net increase (decrease) in cash &				
cash equivalents	15,258	(2,076)	6,553	10,781
Cash & cash equivalents at beginning of year	7,551	24,885	18,332	7,551
Cash & cash equivalents at end of year	$22,809	$22,809	$24,885	$18,332

Reconciliation of Net Income To Net Cash				
Provided by Operating Activities	Total	2002	2001	2000
Net income	$11,358	$7,610	$3,242	$506
Provision for depreciation & amortization	30,700	12,000	9,700	9,000
Provision for losses on accounts receivable	473	170	163	140
Gains on property, plant & equipment				
disposals	(4,620)	(2,000)	(1,120)	(1,500)
Changes in operating assets & liabilities				
Accounts receivable	(5,350)	(2,000)	(1,750)	(1,600)
Inventories:	(8,100)	(3,100)	(2,700)	(2,300)
Other assets	(57)	- -	- -	(57)
Accounts payable	12,300	- -	5,100	7,200
Accrued income taxes	1,200	1,200	- -	- -
Deferred income taxes	5,420	2,000	1,700	1,720
Net cash provided by operating activities	$43,324	$15,880	$14,335	$13,109

262

b. 1. The three-year analysis revealed that 45% of cash flows from operations went into investing activities. The company is not replacing its productive assets.

2. Cash flows used in financing activities are 19% of the cash flows from operating activities. At first glance, one might assume the company is paying down debt. Closer analysis reveals that the company actually increased its debt levels, but payment to stockholders in the form of dividends and share purchases used more cash than was raised in the borrowing. The company is borrowing, and therefore, increasing debt.

3. Further analysis reveals that a substantial part of the borrowing is short-term rather than long-term. Such money is riskier.

c.

Szabo Company
Statement of Cash Flows
For Year Ended December 31, 2002
(Inflow & Outflow by Activity)

	Inflow	Outflow	Inflow %	Outflow %
Cash flows from operating activities:			96.95	
Cash received from customers	$ 173,233			
Cash paid to suppliers & employees		$150,668		83.35
Interest received	132		.08	
Interest paid		191		.11
Income taxes paid		6,626		3.67
Cash flows from operations	173,365	157,485	97.03	87.13
Cash flows from investing activities:				
Capital expenditures		8,988		4.97
Proceeds from property, plant & equipment disposals	1,215		.68	
Cash flows from investing activities	1,215	8,988	.68	4.97
Cash flows from financing activities:				
Net increase (decrease) in short-term debt	- -			
Increase in long-term debt	4,100		2.29	
Dividends paid		6,050		3.35
Purchase of company stock		8,233		4.55
Cash flows from financing activities	4,100	14,283	2.29	7.90
Total cash flows	178,680	$180,756	100.00	100.00
	(180,756)			
Increase (decrease) in cash	$ (2,076)			

d. 1. 97% of cash inflows came from operations, and 2% came from financing activities. Significant cash inflows coming from operations is positive.

   2. 83% of cash outflows were payments to suppliers and employees. 5% of outflows were used for investment in property, plant, and equipment. 8% of cash outflows were used to pay dividends and purchase shares. Almost as much was spent to pay stockholders as for outflows for capital expenditures.

PROBLEM 10-13

Owens appears to be the growth firm. Operating activities may represent a use of cash because of the expansion of receivables and inventory. The expansion of fixed assets would use cash in investing activities. Financing activities are providing cash for expansion.

Alpha appears to be the firm in danger of bankruptcy. Cash is used in operations, capital expenditures appear to be nominal, and financing activities are using instead of providing cash.

Arrow appears to be the older firm expanding slowly. Arrow is generating significant cash from operating activities, while nominal cash is used for investing activities. Financing activities are using cash instead of providing cash (dividends, repayment of long-term debt, etc.).

PROBLEM 10-14

a.

Accounts receivable, January 1, 2002	$ 30,000
Sales	480,000
	510,000
Accounts receivable, December 31, 2002	(40,000)
	$470,000

b. Accounts receivable increased by $10,000 during the year 2002. Thus cash collected from customers was $10,000 less than sales.

PROBLEM 10-15

a.

Revenues from customers	$150,000
Decrease in accounts receivable	8,000
	$158,000

b. No. Depreciation expense is a non-cash charge reducing income.

CASE 10-1 CASH FLOW TALES

(This case provides an opportunity to review the cash flow of Osmonics. Osmonics is a integrated manufacturer of high technology equipment and products that purify water, separate fluids, remove dissolved materials or concentrate wastes from fluids, and enable clean water to be reused or discharged to the environment.)

a. 1.   <u>1995</u>   <u>1994</u>
       Operating Cash Flow/Current
       Maturities Of Long-Term Debt:

       and Current Notes Payable $\dfrac{\$6,569}{\$1,695}$ $\dfrac{\$9,906}{\$744}$

                                                3.88   13.31

There was a substantial coverage of current maturities of long-term debt and current notes payable. The coverage declined significantly in 1995.

2. Operating Cash Flow/Total Debt: $\dfrac{\$6,569}{\$46,587}$ $\dfrac{\$9,906}{\$38,284}$

                                                14.10%   25.88%

Operating cash flow in relation to total debt decreased materially in 1995.

3. $\dfrac{\text{Operating Cash Flow - Preferred Dividends}}{\text{Common Shares Outstanding}}$:

                                          <u>1995</u>   <u>1994</u>

                                   $\dfrac{\$6,569,000}{12,745,000}$ $\dfrac{\$9,906,000}{12,668,000}$

                                        .52¢   .78¢

Operating cash flow per common share was less than net income per share in 1995 and 1994.

4. Operating Cash Flow/Cash Dividends:

	1995	1994
	----------------	----------------
	$6,569	$9,906
	No cash	No cash
	dividend	dividend

Osmonics did not pay a cash dividend in 1995 or 1994.

b. 1. Significant cash inflows came from operations.

    2. There was a significant decrease in cash flows from operations.

    3. Significant cash outflows related to investing activities.

    4. Cash used for investing activities were more than the cash provided by operations.

c. Depreciation has been expensed on the income statement, reducing net income. Since depreciation represents a non-cash expense, it is added to net income as part of the computation of net cash provided by operating activities.

CASE 10-2 WATCH THE CASH

(This case provides an opportunity to review the cash flows of the Arden
Group. Net cash provided by operating activities is presented using the
direct method.)

a.

Arden Group, Inc. and Consolidated Subsidiary
Statements of Cash Flows

(In thousands)	Total	Fiscal Year Ended On Jan. 2, 1999	Fiscal Year Ended On Jan. 3, 1998	Fiscal Year Ended On Dec. 28, 1996
Cash flows from operating activities:				
Cash received from customers	$823,916	$296,751	$274,683	$252,482
Cash paid to suppliers and employees	(775,704)	(278,213)	(254,622)	(242,869)
Sales (purchases) of trading securities, net	7,540	- -	8,851	(1,311)
Interest and dividends received	4,810	1,449	1,683	1,678
Interest paid	(2,334)	(751)	(705)	(878)
Income taxes paid	(13,214)	(6,689)	(3,831)	(2,694
Net cash provided by operating activities	45,014	12,547	26,059	6,408
Cash flows from investing activities:				
Capital expenditures	(24,981)	(4,244)	(7,896)	(12,841)
Deposits for property in escrow	2,664	- -	- -	2,664
Transfer to discontinued operations	(3,031)	- -	(2,575)	(456)
Purchases of available-for-sale securities	(6,995)	(3,793)	(3,202)	- -
Sales of available-for-sale securities	1,648	268	1,380	- -
Proceeds from the sale of property, plant & equipment, liquor licenses and lease-hold interests	5,672	3,171	163	2,338
Payments received on notes from the sale of property, plant and equipment and liquor licenses	56	- -	53	3
Net cash used in investing activities	(24,967)	(4,598)	(12,077)	(8,292)
Cash flows from financing activities:				
Purchase and retirement of stock	(15,579)	- -	(13,966)	(1,613)
Principal payments on long-term debt	(2,739)	(1,188)	(799)	(752)
Principal payments under capital lease obligations	(760)	(230)	(205)	(325)
Loan payments received from officer/director	154	40	114	- -
Proceeds from equipment financing	2,500	- -	2,500	- -
Purchase of Company debentures	(78)	(23)	- -	(55)
Net cash used in financing activities	(16,502)	(1,401)	(12,356)	(2,745)
Net increase (decrease in cash and cash equivalents	3,545	6,548	1,626	(4,629)
Cash and cash equivalents, beginning of period	10,102	7,099	5,473	10,102
Cash and cash equivalents, end of period	$13,647	$13,647	$7,099	$5,473

b. 1. Net cash provided by operating activities increased $45,014,000. (Most of this increase came from cash received from customers.)

2. Net cash used in investing activities increased $24,967,000. (Most of this was for capital expenditures.)

3. Net cash used in financing activities increased $16,502,000. (Most of this was for the purchase and retirement of stock.)

C.

Arden Group, Inc. and Consolidated Subsidiary
Statements of Cash Flows
Inflow & Outflow of Activity
Fiscal Year Ended On January 2, 1999

	Inflow	Outflow	Inflow Percentage	Outflow Percentage
Cash flows from operating activities:			98.37	
Cash received from customers	$296,751			
Cash paid to suppliers and employees	- -	$278,213		94.27
Sales of trading securities	- -	- -	- -	- -
Interest and dividends received	1,449	- -	.48	
Interest paid	- -	751		.25
Income taxes paid	- -	6,689		2.27
Cash provided by operating activities	$298,200	$285,653	98.85	96.79
Cash flows from investing activities:				
Capital expenditures	- -	$4,244		1.43
Deposits for property in escrow	- -	- -		
Transfer to discontinued operations	- -	- -		
Purchase of available-for-sale securities		3,793		1.29
Sales of available-for-sale securities	268		.09	
Proceeds from the sale of property, plant and equipment, liquor licenses and leasehold interests	3,171		1.05	
Payments received on notes from the sale of property, plant and equipment and liquor licenses	- -	- -		
Cash used in investing activities	$3,439	$8,037	1.14	2.72
Cash flows from financing activities:				
Purchase and retirement of stock	- -	- -		
Principal payments on long-term debt	- -	$ 1,188		.40
Principal payments under capital lease obligations	- -	230		.08
Loan payments received from officer/ director	$ 40	- -	.01	
Proceeds from equipment financing	- -	- -		
Purchase of Company debentures		23		.0
Cash used in financing activities	$ 40	$ 1,441	.01	.49
Total	$301,679	$295,131	100.0	100.00

d. 1. Cash received from customers provided 98.37% of the inflow.

 2. Cash paid to suppliers and employees made up 94.27% of the outflow.

CASE 10-3 RAPIDLY EXPANDING

(This case provides the opportunity to review a company that has had rapid growth in a market where there is extensive competition. In the author's opinion, the company did a very good job of presenting its financial results. This is a very interesting case for students to follow up on. This company addressed it's problem. The stock on a split adjusted basis was approximately $3.00 at the end of 1996. On July 1, 1999 the stock price was approximately $70.00. One thing that the company did was reduce the selection of inventory and speed up turnover of inventory.)

a. Liquidity ratios

    1. Current Ratio:

1996	1995
$\dfrac{\$1,560,543,000}{\$974,688,000}$	$\dfrac{\$1,240,667,000}{\$631,618,000}$
= 1.60	= 1.96

    2. Acid-Test Ratio:

1996	1995
$\dfrac{\$86,445,000 + \$121,438,000}{\$974,688,000}$	$\dfrac{\$144,700 + \$84,440}{\$631,618,000}$
= .21	= .36

b. Long-term debt-paying ratios

    1. Times Interest Earned:

1996	1995
$\dfrac{\$122,583,000}{\$43,594,000}$	$\dfrac{\$121,927,000}{\$27,876,000}$
= 2.81 times per year	= 4.37 times per year

2.Debt Ratio:

1996	1995

$$\frac{\$1,890,832,000 - \$431,614,000}{\$1,890,832,000} \qquad \frac{\$1,507,125,000 - \$376,122,000}{\$1,507,125,000}$$

$$= 77.17\% \qquad\qquad\qquad = 75.04\%$$

3.Operating Cash Flow/Total Debt:

1996	1995

$$\frac{\$99,520,000}{\$1,459,218,000} \qquad\qquad \frac{(\$37,411,000)}{\$1,131,003,000}$$

$$= 6.82\% \qquad\qquad = 3.31\% \text{ negative}$$

c. Profitability Ratios

1.Total Asset Turnover:

1996	1995

$$\frac{\$7,217,488,000}{\$1,890,832,000} \qquad\qquad \frac{\$5,079,557,000}{\$1,507,125,000}$$

$$= 3.82 \text{ times per year} \qquad = 3.37 \text{ times per year}$$

2.Return on Assets:

1996	1995

$$\frac{\$48,019,000}{\$1,890,832,000} \qquad\qquad \frac{\$5,079,557,000}{\$1,507,125,000}$$

$$= 2.54\% \qquad\qquad = 3.83\%$$

3.Return on Total Equity:

1996	1995

$$\frac{\$48,019,000}{\$431,614,000} \qquad\qquad \frac{\$57,651,000}{\$376,122,000}$$

$$= 11.13\% \qquad\qquad = 15.33\%$$

4. Operating Cash Flow Per Share:

1996	1995
$\dfrac{\$99,520,000}{\$43,640,000}$	$\dfrac{\$37,411,000}{\$43,471,000}$
= $2.28	= $.86 negative

d. Investor Analysis Ratios

1. Degree of Financial Leverage:

1996	1995
$\dfrac{\$122,583,000}{\$78,989,000}$	$\dfrac{\$121,927,000}{\$94,051,000}$
= 1.55	= 1.30

2. Price/Earnings Ratio:

High Market Price

1996	1995
$\dfrac{29\%}{\$1.10}$	$\dfrac{\$45\ 1/4}{\$1.33}$
= 26.93	= 34.02

Low Market Price

1996	1995
$\dfrac{\$12\ 3/4}{\$1.10}$	$\dfrac{\$22\ 1/8}{\$1.33}$
= 11.59	= 16.64

3. Percentage Of Earnings Retained:

1996	1995
$\dfrac{\$48,019,000}{\$48,019,000}$	$\dfrac{\$57,651,000}{\$57,651,000}$
= 100%	= 100%

4. Book Value:

1996	1995
$\dfrac{\$431,614,000}{42,842,000}$	$\dfrac{\$376,122,000}{42,216,000}$
= \$10.07	= \$8.91

e. Horizontal Common-Size Analysis

Item		1996	1995	1994	1993	1992
1.	Revenues	776%	546%	323%	174%	100%
2.	Gross profit	517%	381%	252%	157%	100%
3.	Selling, general and administrative expenses	502%	350%	162%	153%	100%
4.	Operating income	653%	649%	411%	191%	100%
5.	Net earnings	500%	600%	430%	207%	100%
6.	Number of stores	344%	279%	207%	152%	100%
7.	Average revenue per store	217%	199%	158%	123%	100%
8.	Total assets	561%	447%	282%	130%	100%
9.	Shareholders' equity	274%	239%	198%	116%	100%

f. Executive Summary

Liquidity

Liquidity declined in 1996 and appears to be relatively low. This is indicated by the current ratio and the acid-test ratio.

There is a substantial improvement in cash provided by operations, but this improvement substantially came from increasing accounts payable.

Debt

The debt position declined in 1996 and appears to be high. This is indicated by the times interest earned and the debt ratio.

There is a substantial improvement in operating cash flow/total debt, but this improvement substantially came from increasing accounts payable.

Profitability

In general, profitability declined in 1996. This is indicated by the return on assets and the return on total equity. There was an improvement in the total asset turnover.

Sales volume is very good, as is revenues per store. There is a problem in having profitability increase in relation to volume of sales. A major contributing factor to the reduced profitability in relation to revenues is a declining gross profit percentage.

Investor Analysis

The stock price substantially decreased in 1996 consistent with our analysis of liquidity, debt, and profitability. In the short run, the increase in accounts payable could be a major problem.

In the author's opinion, it is difficult to see a major rise in the stock price until the areas of concern in liquidity, debt, and profitability are improved.

CASE 10-4   THE RETAIL MOVER

(This case represents a firm on the verge of bankruptcy. The company is W.T. Grant. The actual years represented in this case were 1969 (1994), 1970 (1995), 1973 (1997), and 1974 (1998).

a. 1.

	1994	1995	1997
Total current assets	$628,408,895	$719,478,441	$924,781,000
Total current liabilities	$366,718,656	$458,999,682	$661,058,000
Working capital	$261,690,239	$260,478,759	$263,723,000

Comment

Working capital was fairly constant while current assets and current liabilities increased significantly.

2.

Current ratio	1994	1995	1997
$\dfrac{\text{Current Assets}}{\text{Current Liabilities}} =$	1.71	1.57	1.40

Comment

The absolute current ratios appear to be too low. There was a substantial decline in the current ratio between 1994 and 1997. The absolute current ratios appear to be too low.

b.

	1995	1997
Net income	$39,577,000	$10,902,000
Cash (outflow) from operating activities	($15,319,217)	($93,204,000)

A net increase in receivables and inventories were the major reasons for the substantial difference between net income and cash (outflow) from operating activities in both 1995 and 1997.

c. There was an apparent write down in customers' installment accounts receivable and merchandise inventories. There was also a substantial increase in allowance for doubtful accounts.

The substantial decrease in deferred finance income is apparently related to the write down in customers' installment accounts receivable.

d. ## Company perspective
The company was apparently desperate for liquidity. The company would have preferred a longer term, but under the circumstances would take whatever they could get.

Bank perspective
This loan appears to be a major blunder on the part of the bank. Apparently the short-term commercial notes were no longer available, probably because of the financial condition of the company.

CASE 10-5   NON-CASH CHARGES

(Companies frequently announce non-cash charges. This case provides an opportunity to discuss if non-cash charges are non-cash charges in the long run.)

a.   True

     Cash inflow from operations will equal the revenue from operations in the long run.

b.   1992 — $800 million

     1992 - 1999   It was estimated that the accrual would be sufficient to cover the company's uninsured costs for cases received until the year 2000.

c. $545 million in 1996

     Cash payments associated with charge will begin after the year 2000 and will be spread over 15 years or more.

d.   Cash inflow will be recorded when received.

     The related revenue will likely be recorded in the same period that the cash is received. This is an example of conservatism.

e.   If they do not win the suit the expenses (cash outflow) for asbestos claims will likely be substantially higher than previously provided for.

f.   Asbestos related expenses (cash outflow) will likely be more than previously estimated.

     g.1. 1996 — $875,000,000

        2. 1997 — $97,000,000
           1996 — $101,000,000
           1995 — $251,000,000

        3. 1997 — $300,000,000
           1996 — $267,000,000
           1995 — $308,000,000

CASE 10-6 CASH MOVEMENTS AND PERIODIC INCOME DETERMINATION

a. Income determination is not an exact science. A substantial amount of subjectivity is used in income determination. Many estimates are typically involved when determining income.

b. Cash flow is determined in an objective manner.

c. In theory, this is a true statement.
United States accounting principles provide for by-passing the income statement for some apparent revenue or expense items. The balance of these items is presented in shareholders' equity in the balance sheet. Examples are net unrealized loss in noncurrent marketable equity securities, cumulative translation adjustments, and cumulative pension liability adjustments. In the long run the revenue (expense) from these items go through the income statement.

An exception in U.S. accounting standards is that compensation expense related to options is usually not recognized in the income statement.

d. In the short run, a negative cash flow from operations could be compensated for by cash flow from investing and financing activities.

e. Revenue and expense items that were more positive for income in the past than they were for cash flow will need to materialize in future cash flow. An example would be sales on account (credit). Collection will need to be made.

Chapter 11
Expanded Analysis

QUESTIONS

11- 1.   Based on the study reported in the text, liquidity and
         debt ratios are regarded as the most significant ratios
         by commercial loan officers.

11- 2.   (a) Debt/equity, current ratio
         (b) Debt/equity, current ratio

11- 3.   The dividend payout ratio does not primarily indicate
         liquidity, debt, or profitability. It is a ratio that is
         of interest to investors because it indicates the
         percentage of earnings that is being paid out in
         dividends. From a view of controlling a loan and
         preventing the stockholders from being paid before the
         bank is paid, the dividend payout ratio can be used as an
         effective ratio.

11- 4.   Based on the study reported in the text, financial
         executives do regard profitability ratios as the most
         significant ratios.

11- 5.   (a) Return on equity   (b) Return on assets
         (c) Net profit margin   (d) Earnings per share
         (e) Return on capital

         Each of these ratios would be considered a measure of
         profitability.

11- 6.   The CPAs gave the highest significance rating to two
         liquidity ratios. These ratios are the current ratio and
         the accounts receivable turnover days. The highest-rated
         profitability ratio was after-tax net profit margin,
         while the highest-rated debt ratio was debt/equity.

11- 7.   According to the study reported in this book, financial
         ratios are not used extensively in annual reports to
         interpret and explain financial statements. Likely
         reasons for this are that management does not want to
         interpret and explain the financial statements to the
         users, or management is of the opinion that
         interpretations and explanations can be made more
         effectively in a descriptive way rather than by the use
         of financial ratios. Also, there are no authoritative

guidelines as to what financial ratios should be included in the annual report, except for earnings per share.

11- 8. (a) Financial summary   (b) Financial highlights
        (c) Financial review   (d) President's letter
        (e) Management discussion

11- 9. Profitability ratios and ratios related to investing are the most likely to be included in annual reports.

Profitability ratios are the most popular ratios with management. Ratios related to investing are logical to be included in the annual report because one of the major objectives of the annual report is to inform stockholders.

11-10. Earnings per share is the only ratio that is required to be disclosed in the annual report. It must be disclosed at the bottom of the income statement.

11-11. Presently, no regulatory agency such as the Securities and Exchange Commission or the Financial Accounting Standards Board accepts responsibility for determining either the content of financial ratios or the format of presentation for annual reports. The exception to this is earnings per share.

There are many practical and theoretical issues related to the computation of financial ratios. As long as each individual is allowed to exercise his/her opinion as to the practical and theoretical issues, there will be a great divergence of opinion on how a particular ratio should be computed.

11-12. Accounting policies that result in the slowest reporting of income are the most conservative.

11-13.

	Conservative Yes	No
(a)	X	
(b)		X
(c)	X	
(d)		X
(e)	X	
(f)		X
(g)	X	
(h)	X	
(i)	X	
(j)		X
(k)	X	

11-14. Substantial research and development will result in more conservative earnings because research and development expenses are charged to the period in which they are incurred.

11-15. Such a model could be used by management to take preventive measures. Such a model could aid investors in selecting and disposing of stocks. Banks could use this model to aid in loan decision making and in monitoring loans. Firms could use this model in making credit decisions and in monitoring accounts receivable. An auditor could use such a model to aid in the determination of audit procedures and in making a decision as to whether the firm will remain as a going concern.

11-16. There are many definitions or descriptions of financial failure. Financial failure can include liquidation, deferment of payments to short-term creditors, deferment of payment of interest on bonds, deferment of payment of principal on bonds, and the omission of a preferred dividend.

11-17. (a) Cash flow/Total debt
(b) Net income/Total assets (return on assets)
(c) Total debt/Total assets (debt ratio)

11-18. (a) cash - low   (b) accounts receivable - high
(c) inventory - low

11-19. Firms that scored below 2.675 are assumed to have similar characteristics of past failures.

11-20. Variable X_4 in the model requires that the market value of the stock be determined. Determining the market value of the stock of a closely held company can be difficult if not impossible.

11-21. False. These studies help substantiate that firms that have weak ratios are more likely to go bankrupt than firms that have strong ratios.

11-22. The abnormally low turnover for accounts receivable indicates that a very detailed audit of accounts receivable should be performed to satisfy ourselves of the collectibility of the receivables.

11-23. A proposed comprehensive budget should be compared with financial ratios that have been agreed upon as part of the firm's corporate objectives. If the proposed comprehensive budget will not result in the firm achieving its objectives, then attempts should be made to change the game plan in order to achieve the corporate objectives.

11-24. 1. Line
2. Column
3. Bar
4. Pie

11-25. 1. Not extending the vertical axis to zero
2. Having a broken vertical axis

11-26. Visually, a pie graph can mislead. Also, some accounting data do not fit on a pie graph.

11-27. The surveyed analysts gave the highest significance ratings to profitability ratios.

11-28. This statement is not true. Chartered Financial Analysts gave relatively low significance ratings to liquidity ratios.

TO THE NET

1. a. Retail - grocery stores

   b.

	January 2, 1999	December 27, 1997
Total current assets	$2,673,100,000	$2,640,551,000

   c. Inventories

   d.

	January 2, 1999	December 27, 1997
Accounts payable	$1,785,630,000	$1,781,527,000

   e. Accounts payable

   f. Inventories
   Inventories are stated at the lower of cost or market. Approximately 95% of inventories for 1998 and 90% of inventories for 1997 were valued using the LIFO method. Cost for the balance of the inventories is determined using the FIFO method.

   g.

	January 2, 1999	December 27, 1997
Total current assets (a)	$2,673,180,000	$2,640,551,000
Total current liabilities (b)	$3,192,068,000	$2,943,516,000
Current ratio (a÷b)	.84	.90

   h.

	January 2, 1999	December 27, 1997
Total current assets	$2,673,180,000	$2,640,551,000
LIFO reserve	471,932,000	467,931,000
Adjusted current assets (a)	$3,145,112,000	$3,108,482,000
Total current liabilities (b)	$3,192,068,000	$2,943,516,000
Adjusted current ratio (a÷b)	.99	1.06

   Yes.

   By adding back the LIFO reserve we have the inventory at approximately the FIFO cost. At FIFO cost the inventory is at approximately the current cost. This gives a more realistic coverage.

i. The current ratio is acceptable. Receivables are relatively low because of the nature of the industry. The major current asset is inventories, which would be relatively liquid in the grocery industry.

   A current ratio of approximately 1 would be acceptable but likely on the low side.

2. a. Tires and inner tubes

   b. 1. $126,967,000

       2. a. $60,627,000
           b. $47,897,000

       3. 35.9%

   c. 1998 net income $126,967,000

       Net decrease in inventory reserve:

1998	$ 47,897,000
1997	60,627,000
	(a) $ 12,730,000
Effective tax rate	(b) 35.9%
Decrease in taxes [(a)x(b)]	(c) $ 4,570,070

       Net decrease in income
       [$12,730,000 - $4,570,070]   8,159,930

       Approximate income for 1998 if
       inventory had been valued at
       approximate current cost
       ($126,967,000 - $8,159,930) $118,807,070

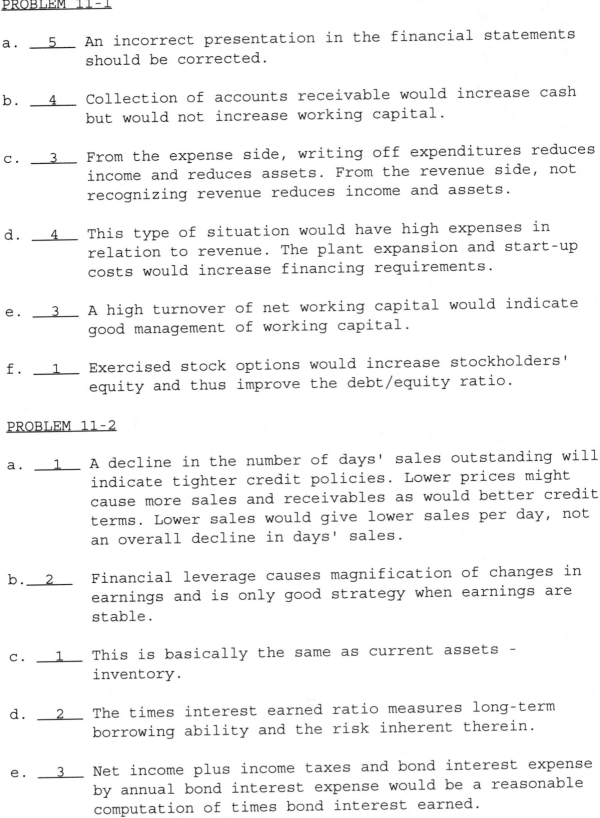

PROBLEMS

PROBLEM 11-1

a. __5__ An incorrect presentation in the financial statements should be corrected.

b. __4__ Collection of accounts receivable would increase cash but would not increase working capital.

c. __3__ From the expense side, writing off expenditures reduces income and reduces assets. From the revenue side, not recognizing revenue reduces income and assets.

d. __4__ This type of situation would have high expenses in relation to revenue. The plant expansion and start-up costs would increase financing requirements.

e. __3__ A high turnover of net working capital would indicate good management of working capital.

f. __1__ Exercised stock options would increase stockholders' equity and thus improve the debt/equity ratio.

PROBLEM 11-2

a. __1__ A decline in the number of days' sales outstanding will indicate tighter credit policies. Lower prices might cause more sales and receivables as would better credit terms. Lower sales would give lower sales per day, not an overall decline in days' sales.

b. __2__ Financial leverage causes magnification of changes in earnings and is only good strategy when earnings are stable.

c. __1__ This is basically the same as current assets - inventory.

d. __2__ The times interest earned ratio measures long-term borrowing ability and the risk inherent therein.

e. __3__ Net income plus income taxes and bond interest expense by annual bond interest expense would be a reasonable computation of times bond interest earned.

PROBLEM 11-3

a. The current ratio has all current assets in the numerator, while in the acid test ratio, inventory is removed. A large inventory would cause the decline in the acid-test ratio. The decline in the inventory turnover supports this conclusion.

b. Financial leverage is the extent to which fixed costs of financing are used, namely debt. The greater the financial leverage, the greater the magnification of changes in earnings. The measures of debt, as indicated by total debt to total assets and long-term debt to total assets, have declined. This increases financial leverage. However, the firm does have leverage and the decline in profit to shareholders is magnified by it.

c. The fixed asset turnover has risen, generally indicating either a rise in sales or a decline in fixed assets. Sales as a percent of 1999 sales are given. Assume 1999 sales were $100; 2000, $103, and 2001, $106.

   If $100/fixed assets = 1.75, then fixed assets = $57 in 1999

   If $103/fixed assets = 1.88, then fixed assets = $55 in 2000

   If $106/fixed assets = 1.99, then fixed assets = $53 in 2001

   There has actually been a slight decline in net fixed assets.

PROBLEM 11-4

a. 1. Rate of Return on Total Assets:

$$\frac{\text{Net Income Before Minority Share Of Earnings And Nonrecurring Items}}{\text{Average Total Assets}} = \frac{- \$.2}{(\$19.7 + 19.4) \div 2} = \frac{(-1.0\%)}{\text{Negative}}$$

   The rate of return on total assets is negative in 2001, due to the negative net income figure.

   2. Acid-Test Ratio:

$$\frac{\text{Cash Equivalents + Marketable Securities + Net Receivables}}{\text{Current Liabilities}} = \frac{\$13.5 - \$2.8 - \$.6}{\$9.3} = 1.09$$

3. Return on Sales:

$$\frac{\text{Net Income Before Minority Share Of Earnings And } \underline{\text{Nonrecurring Items}}}{\text{Net Sales}} = \frac{\$-.2}{\$24.9} = (-.8\%) \text{ Negative}$$

4. Current Ratio :

$$\frac{\text{Current Assets}}{\text{Current Liabilities}} = \frac{\$13.5}{\$24.9} = (-.8\%) \text{ Negative}$$

5. Inventory Turnover:

$$\frac{\text{Cost of Goods Sold}}{\text{Average Inventory}} = \frac{\$18.0}{(\$3.2 + \$2.8)/2} = 6 \text{ times per year}$$

b. 1. Rate Of Return On Total Assets:

Unfavorable - The rate is low and has been declining.

2. Return on Sales:

Unfavorable - The rate is low and has been declining.

3. Acid-Test Ratio:

Favorable - The direction of change is unfavorable, but it is probably more than adequate.

4. Current Ratio:

Unfavorable - The decline has been sharp, and the ratio is probably too low.

5. Inventory Turnover:

Neutral - Inventory turnover has been fairly constant, and we don't know enough about the business to determine if the turnover is adequate.

6. Equity Relationships:

Unfavorable - The trend towards a heavy reliance on current liabilities is unfavorable. This high proportion of current liabilities could result in short-term liquidity problems.

7. Asset Relationships:
   Neutral - The reduction in the proportion of assets that are current could indicate that the firm is working its current assets harder. The reduction in the proportion of assets that are current could also indicate that there has been an expansion in property, plant, and equipment, without an adequate increase in current assets.

c. The facts available from the problem are inadequate to make final judgment; additional information as listed in Part D would be necessary. However, the facts given do not present an overall good picture of D. Hawk. The company doesn't appear to be in serious trouble at the moment, but most of the trends reflected in figures are unfavorable. The company appears to be developing liquidity problems:

   1. Cash and securities are declining.

   2. Inventories and plant and equipment are an increasing portion of the assets.

   3. Current liabilities are an increasing portion of capital.

   The operations of the company also show unfavorable trends:

   1. Cost of goods sold is increasing as a percent of sales.

   2. Administrative expenses are increasing as a percent of sales.

   3. Recognizing that prices have risen, it appears that physical volume at D. Hawk might have actually decreased.

   On the basis of these observations and the fact that D. Hawk would be a very large customer (thus a potentially large loss if the accounts become uncollectible), credit should be extended to D. Hawk only under carefully controlled and monitored conditions.

d. Additional information would be:

   1. Quality of management of D. Hawk Company.

   2. The locations of the D. Hawk stores.

   3. The current activities of D. Hawk, which have increased plant and equipment but not inventories.

4. Industry position of D. Hawk Company.

5. Credit rating of the D. Hawk Company.

6. Current economic conditions.

7. Capacity of L. Konrath Company to handle such a large single account.

8. Normal ratios for the industry.

PROBLEM 11-5

a.

Liquidity Ratios:

1. Days' Sales in Inventory = $\dfrac{\text{Ending Inventory}}{\text{Cost Of Goods Sold}/365}$

$$\frac{\$63,414}{\$495,651/365} = \frac{\$63,414}{\$1,357.95} = 46.70 \text{ days}$$

2. Merchandise Inventory Turnover = $\dfrac{\text{Cost of goods sold}}{\text{Average inventory}}$

$$\frac{\$495,651}{\$(63,414 + \$74,890)/2} = \frac{\$495,651}{\$69,152} = 7.17 \text{ times per year}$$

3. Inventory Turnover in Days = $\dfrac{\text{Average Inventory}}{\text{Cost Of Goods Sold}/365}$

$$\frac{\$63,414 + \$74,890)/2}{\$495,651/365} = \frac{\$69,152}{\$1,357.95} = 50.92 \text{ days}$$

4. Operating Cycle = $\begin{array}{c}\text{Accounts Receivable} \\ \text{Turnover in Days}\end{array}$ + $\begin{array}{c}\text{Inventory Turnover} \\ \text{in Days}\end{array}$

$\begin{array}{l}\text{Accounts Receivable} \\ \text{Turnover in Days}\end{array}$ = $\dfrac{\text{Average Gross Receivables}}{\text{Net Sales}/365}$

$$\frac{(\$99,021 + \$750 + \$83,575 + \$750)/2}{\$578,530/365} =$$

$$\frac{\$92,048}{\$1,585.01} = 58.07 \text{ days}$$

58.07 days + 50.92 days = 108.99 days

5. Working Capital = Current Assets - Current Liabilities

$227,615 - $73,730 = $153,885

6. Current Ratio = $\dfrac{\text{Current Assets}}{\text{Current Liabilities}}$

$\dfrac{\$227,615}{\$\ 73,730} = 3.09$

7. Acid-Test Ratio = $\dfrac{\text{Cash Equivalents + Marketable Securities} + \text{Current Liabilities}}{\text{Current Liabilities}}$

$\dfrac{\$64,346 + \$99,021}{\$73,730} = 2.22$

8. Cash Ratio = $\dfrac{\text{Cash Equivalents + Marketable Securities}}{\text{Current Liabilities}}$

$\dfrac{\$64,346}{\$73,730} = .87$

Debt:

1. Debt Ratio = $\dfrac{\text{Total Liabilities}}{\text{Total Assets}}$

$\dfrac{\$370,264 - \$198,084}{\$370,264} = \dfrac{\$172,180}{\$370,264} = 46.50\%$

2. Debt/Equity = $\dfrac{\text{Total Liabilities}}{\text{Shareholders' Equity}}$

$\dfrac{\$370,264 - \$198,084}{\$198,084} = \dfrac{\$172,180}{\$198,084} = 86.92\%$

3. Times Interest Earned = $\dfrac{\text{Recurring Earnings, Excluding INterest Expense, Tax Expense, Equity Earnings, and Minority Income}}{\text{Interest Expense, Including Capitalized Interest}}$

$\dfrac{\$43,138 + \$4,308}{\$4,308} = \dfrac{\$47,446}{\$4,308} = 11.01$ times per period

Profitability:

1. Net Profit Margin = Net Income Before Minority
                            Share Of Earnings And
                            <u>Nonrecurring Items</u>
                               Net Sales

$$\frac{\$ 23,018}{\$578,530} = 3.98\%$$

2. Total Asset Turnover = $\dfrac{\text{Net Sales}}{\text{Average Total Assets}}$

$$\frac{\$578,530}{(\$370,264 + \$295,433)/2 = \$332,848.5} \quad \frac{\$578,530}{\$332,848.5} = 1.74 \text{ times per year}$$

3. Return on Assets = $\dfrac{\begin{array}{c}\text{Net Income Before Minority}\\ \text{Share of Earnings And}\\ \text{Nonrecurring Items}\end{array}}{\text{Average Total Assets}}$

$$\frac{\$23,018}{\$370,264 + \$295,433)/2} = \frac{\$23,018}{\$332,848.5} = 6.92\%$$

4. Return on Total Equity = $\dfrac{\begin{array}{c}\text{Net Income Before Nonrecurring}\\ \text{Items - Dividends On Redeemable}\\ \text{Preferred Stock}\end{array}}{\text{Average Total Equity}}$

$$\frac{\$23,018}{\$198,084 + \$175,583/2} = \frac{\$23,018}{\$186,833.5} = 12.32\%$$

b. Approximate income for 2001 if inventory had been valued at approximate current cost:

2001 net income as reported		$ 23,018
Net decrease in inventory reserve		
2001	$35,300	
2000	41,100	
(a)	$ 5,800	
(b) Effective tax rate	36.6%	
(c) Decrease in taxes (a) x (b)	$ 2,123	
(d) Net decrease in income		
[(a) - (c)]		
$5,800 - $2,123		(3,677)
Approximate income for 2001 if inventory had been valued at approximate current cost		$ 19,341

290

Inventory adjusted:

As disclosed on the balance sheet	$ 63,414
Increase in inventory	35,300
	$ 98,714

Deferred current tax liability:
   Increase related to inventory reserve
   $35,300 x 36.6% =   12,920

Retained earnings adjusted:

As disclosed on the balance sheet	$154,084
Increase related to inventory reserve ($35,300 x 36.6%)	22,380
	$176,464

Liquidity:

1. Days' Sales In Inventory

$$\frac{\$63,414 + \$35,300}{\$495,651/365} = \frac{\$98,714}{\$1,357.95} = 72.69 \text{ days}$$

2. Merchandise Inventory Turnover

$$\frac{\$495,651}{(\$63,414 + \$35,300 + \$74,890 + \$41,100)/2} = \frac{\$495,651}{\$107,352}$$

$$= 4.62 \text{ times per year}$$

3. Inventory Turnover In Days

$$\frac{\$107,352}{\$495,651/365} = \frac{\$107,352}{\$1,357.95} = 79.05 \text{ days}$$

4. Operating Cycle

58.07 days + 79.05 days = 137.12 days

5. Working Capital

($227,615 + $35,300) - ($73,730 + $12,920)* = $176,265
   *$35,300 X 36.6% = $12,920

6. Current Ratio

$$\frac{\$262,915}{\$86,650} = 3.03$$

7. Acid-Test Ratio

$$\frac{\$64,346 + \$99,021}{\$73,730 + \$12,920} = \frac{\$163,367}{\$86,650} = 1.89$$

8. Cash Ratio

$$\frac{\$64,346}{\$73,730 + \$12,920} = \frac{\$64,346}{\$86,650} = .74$$

Debt:

1. Debt Ratio

$$\frac{\$370,264 - \$198,084 + \$12,920}{\$370,264 + \$35,300} = \frac{\$185,100}{\$405,564} = 45.64\%$$

2. Debt/Equity

$$\frac{\$370,264 - \$198,084 + \$12,920}{\$198,084 + \$22,380} = \frac{\$185,100}{\$220,464} = 83.96\%$$

3. Times Interest Earned

$$\frac{\$43,138 + \$4,308 - \$5,800}{\$4,308} = \frac{\$41,646}{\$4,308} = 9.67 \text{ times per year}$$

Profitability:

1. Net Profit Margin

$$\frac{\$23,018 - \$3,677}{\$578,530} = \frac{\$19,341}{\$578,530} = 3.34\%$$

2. Total Asset Turnover

$$\frac{\$578,530}{(\$370,264 + \$295,433 + \$35,300 + \$41,100)/2} =$$

$$\frac{\$578,530}{\$742,097/2} = \frac{\$578,530}{\$371,049} = 1.56 \text{ times per year}$$

3. Return On Assets

$$\frac{\$23,018 - \$3,677}{(\$370,264 + \$295,433 + \$35,300 + \$41,100)/2}$$

$$\frac{\$19,341}{\$371,049} = 5.21\%$$

4. Return On Total Equity

$$\frac{\$19,341}{(\$198,084 + \$175,583 + \$22,380 + \$28,482*)/2}$$

$$*\$41,100 \times (1 - 30.7\%)$$
$$\$41,100 \times 69.30\% = \$28,482.30$$

$$\frac{\$19,341}{\$212,265} = 9.11\%$$

c.

Ratio	Without considering the LIFO reserve	Considering the LIFO reserve
Liquidity:		
Days' sales in inventory	46.70 days	72.69 days
Merchandise inventory turnover	7.17 times per year	4.62 times per year
Inventory turnover in days	50.92 days	79.05 days
Operating cycle	108.99 days	137.12 days
Working capital	$153,885	$176,265
Current ratio	3.09	3.03
Acid-test ratio	2.22	1.89
Cash ratio	.87	.74
Debt:		
Debt ratio	46.50%	45.64%
Debt/equity	86.92%	83.96%
Times interest earned	11.01 times per year	9.67 times per year
Profitability:		
Net profit margin	3.98%	3.34%
Total asset turnover	1.74 times per year	1.56 times per year
Return on assets	6.92%	5.21%
Return on total equity	12.32%	9.11%

All but one liquidity ratio was less favorable when considering the LIFO reserve. Some of the liquidity ratios declined substantially. The only liquidity indicator to improve was working capital.

Debt ratios were slightly more favorable when considering the LIFO reserve. Profitability declined moderately when the LIFO reserve was considered.

PROBLEM 11-6

1. Decreases retained earnings, increases payables.

   a, c, g, i, j

2. Reduces retained earnings, increases common stock.
   f, g, i

3. Increases cash, increases retained earnings.

   b, d, h

4. This creates an arrearage, which would increase the amount for preferred stock in calculating book value for common.

   i

5. This merely increases the number of shares. No effect until the stock is sold.

   d (Assumption that the preferred shares would be held as a temporary investment)

6. Decreases cash, decreases dividends payable. Increases current ratio if originally more than 1:1.

   d

7. No change in equity, but more shares. Therefore reduces equity per share of common stock.

   i

PROBLEM 11-7

a.

Argo Sales Corporation
Balance Sheet
December 31, 2001

	Current assets:		
	Cash	$ 20,000 (6)	
	Marketable securities	80,000 (7)	
	Accounts receivable	150,000 (5)	
	Inventory	120,000 (8)	
	Prepaid expenses	5,000 (11)	
(10)	Total current assets		$375,000
	Fixed assets:		
	Land, buildings, and equipment	$292,500 (15)	
	Less accumulated depreciation	97,500 (16)	
(14)	Total fixed assets		195,000
(13)	Intangible assets		30,000
(12)	Total assets		$600,000
	Current liabilities:		
	Accounts payable	$100,000 (17)	
	Accrued expenses payable	25,000 (18)	
(9)	Total current liabilities		$125,000
	Long-term liabilities:		
(21)	5% Bonds payable - due 2010		75,000
(20)	Total liabilities		$200,000
	Stockholders' Equity:		
	6% Preferred stock, $100 par value,		
	500 shares authorized, issued		
	and outstanding (25)	$ 50,000 (24)	
	Common stock, $10 par value,		
	$22,500 shares authorized,		
	issued and outstanding (22)	225,000 (23)	
	Contributed capital in excess		
	of par value	27,500 (26)	
	Retained earnings	97,500 (27)	
(19)	Total stockholders' equity		400,000
(28)	Total liabilities and stockholders' equity		$600,000

Argo Sales Corporation
Income Statement
For the Year Ended December 31, 2001

(1)	Net sales	$1,200,000
(3)	Less cost of goods sold	720,000
(2)	Gross profit on sales	480,000

Selling expenses	$240,000	(4)
Administrative expenses	116,250	(30)
Interest expense	3,750	(29) 360,000
Net income		$ 120,000

Notes: Supporting Computations for Amounts on Financial Statements

(1)   Sales = $\dfrac{\text{Net Income}}{\text{Net Profit Rate}}$ = $\dfrac{\$120,000}{.10}$ = $1,200,000

(2)   Gross Profit:

Sales x Gross Profit Rate = $1,200,000 x .40 = $480,000

(3)   Cost Of Goods Sold:

Sales - Gross Profit = $1,200,000 - $480,000 = $720,000

(4)   Selling Expenses:

Sales x Selling Expenses Rate: $1,200,000 x .20 = $240,000

(5)   Accounts Receivable:

$\dfrac{\text{Sales}}{\text{Accounts Receivable Turnover}}$ = $\dfrac{\$1,200,000}{8}$ = $150,000

(6)   Cash:

Quick Assets = $\dfrac{\text{Accounts Receivable}}{\text{\% Of Quick Assets In Accounts Receivable}}$

= $\dfrac{\$150,000}{.60}$ = $250,000

Cash = Quick Assets x % of Quick Assets In Cash

= $250,000 x .08 = $20,000

(7) Marketable Securities:

Quick Assets x % Of Quick Assets In Securities

= $250,000 x .32 = $80,000

(8) Inventory = $\dfrac{\text{Cost Of Goods Sold}}{\text{Inventory Turnover}} = \dfrac{\$720,000}{6} = \$120,000$

(9) Current Liabilities = $\dfrac{\text{Quick Assets}}{2\ *} = \dfrac{\$250,000}{2} = \$125,000$

*From Acid-Test Ratio

(10) Current Assets:

Current Liabilities x 3* = $125,000 x 3 = $375,000

*From Current Ratio

(11) Prepaid Expenses:

Current Assets - (Cash + Securities + Receivables + Inventory) =

$375,000-($20,000+$80,000+$150,000+$120,000) = $5,000

(12) Total Assets = $\dfrac{\text{Sales}}{\text{Asset Turnover}} = \dfrac{\$1,200,000}{2} = \$600,000$

(13) Intangible Assets = $\dfrac{\text{Total Assets}}{20\ *} = \dfrac{\$600,000}{20} = \$30,000$

*From Ratio Of Total Assets To Intangibles

(14) Fixed Assets (Net):

Total Assets - (Current Assets + Intangibles)
$600,000 - ($375,000 + $30,000) = $195,000

(15) Land, Buildings, and Equipment:

Let: A = land, buildings, and equipment
      D = accumulated deprecation
      N = net fixed assets
A-D = N A-[(A/3*)] = $195,000 x 2/3A = $195,000 A = $292,500

*From Ratio Of Depreciation To Cost

(16)   Accumulated Depreciation:

$$\frac{\underline{Land,\ Buildings\ and\ Equipment}}{3*} = \frac{\$292,500}{3} = \$97,500$$

   *From Ratio Of Depreciation To Cost

(17)   Accounts Payable $= \dfrac{\text{Accounts Receivable}}{1.5\ *} = \dfrac{\$150,000}{1.5} = \$100,000$

   *From Ratio Of Accounts Receivable To Accounts Payable

(18)   Accrued Expenses Payable:

   Current Liabilities - Accounts Payable = $125,000 - $100,000 = $25,000

(19)   Total Stockholders' Equity:

   Working Capital x 1.6* = 1.6 x($375,000-$125,000) = $400,000

   *From Ratio Of Working Capital To Stockholders' Equity

(20)   Total Liabilities:

   Total Assets - Stockholders' Equity = $600,000 - $400,000
                                        = $200,000

(21)   5% Bonds Payable - Due 2010:

   Total Liabilities - Current Liabilities
   = $200,000 - $125,000 = $75,000

(22)   Common Stock Shares $= \dfrac{\underline{Net\ Income\ -\ Preferred\ Dividends}}{Earnings\ Per\ Share}$

$$= \frac{\$120,000 - \$3,000}{\$5.20} = 22,500\ shares$$

(23)   Common Stock Shares x Par Value = $22,500 x $10 = $225,000

(24) Preferred Stock $= \dfrac{\underline{Preferred\ Dividends}}{Dividend\ Rate} = \dfrac{\$3,000}{.06} = \$50,000$

(25)   Preferred Stock Shares $= \dfrac{\underline{Preferred\ Stock}}{Par\ Value} = \dfrac{\$50,000}{\$100} = 500$ shares

(26)   Contributed Capital In Excess Of Par Value:

Common x % Premium   = $225,000 x .10 = $22,500
Preferred x % Premium = $ 50,000 x .10   5,000
                                          $27,500

(27)   Retained Earnings:

Stockholders' Equity - (Common + Preferred + Premium)
= $400,000 - ($225,00 + $50,000 + $27,500) = $97,500

(28)   Total Liabilities and Stockholders' Equity:

Total Assets = Total liabilities And Stockholders' Equity

Total Assets = $600,000 (from 12)

(29)   Interest Expense:

Bonds Payable x Interest Rate = $75,000 x .05 = $3,750

(30)   Administrative Expenses:

Gross profit		$480,000
Less net income		120,000
Total expenses		360,000
Less: Selling expenses	$240,000	
Interest	3,750	
Administrative expenses		243,750
		$116,250

Proof statistics supplied:

1.   Debt To Equity Ratio = $200,00 to $400,000 = 1 to 2

2.   Times Interest Earned =

$$\frac{\text{Recurring Earnings, Excluding Interest Expense, Tax Expense, Equity Earnings, And Minority Income}}{\text{Interest Expense, Including Capitalized Interest}} = \frac{\$120,000 + \$3,750}{\$3,750} = \text{33 times per year}$$

b.   1.   Rate Of Return On Stockholders' Equity:

$$\frac{\text{Net Income Before Nonrecurring Items}}{\text{Total Equity}} = \frac{\$120,000}{\$400,000} = 30\%$$

2. Price-Earnings Ratio For Common Stock:

Market Value Per Share To Earnings Per Share
$78.00 to $5.20 = 15 to 1

3. Dividends Paid Per Share Of Common Stock:

Net income	$120,000
Less dividends on preferred stock	3,000
Dividends on common stock	$117,000

$$\frac{\text{Dividends On Common}}{\text{Shares of Common}} = \frac{\$117,000}{22,500} = \$5.20$$

4. Dividends Paid Per Share Of Preferred Stock:

$$\frac{\text{Dividends On Preferred}}{\text{Shares Of Preferred}} = \frac{\$3,000}{500 \text{ shares}} = \$6$$

5. Yield On Common Stock:

$$\frac{\text{Dividends Per Share}}{\text{Market VAlue}} = \frac{\$5.20}{\$78.00} = 6 \ 2/3\%$$

PROBLEM 11-8

a. 1. Current Ratio: $\frac{\text{Current Assets}}{\text{Current Liabilities}}$

2000	2001
$\frac{\$235,000}{\$132,500} = 1.77 \text{ to } 1$	$\frac{\$290,000}{\$145,000} = 2.00 \text{ to } 1$

2. Quick Ratio: $\frac{\text{Cash Equivalents + Marketable Securities + Net Receivables}}{\text{Current Liabilities}}$

2000	2001
$\frac{\$185,000}{\$132,500} = 1.40 \text{ to } 1$	$\frac{\$210,000}{\$145,000} = 1.45 \text{ to } 1$

300

3. Inventory Turnover: $\dfrac{\underline{\text{Cost Of Goods Sold}}}{\text{Average Inventory}}$

    2001

    $$\frac{\$1,902,500}{\$50,000 + \$80,000)/2} = 29 \text{ times per year}$$

4. Return on Assets: $\dfrac{\text{Net Income Before Minority Share Of}}{\underline{\text{Earnings And Nonrecurring Items}}}$
    $$\text{Average Total Assets}$$

    2000

    $\dfrac{\underline{\$120,000}}{\$881,000} = 13.62\%$ (Average Assets Not Available)

    2001

    $$\frac{\$151,000}{\$881,000 + \$970,000/2} = 16.37\%$$

5. Percent Changes:

Amounts
(000s omitted)

	2001	2000	Percent
Sales	$3,000.0	$2,700.0	$\dfrac{\$300.0}{\$2,700.0} = 11.11\%$
Cost of goods sold	$1,902.5	$1,720.0	$\dfrac{\$182.5}{\$1,720.0} = \$10.61\%$
Gross profit	$1,097.5	$980.0	$\dfrac{\$117.5}{\$980.0} = 11.99\%$
Net income after taxes	$151.5	$120.0	$\dfrac{\$31.5}{\$120.0} = 26.25\%$

b. Other financial reports and financial analyses which might be helpful to the commercial loan officer of Bell National Bank include:

-   Statement of cash flows would highlight the amount of cash flows from operations, investing, and financing activities.

-   Projected financial statements for 2002. In addition, a review of Warford's comprehensive budgets might be useful. These items would present management's estimates of operations for the coming year, as well as investing, and financing activities.

- A closer examination of Warford liquidity by calculating some additional ratios such as days' sales in receivables, accounts receivable turnover, and days' sales in inventory.

- An examination as to the extent that leverage is being used by Warford.

c. Warford Corporation should be able to finance the plant expansion from internally generated funds as shown in the calculations presented below.

| | (000's omitted) | | |
	2001	2002	2003
Sales	$3,000.0	$3,333.3	$3,703.6
Cost of goods sold	1,902.5	2,104.3	2,327.6
Gross profit	$1,097.5	$1,229.0	$1,376.0
Operating expenses	845.0	915.4	991.7
Income before taxes	$ 252.5	$ 313.6	$ 384.3
Income taxes (40%)	101.0	125.4	153.7
Net income	$ 151.5	$ 188.2	$ 230.6
Add:			
Depreciation		102.5	102.5
Deduct:			
Dividends		(75.0)	(75.0)
Note interest and repayments		(7.0)	(60.0)
Funds available for			
plant expansion		$208.7	$198.1
Plant expansion		(150.0)	(150.0)
Excess funds		$ 58.7	$ 48.1

Assumptions:

- Sales increase at a rate of 11.1%.

- Cost of goods sold increases at a rate of 10.6%.

- Other operating expenses increase at the same rate experienced from 2000 to 2001, i.e., at 8.3%.

- Depreciation remains constant at $102,500.

- Dividends remain at $1.25 per share.

- Plant expansion is financed equally over the two years ($150,000 each year).

- Loan extension is granted.

d. Bell National Bank should probably grant the extension of the loan, if it is really required, because the projected cash flows for 2002 and 2003 indicate that an adequate amount of cash will be generated from operations to finance the plant expansion and repay the loan. In actuality, there is some question whether Warford needs the extension because the excess funds generated from 2002 operations might cover the $60,000 loan repayment. However, Warford may want the loan extension to provide a cushion because their cash balance is low. The financial ratios indicate that Warford has a solid financial structure. If the bank wanted some extra protection, it could require Warford to appropriate retained earnings for the amount of the loan and/or restrict cash dividends for the next two years to the 2001 amount of $1.25 per share.

PROBLEM 11-9

a. __2__ $$\frac{\text{Cash Equivalents + Marketable Securities + Net Receivables}}{\text{Current Liabilities}}$$

$$\frac{\$400 + \$1,700}{\$2,400} = \frac{\$2,100}{\$2,400} = .88$$

b. __3__ $$\frac{\text{Average Gross Receivables}}{\text{Net Sales/365}} = \frac{(\$1,500 + \$1,700) \div 2}{\$28,800/365} = 20.28 \text{ days}$$

c. __5__ $$\frac{\text{Recurring Earnings Before Interest and Tax}}{\text{Interest Expense}} = \frac{\$1,200 + \$400 + \$800}{\$28,800/365} = 6.00 \text{ times per year}$$

d. __1__ $$\frac{\text{Net Sales}}{\text{Average Total Assets}} = \frac{\$28,800}{(\$8,500 + \$9,500 \div 2)} = 3.2 \text{ times per year}$$

e. __4__ $$\frac{\text{Cost of Goods Sold}}{\text{Average Inventory}} = \frac{\$15,120}{(\$2,120 + \$2,200) \div 2} = 7.0 \text{ times per year}$$

f. __5__ $$\frac{\text{Operating Income}}{\text{Net Sales}} = \frac{\$1,200 + \$800 + \$400}{\$28,80} = 8.3\%$$

g. __5__ Dividends Per Share
        Fully Diluted Earnings Per Share

        = The data for this formula is not provided. Since there
          is no preferred stock, the following formula will also
          give the correct answer:

$$\frac{\text{Cash Dividends}}{\text{Net Income}} = \frac{\$400}{\$1,200} = 33.3\%$$

PROBLEM 11-10

a. __2__ Current Ratio = $\frac{\text{Current Assets}}{\text{Current Liabilities}}$

$$\frac{\$30,000 - \$2,000}{\$12,000 - \$2,000} = \frac{\$28,000}{\$10,000} = 2.8 \text{ to } 1.00$$

b. __1__ Quick (Acid-Test) Ratio = $\frac{\text{Cash Equivalents + Marketable Securities + Net Receivables}}{\text{Current Liabilities}}$

$$\frac{\$6,000 + \$6,600 - \$2,000}{\$12,000 - \$2,000} = \frac{\$10,600}{\$10,000} = 1.06 \text{ to } 1.00$$

c. __1__ A two-for-one common stock split would result in
        doubling the number of common shares. It would result
        in the par value being reduced from $1.00 to 50¢. It
        would not influence retained earnings or total
        stockholders' equity.

        Each $1,000 bond that was convertible into 300 shares
        of common stock would now be convertible into 600
        shares of common stock.

d. __3__ $$\frac{\$36,000 - \$6,000}{20} = \frac{\$30,000}{20} = \$1,500 \text{ Per Year}$$

        $13,500 ÷ $1,500 = 9

e. __4__ Book Value = $\frac{\text{Total Stockholders' Equity - Preferred Stock Equity}}{\text{Number Of Common Shares Outstanding}}$

$$\frac{\$48,200 - 0}{20,000 \text{ Shares}} = \$2.41$$

f. __2__
Sales	$90,000,000
Gross profit	20 percent
Cost of goods sold	80 percent
Cost of goods sold	$72,000,000
Divided by turnover	5
Average inventory	14,400,000

Ending inventory	$16,000,000	
Beginning inventory	?	(a)
Total	?	(b)

Total inventory = Average inventory x 2 = $14,400,000 x 2 = $28,800,000

= ($28,800,000) less ending inventory ($16,000,000)
= Beginning inventory $12,800,000

g. __3__   Payout ratio of 80 percent (this is, 80 percent of net income is being paid out in dividends):

$4,000,000 = .8X
X = $5,000,000 (Net income)

Retained earnings, November 30, 2001	$16,000
Less net income for year	(5,000)
Plus dividends	4,000
Retained earnings, December 1, 2000	$15,000

PROBLEM 11-11

a.

Calcor Company
Pro Forma Income Statement
For the Year Ending November 30, 2002

Net sales ($8,400,000 x 1.05 x 1.10)	$9,702,000
Expenses:	
Cost of goods sold ($6,300,000 x 1.05 x 1.04)	6,879,600
Selling expense ($780,000 + $420,000)	1,200,000
Administrative expense	900,000
Interest expense [$140,000 + ($300,000 x .10)]	170,000
Total expense	9,149,600
Income before income taxes	552,400
Income taxes	220,960
Net income	$ 331,440

b. President Kuhn's entire goal is not achieved because the return on sales (8 percent) and the turnover of average assets (5 times per year) are not met. However, the return on average assets before interest and taxes, which is a multiplication of the first two ratios, would be achieved. This is reflected by the calculation of the following ratios.

1. $\dfrac{\text{Return on Sales Before}}{\text{Interest and Taxes}} = \dfrac{\text{Income Before Interest and Taxes}}{\text{Sales}}$

$$= \frac{\$552400 + \$170,000}{\$9,702,000}$$

$$= \frac{\$722,400}{\$9,702,000} = 7.4\%$$

The goal of an 8 percent return on sales before interest and taxes would not be achieved (7.4% < 8%).

2. $\dfrac{\text{Turnover of Average}}{\text{Assets}} = \dfrac{\text{Sales}}{\text{Average assets}}$

$$= \frac{\$9,702,000}{\$2,100,000* + \$300,000}$$

$$= 4.0425 \text{ times per year}$$

$* \ 2001 \text{ Average Assets } \dfrac{2001 \text{ Sales}}{2001 \text{ Turnover of Average Assets}}$

$$= \frac{\$8,400,000}{4}$$

$$= \$2,100,000$$

The goal of a turnover of average assets of 5 times would not be achieved (4.0425 < 5).

3. $\dfrac{\text{Return On Average Assets}}{\text{Before Interest and Taxes}} = \dfrac{\text{Income Before Interest And Taxes}}{\text{Average Assets}}$

$$= \frac{\$552,400 + \$170,000}{\$2,100,000 + \$300,000}$$

$$= \frac{\$722,400}{\$2,400,000}$$

$$= 30.1\%$$

The goal of return on average assets before interest and taxes of 30 percent would be achieved.

c. No. Return on average assets before interest and taxes (third goal) is equal to return on sales before interest and taxes (first goal) times turnover of average assets (second goal). If Calcor Company achieved the first two goals, the return on average assets before interest and taxes would be at least 40 percent (.08 x 5), which is greater than the goal of 30 percent.

PROBLEM 11-12

a. <u>A Company Z Score</u>

$$X_1 = \frac{\text{Working Capital}}{\text{Total Assets}} \qquad X_1 = \frac{\$90,000}{\$300,000} = 30.00$$

$$X_2 = \frac{\text{Retained Earnings}}{\text{Total Assets}} \qquad X_2 = \frac{\$80,000}{\$300,000} = 26.67$$

$$X_3 = \frac{\text{E.B.I.T.}}{\text{Total Assets}} \qquad X_3 = \frac{\$70,000}{\$300,000} = 23.33$$

$$X_4 = \frac{\text{Market Value of Equity}}{\text{Book Value of Total Debt}} \qquad X_4 = \frac{\$180,000}{\$30,000} = 600.0$$

$$X_5 = \frac{\text{Sales}}{\text{Total Assets}} \qquad X_5 = \frac{\$430,000}{\$300,000} = 143.33$$

$$Z = .012X1 + .014X2 + .033X3 + .006X4 + .010X5$$

$$
\begin{aligned}
Z =\ & 0.012 \times 30.00 \\
+\ & 0.014 \times 26.67 \\
+\ & 0.033 \times 23.33 \\
+\ & 0.006 \times 600.00 \\
+\ & 0.010 \times 143.33
\end{aligned}
$$

$$
\begin{aligned}
Z =\ & 0.36 \\
+\ & 0.37 \\
+\ & 0.77 \\
+\ & 3.60 \\
+\ & 1.43
\end{aligned}
\qquad Z = \underline{6.53}
$$

B Company Z Score

$$X_1 = \frac{\text{Working Capital}}{\text{Total Assets}} \qquad X_1 = \frac{\$120,000}{\$280,000} = 42.86$$

$$X_2 = \frac{\text{Retained Earnings}}{\text{Total Assets}} \qquad X_2 = \frac{\$90,000}{\$280,000} = 32.14$$

$$X_3 = \frac{\text{E.B.I.T.}}{\text{Total Assets}} \qquad X_3 = \frac{\$60,000}{\$280,000} = 21.43$$

$$X_4 = \frac{\text{Market Value of Equity}}{\text{Book Value of Total Debt}} \qquad X_4 = \frac{\$168,750}{\$50,000} = 337.50$$

$$X_5 = \frac{\text{Sales}}{\text{Total Assets}} \qquad X_5 = \frac{\$400,000}{\$280,000} = 142.86$$

$$Z = .012X1 + .014X2 + .033X3 + .006X4 + .010X5$$

$$
\begin{aligned}
Z = \ & 0.012 \ \times \ 42.86 \\
+ \ & 0.014 \ \times \ 32.14 \\
+ \ & 0.033 \ \times \ 21.43 \\
+ \ & 0.006 \ \times \ 337.50 \\
+ \ & 0.010 \ \times \ 142.86
\end{aligned}
$$

$$
\begin{aligned}
Z = \ & 0.51 \qquad Z = \underline{5.13} \\
+ \ & 0.45 \\
+ \ & 0.71 \\
+ \ & 2.03 \\
+ \ & 1.43
\end{aligned}
$$

C Company Z Score

$$X_1 = \frac{\text{Working Capital}}{\text{Total Assets}} \qquad X_1 = \frac{\$150,000}{\$250,000} = 60.00$$

$$X_2 = \frac{\text{Retained Earnings}}{\text{Total Assets}} \qquad X_2 = \frac{\$60,000}{\$250,000} = 24.00$$

$$X_3 = \frac{\text{E.B.I.T.}}{\text{Total Assets}} \qquad X_3 = \frac{\$50,000}{\$250,000} = 20.00$$

$$X_4 = \frac{\text{Market Value of Equity}}{\text{Book Value of Total Debt}} \qquad X_4 = \frac{\$148,500}{\$80,000} = 185.63$$

$$X_5 = \frac{\text{Sales}}{\text{Total Assets}} \qquad\qquad X_5 = \frac{\$200,000}{\$250,000} = 80.00$$

$$Z = .012X1 + .014X2 + .033X3 + .006X4 + .010X5$$

$$
\begin{aligned}
Z \quad &= 0.012 \quad x \quad 60.00 \\
&+ 0.014 \quad x \quad 24.00 \\
&+ 0.033 \quad x \quad 20.00 \\
&+ 0.006 \quad x \quad 185.63 \\
&+ 0.010 \quad x \quad 80.00
\end{aligned}
$$

$$
\begin{aligned}
Z = 0.72 \qquad\qquad &Z = \underline{3.63} \\
+ 0.34 \\
+ 0.66 \\
+ 1.11 \\
+ 0.80
\end{aligned}
$$

b. All of these companies appear to have good financial condition. The company with the lowest score is Company C; therefore, Company C is most likely to experience financial failure.

PROBLEM 11-13

a. $X_1 = \dfrac{\text{Working Capital}}{\text{Total Assets}} \qquad X_1 = \dfrac{\$152,800}{\$494,500} = 30.90$

$X_2 = \dfrac{\text{Retained Earnings}}{\text{Total Assets}} \qquad X_2 = \dfrac{\$248,000}{\$494,500} \ 50.15$

$X_3 = \dfrac{\text{E.B.I.T.}}{\text{Total Assets}} \qquad X_3 = \dfrac{\$84,000}{\$494,500} = 16.99$

$X_4 = \dfrac{\text{Market Value of Equity}}{\text{Book Value of Total Debt}} \qquad X_4 = \dfrac{\$690,000}{\$200,500} = 344.14$

$X_5 = \dfrac{\text{Sales}}{\text{Total Assets}} \qquad X_5 = \dfrac{\$860,000}{\$494,500} = 173.91$

$$Z = .012X1 + .014X2 + .033X3 + .006X4 + .010X5$$

$$
\begin{aligned}
Z \quad &= 0.012 \quad x \quad 30.90 \\
&+ 0.014 \quad x \quad 50.15 \\
&+ 0.033 \quad x \quad 16.99 \\
&+ 0.006 \quad x \quad 344.14 \\
&+ 0.010 \quad x \quad 173.91
\end{aligned}
$$

```
Z  = 0.37              Z = 5.43
   + 0.70
   + 0.56
   + 2.06
   + 1.74
```

b. No. In a study using 1970-1973, a Z score of 2.675 was
    established as a practical cutoff point. The Z score for
    General Company is substantially above 2.675.

PROBLEM 11-14

2001 Net Income As Reported		$90,200,000
Net Change In Inventory Reserve:		
2001	$50,000,000	
2000	46,000,000	
(a)	$ 4,000,000	
(b) Effective Federal Tax Rate		37.9%
(c) Change In Taxes (a x b)	$ 1,516,000	
(d) Net Change In Income (a-c)		2,484,000
2001 Approximate Income If Inventory Had Been Valued At Approximate Current Cost		$92,684,000

PROBLEM 11-15

2000 Net Income As Reported		$45,000,000
Net Change In Inventory Reserve:		
2000	$20,000,000	
1999	28,000,000	
(a)	($8,000,000)	
(b) Effective Federal Tax Rate		23.7%
(c) Change In Taxes (axb)	1,896,000)	
(d) Net Change In Income (a-c)		(6,104,000)
2000 Approximate Income If Inventory Had Been Valued At Approximate Current Cost		$38,896,000

PROBLEM 11-16

The vertical axis does not start at zero.

CASES

CASE 11-1 WHAT POSITION?

(This case provides an opportunity to examine the impact of the LIFO reserve and consider the likelihood of bankruptcy.)

a. LIFO inventory liquidations increased consolidated net income by approximately $89,000 ($.04 per share) in 1995 and $75,000 ($.03 per share) in 1994.

b. LIFO Reserve:

August 26, 1995	$18,157,000
August 27, 1994	$17,576,000
Increased reduction in inventory (Increased cost of merchandise sold reduces income)	$ 581,000

Estimate the tax rate to determine the influence to net income:

Provision for income taxes	$2,715,000 = 37.73%
Income before income taxes	$7,195,000

(1-37.73%) x $581,000 = $ 361,789

With FIFO, the reported net income would have been ($4,480,000 + $361,789) = $4,841,789

c. 1. Days' Sales In Inventory = $\dfrac{\text{Ending Inventory}}{\text{Cost of Goods Sold}/365}$

$$\dfrac{\$44,064,000}{\$418,128,000/365} = 38.47 \text{ days}$$

2. Working Capital = Current Assets - Current Liabilities

$63,635,000 - $57,549,000 = $6,086,000

3. Current Ratio = $\dfrac{\text{Current Assets}}{\text{Current Liabilities}}$

$$\dfrac{\$63,635,000}{\$57,549,000} = 1.11$$

$$\text{Acid-Test Ratio} = \frac{\text{Cash Equivalents} + \text{Marketable Securities} + \text{Net Receivables}}{\text{Current Liabilities}}$$

$$\frac{\$7,402,000 + \$6,587,000}{\$57,549,000} = .24$$

5. $$\text{Debt Ratio} = \frac{\text{Total Liabilities}}{\text{Total Assets}}$$

$$\frac{\$154,001,000 - \$40,731,000}{\$154,001,000} = 73.55\%$$

d. Addition to inventory $18,157,000

Addition to deferred taxes (liability)
   37.73% x $18,157,000 =$ 6,850,636

Addition to retained earnings
   ($18,157,000 - $6,850,636) $11,306,364

Increased Net Income (Eliminate LIFO reserve):

Net income reported $4,480,000

Increase in reserve ($581,000)

Tax rate (37.73%)

Net increase to income

($581,000 x (1 - 37.73) =   <u>361,789</u>
                                                      <u>$4,841,789</u>

1. $$\text{Days' Sales In Inventory} = \frac{\text{Ending Inventory}}{\text{Cost of Goods Sold}/365}$$

$$\frac{\$44,064,000 + \$18,157,000}{(\$418,128,000 - \$581,000)\,/\,365} = 54.39 \text{ days}$$

2. Working Capital = Current Assets - Current Liabilities

    ($63,635,000 + $18,157,000) - ($57,549,000 + $6,850,636)

    = $17,392,364

3. Current Ratio $= \dfrac{\text{Current Assets}}{\text{Current Liabilities}}$

$$= \frac{\$63,635,000 + \$18,157,000)}{(\$57,549,000 + \$6,850,636)} = 1.27$$

4. Acid-Test Ratio $= \dfrac{\text{Cash Equivalents} + \text{Marketable Securities} + \text{Net Receivables}}{\text{Current Liabilities}}$

$$= \frac{(\$7402,000 + \$6,587,000)}{\$57,549,000 + \$6,850,636)} = .22$$

5. Debt Ratio $= \dfrac{\text{Total Liabilities}}{\text{Total Assets}}$

$$\frac{\$57,549,000 + \$48,399,000 + \$5,276,000 + \$2,046,000 + \$6,850,636}{\$154,001,000 + \$18,157,000} = 69.77\%$$

e.

	Ratios in (c)	Ratios in (d)
Days' Sales in Inventory	38.47 Days	54.39 Days
Working Capital	$6,086,000	$17,392,364
Current Ratio	1.11	1.27
Acid-Test Ratio	.24	.22
Debt Ratio	73.55%	69.77%

Material increase to days' sales in inventory, working capital, and the current ratio. Acid-test ratio decreased slightly. The debt ratio decreased moderately.

f. 1. Cash Flow/Total Debt $= \dfrac{\$19,829,000}{\$154,001,000 - \$40,731,000} = 17.51\%$

2. Net Income/Total Assets $= \dfrac{\$4,480,000}{\$154,001,000} = 2.91\%$

3. Debt Ratio (See part (c))   73.55%

This company is apparently not in any immediate danger of financial failure. On the other hand, any major disruption in profits could be a problem.

g. Z score for 1995

$$
\begin{aligned}
Z = \ & .012 \ (\text{Working Capital/Total Assets}) \\
+\ & .014 \ (\text{Retained Earnings [balance sheet]/Total Assets}) \\
+\ & .033 \ (\text{Earnings Before Interest and Taxes/Total Assets}) \\
+\ & .006 \ (\text{Market Value of Equity/Book Value of Total Debt}) \\
+\ & .010 \ (\text{Sales/Total Assets})
\end{aligned}
$$

$$
\begin{aligned}
Z = \ & .012 \ (\$6,086,000/\$154,001,000) \\
+\ & .014 \ (\$35,664,000/\$154,001,000) \\
+\ & .033 \ [(\$7,195,000 + \$4,469,000)/\$154,001,000] \\
+\ & .006 \ [(\$16.25 \times 2,193,352)/(\$154,001,000-\$40,731,000] \\
+\ & .010 \ (\$559,244,000/\$154,001,000)
\end{aligned}
$$

$$
\begin{aligned}
Z = \ & .012 \ (3.95) \\
+\ & .014 \ (23.16) \\
+\ & .033 \ (7.57) \\
+\ & .006 \ (31.47) \\
+\ & .010 \ (363.14)
\end{aligned}
$$

$$Z = .05 + .32 + .25 + .01 + 3.63$$

$$Z = 4.26$$

Comment   The 4.26 Z score is somewhat better than the 2.675 guideline related in the book. If this is a reasonable comparison, then there is no immediate danger of financial failure.

Chapter 12
Special Industries: Banks, Utilities, Oil and Gas, Transportation, Insurance, Real Estate Companies

QUESTIONS

12- 1.   Interest income, service charges, and earnings in investments are the main sources of revenue for banks.

12- 2.   Loans are assets because they are an investment of the banks, money. They are like receivables; money is owed to the bank, not by it.

12- 3.   Savings accounts are liabilities because they hold cash owed to customers.

12- 4.   Loans/deposits is a type of debt coverage, since loans are a main amount to repay depositors.

12- 5.   Banks report to the Comptroller of the Currency, the Federal Reserve, the Federal Deposit Insurance Corporation (FDIC), and to their shareholders, and they must publish their reports in newspapers for the general public.

12- 6.   Bank holding companies own banks and other types of subsidiaries that may not be financially related. These holdings can affect the special bank ratios.

12- 7.   Interest expense will usually be the biggest expense item for banks.

12- 8.   Total deposits times capital is a measure of liabilities to equity, of creditors' to owners' funds.

12- 9.   Interest margin to average assets, earnings per share, return on equity, and return on assets are all ratios that indicate a bank's profitability.

12-10.   Earning assets are those that generate interest from which the firm earns its profits.

12-11.   The loan loss coverage ratio measures the quality of the loans and the level of protection related to loan payment.

12-12.   Deposits times capital is a type of debt to equity or
         leverage ratio.

12-13.   A review of assets may indicate that the bank has a
         substantial investment in long-term bonds. Such an
         investment could reflect substantial risk if interest
         rates increase. Another example would be a bank holding
         long-term fixed rate mortgages. The value of these
         mortgages could decline substantially if interest rates
         increase.

12-14.   This review may indicate that investments have a market
         value that is substantially above or below the book
         amount.

12-15.   In general, foreign loans are perceived as being more
         risky than domestic loans.

12-16.   It may indicate a significant change and/or significant
         losses charged.

12-17.   In general, nonperforming assets are assets that the bank
         is not receiving income on or receiving inadequate
         income. The amount and trend of nonperforming assets
         should be observed closely. This can be an early
         indication of troubles to come for a bank.

12-18.   A decreasing amount in savings deposits would indicate
         that the bank is losing one of its cheapest source of
         funds.

12-19.   This footnote may reveal significant additional
         commitments and contingent liabilities.

12-20.   Utilities have heavy investment in fixed assets,
         necessitating long-term debt. Further, they are able to
         use leverage favorably, since their profits are
         controlled and are reasonably stable, due to the control
         and to the nature of the product.

12-21.   Demand for utilities is inelastic; there are no
         substitute services. There is virtually no competition.

12-22. Plant and equipment are listed first because the uniform accounting system recognized their importance in the operation. Current assets are a very small part of total assets.

12-23. Inventory ratios have little meaning for utilities, because they are unable to store their finished product.

12-24. Funded debt to operating property is a type of debt coverage ratio. It tells how funds are supplied for long-term investment.

12-25. Yes, the times interest earned ratio is meaningful for utilities, since they have such a heavy use of debt.

12-26. No. Long-term capitalization, the major source of funds, including long-term debt, is presented first. Current liabilities are quite unimportant.

12-27. Electric utilities that have substantial construction work in progress are usually viewed as being more risky investments than electric utilities that do not have substantial construction work in progress.

Most utility commissions allow no or only a small amount of construction work in progress in the rate base. Therefore the utility rates essentially do not reflect the construction work in progress.

It is possible that the utility commission will not allow all of this property and plant in the rate base. The utility commission may rule that part of the cost was due to inefficiency and disallow this cost. The utility commission may also disallow part of the cost on the grounds that the utility used bad judgment and provided for excess capacity.

For the costs that are allowed, the risk is that the utility commission will not allow a reasonable rate of return.

12-28. The account allowance for equity funds used during construction represents an assumed rate of return on equity funds used for construction. The account allowance for borrowed funds used during construction represents the cost of borrowed funds that are used for construction.

12-29. Each relates to accounting for exploration costs. Successful efforts capitalizes only those costs of successful projects. Full cost capitalizes the outlays for both successful and unsuccessful projects.

12-30. Regulation makes their accounting systems uniform, and their revenues are controlled by rate structure.

12-31. A variation of one of two costing methods is used by an oil or gas company to account for exploration and production costs. These methods are the successful-efforts method and the full-costing method. The selection has a significant influence on the financial statements.

   The successful-efforts method places only exploration and production costs of successful wells on the balance sheet under property, plant, and equipment. Exploration and production costs of unsuccessful (or dry) wells are expensed when it is determined that there is a dry hole. With the full-costing method, exploration and production costs of all, the wells are placed on the balance sheet under property, plant, and equipment.

12-32. Major items on this schedule are typically revisions of previous estimates, improved recovery, discoveries and other additions, and production. This information can be significant in terms of the companies' reserves.

12-33. This is a true statement. One of the reasons is that large sums can be spent for exploration and development years in advance of revenue from the found reserves. The other reason is that there can be significant differences between when expenses are deducted on the financial statements and when they are deducted on the tax return.

12-34. A decreasing operating ratio means a lower proportion of expenses and more profits.

12-35. Operating revenue to operating property is a turnover ratio. Because of the heavy investment in fixed assets, this ratio will usually be less than 1 to 1 for a utility.

12-36. Fixed assets is the most important asset category.

12-37. Revenue is divided into categories by type or function of service, such as passenger, freight, mail, etc.

12-38. Differences in traffic volume and distance traveled will change revenues. The price level, type of service and effectiveness of asset use will change expenses for a transportation firm.

12-39. Higher revenue per passenger mile basically indicates higher rates on fares.

12-40. The passenger load factor indicates utilization of capacity. The greater the utilization, the lower the fixed charge per passenger and the higher the profit.

12-41. In this publication, data are compiled by composite carrier groups. It includes industry total dollars for income statement accounts, such as total revenue.

12-42. The annual reports filed with the state insurance departments are in accordance with Statutory Accounting Practices (SAP).

12-43. Annual reports that insurance companies issue to the public are in accordance with generally accepted accounting principles (GAAP).

12-44. Real estate investments are reported at cost less accumulated depreciation and an allowance for impairment in value. An insurance company with substantial real estate investments is risky because there is a great deal of subjectivity in establishing the allowance for impairment in value.

12-45. Under GAAP, these costs are deferred and charged to expense over the premium-paying period. Under SAP, these costs are charged to expense as incurred.

12-46. Intangibles are recognized as an asset under GAAP, while intangibles are not recognized as an asset under SAP.

12-47. For short-duration contracts, revenue is ordinarily recognized over the period of the contract in proportion to the amount of insurance protection provided. When the risk differs significantly from the contract period, revenue is recognized over the period of risk in proportion to the amount of insurance protection.

12-48. Insurance company, specific ratios are frequently based on SAP financial reporting to the states and not GAAP financial reporting that is used for the annual report and SEC reporting.

12-49. Insurance is a highly regulated industry that some perceive as having relatively low growth prospects. It is also an industry with substantial competition.

The accounting environment probably also contributes to the relatively low market price for insurance company stocks.

12-50. Conventional accounting recognizes depreciation but not the value of the property. This potentially presents a problem to investors in judging the value of the company. Some real estate companies have sold substantial portions of their property in order to realize value for their investors, while some have attempted to reflect value by disclosing current value in addition to the conventional accounting.

TO THE NET

1. a.   2911

   b.   Net proved reserves of crude oil and natural gas
        liquids. (Millions of Barrels)

	Worldwide
Developed reserves	2,082
Undeveloped reserves	576
As of December 31, 1995	2,658
Developed reserves	2,087
Undeveloped reserves	617
As of December 31, 1996	2,704
Developed reserves	2,455
Undeveloped reserves	812
As of December 31, 1997	3,267
Developed reserves	2,646
Undeveloped reserves	927
As of December 31, 1998	3,573

   c.   Net proved reserves of crude oil and natural gas
        liquids. (Millions of Barrels)

	As of December 31, 1998	As of December 31, 1997	As of December 31, 1996	As of December 31, 1995
Developed reserves	127.1	117.9	100.2	100.0
Undeveloped reserves	160.9	141.0	107.1	100.0
Total	134.4	122.9	101.7	100.0

   d.   There has been a substantial increase in proved
        reserves oil and natural gas liquids. This is
        especially true for undeveloped reserves.

2. a. Electric and other services combined.

   b. Construction in progress $391,100,000.

   c. Allowance for borrowed funds used during construction
       $17,347,000.

   d. Balance Sheet
       The interest on the borrowed funds used during
       construction increases construction in progress and
       reduces cash.

       Statement of Income
       No net effect. Interest expense is increased and
       this is offset with the account allowance for
       borrowed funds used during construction.

       Statements of Cash Flows
       Cash outflow is increased by the interest payment.

PROBLEMS

PROBLEM 12-1

			2001	2000
a. Total Deposits Times Capital	=	Average Total Deposits Average Total Capital	$24,000,000 $ 1,850,000	$20,000,000 $ 1,600,000
			= 12.97	= 12.50
b. Loans To Total Deposits	=	Average Loans Average Total Deposits	$16,000,000 $24,000,000	$13,200,000 $20,000,000
			= 66.7%	= 66.0%

e. McEttrick National Bank has experienced a faster rise in deposits than in capital. This has caused the deposits to capital to rise. Loans have risen faster than deposits, so that loans to total deposits has risen. Capital to total assets has dropped, probably due to a faster rise in deposits. The interest margin to average total assets has dropped, which indicates a drop in profitability.

PROBLEM 12-2

a. 1. Earning Assets to Total Assets = $\dfrac{\text{Average Earning Assets}}{\text{Average Total Assets}}$

2001	2000	1999
$50,000,000 $58,823,529	$45,000,000 $54,216,867	$43,000,000 $52,000,000
= 85.00%	= 83.00%	= 82.69%

2. Interest Margin to Average Earning Assets = $\dfrac{\text{Interest Margin}}{\text{Average Earning Assets}}$

2001	2000	1999
$ 2,550,000 $50,000,000	$ 2,200,000 $45,000,000	$ 2,020,000 $43,000,000
= 5.10%	= 4.89%	= 4.70%

Pretax Income (Before Security Transactions) + Provision For

3. Loan Loss Coverage Ratio = $\frac{\text{Loan Losses}}{\text{Net Charge-Offs}}$

2001	2000	1999
$\frac{(\$562,000 + \$190,000)}{\$180,000}$	$\frac{(\$480,500 + \$160,000)}{\$162,000}$	$\frac{(\$440,000 + \$142,000)}{\$160,000}$
= 4.17 times per year	= 3.95 times per year	= 3.64 times per year

4. Equity to Total Assets = $\frac{\text{Average Equity}}{\text{Average Total Assets}}$

2001	2000	1999
$\frac{\$4,117,600}{\$58,823,529}$	$\frac{\$3,524,000}{\$54,216,867}$	$\frac{\$3,120,000}{\$52,000,000}$
= 7.00%	= 6.50%	= 6.00%

5. Deposits Times Capital = $\frac{\text{Average Deposits}}{\text{Average Stockholders' Equity}}$

2001	2000	1999
$\frac{\$52,500,000}{\$4,117,600}$	$\frac{\$42,500,000}{\$3,524,000}$	$\frac{\$37,857,000}{\$3,120,000}$
= 12.75 times per year	= 12.06 times per year	= 12.13 times per year

6. Loans to Deposits = $\frac{\text{Average Net Loans}}{\text{Average Deposits}}$

2001	2000	1999
$\frac{\$32,500,000}{\$52,500,000}$	$\frac{\$26,000,000}{\$42,500,000}$	$\frac{\$22,500,000}{\$37,857,000}$
= 61.90%	= 61.18%	= 59.43%

b. Earning assets to total assets has increased. This indicates that management has improved in putting bank assets to work. Interest margin to average earning assets have increased. This indicates improved profitability.

The loan loss coverage ratio has increased, indicating an improved level of protection of loans.

Equity to total assets increased, indicating an improved cushion against the risk of using debt and leverage.

Deposits times capital increased, indicating a prospect of higher return to shareholders.

Loans to deposits increased, indicating increased risk.

PROBLEM 12-3

a.

	2001	2000
Operating Ratio:		
Operating expense	$20,340,000	$18,125,000
Operating revenue	$22,830,000	$20,500,000
	= 89.1%	= 88.4%

Operating expenses as a percent of revenue have increased.

b. Times Interest Earned = $\dfrac{\text{Operating Income}}{\text{Interest Expense}}$

	2001	2000
Operating income (after tax)	$2,490,000	$2,375,000
Income tax	3,200,000	3,000,000
Operating income (before tax)	$5,690,000	$5,375,000
Interest expense	$1,200,000	$1,000,000
Times interest earned	4.74	5.38

This utility has experienced a heavy increase in interest expense, causing a decline in the times interest earned.

c. Vertical common-size analysis:

	2001		2000	
Residential	$11,800,000	51.7%	$10,000,000	48.8%
Commercial	10,430,000	45.7%	10,000,000	48.8%
Other	600,000	2.6%	500,000	2.4%
Total	$22,830,000	100.0%	$20,500,000	100.0%

There has been a rise in residential usage, and this causes a proportionate increase in revenue from this source. Commercial use has not fallen.

PROBLEM 12-4

a. 1. Operating Ratio = $\dfrac{\text{Operating Expenses}}{\text{Operating Revenues}}$

2001	2000	1999
$\dfrac{\$850,600}{\$1,080,500}$	$\dfrac{\$820,200}{\$1,037,200}$	$\dfrac{\$780,000}{\$974,000}$
= 78.72%	= 79.08%	= 80.08%

2. Funded Debt to Operating Property = $\dfrac{\text{Funded Debt (Long - Term)}}{\text{Operating Property}}$

2001	2000	1999
$\dfrac{\$1,500,000}{\$3,900,000}$	$\dfrac{\$1,480,000}{\$3,750,000}$	$\dfrac{\$1,470,000}{\$3,600,000}$
= 38.46%	= 39.47%	= 40.83%

3. Percent Earned on Operating Property = $\dfrac{\text{Net Income}}{\text{Operating Property}}$

2001	2000	1999
$\dfrac{\$280,000}{\$3,900,000}$	$\dfrac{\$260,000}{\$3,750,000}$	$\dfrac{\$230,000}{\$3,600,000}$
= 7.18%	= 6.93%	= 6.39%

4. Operating Revenue to Operating Property = $\dfrac{\text{Operating Revenue}}{\text{Operating Property}}$

2001	2000	1999
$\dfrac{\$1,080,500}{\$3,900,000}$	$\dfrac{\$1,037,200}{\$3,750,000}$	$\dfrac{\$974,000}{\$3,600,000}$
= 27.71%	= 27.66%	= 27.06%

b. The operating ratio decreased, indicating improved efficiency. Funded debt to operating property decreased, indicating less risk because a lower percentage of funds were supplied by funded debt.

Percent earned to operating property increased, indicating improved profitability.

Operating revenue to operating property increased, indicating improved profitability.

c. Cash flow per share has increased much more than earnings per share. This would be considered to be positive.

PROBLEM 12-5

a. Operating Ratio = $\dfrac{\text{Operating Expense}}{\text{Operating Revenue}}$

2001	2000
$\dfrac{\$625,000}{\$624,000} = 100.2\%$	$\dfrac{\$617,000}{\$618,000} = 99.8\%$

This firm is having profit problems. Expenses have increased faster than revenues.

b. Long-Term Debt to Operating Property = $\dfrac{\text{Long - Term Debt}}{\text{Operating Property}}$

2001	2000
$\dfrac{\$280,000}{\$365,000} = 76.7\%$	$\dfrac{\$270,000}{\$360,000} = 75.0\%$

This firm is using more debt in absolute terms and in relation to operating property.

c. Operating Revenue to Operating Property = $\dfrac{\text{Operating Revenue}}{\text{Operating Property}}$

<u>2001</u>

$\dfrac{\$624,000}{\$365,000}$ = 1.71 times per year

<u>2000</u>

$\dfrac{\$618,000}{\$360,000}$ = 1.72 times per year

The turnover has remained relatively constant.

d. Revenue per Passenger Mile:

<u>2001</u>

$\dfrac{\$624,000}{\$7,340,000}$ = 8.5¢/Mile

<u>2000</u>

$\dfrac{\$618,000}{\$7,600,000}$ = = 8.1¢/Mile

The firm is generating more revenue per passenger mile, but is suffering from a serious decline in passenger miles.

PROBLEM 12-6

a. 1. Operating Ratio = <u>Operating Expenses</u>
   Operating Revenues

<u>2001</u>	<u>2000</u>	<u>1999</u>
<u>$1,550,000</u>	<u>$1,520,000</u>	<u>$1,480,000</u>
$1,840,000	$1,670,400	$1,620,700
= 84.24%	= 91.00%	= 91.32%

2. Long-Term Debt To Operating Property = <u>Long-Term Debt</u>
   Operating Property

<u>2001</u>	<u>2000</u>	<u>1999</u>
<u>$910,000</u>	<u>$900,500</u>	<u>$895,000</u>
$995,000	$990,000	$985,000
= 91.46%	= 90.96%	= 90.86%

3. Operating Revenue to Operating Property = $\frac{\text{Operating Revenue}}{\text{Operating Property}}$

2001	2000	1999
$\frac{\$1,840,000}{\$\ \ 995,000}$	$\frac{\$1,670,400}{\$\ \ 990,000}$	$\frac{\$1,620,700}{\$\ \ 985,000}$
= 184.92%	= 168.73%	= 164.54%

b. The operating ratio decreased significantly, indicating improved profitability.

Long-term debt to operating property increased slightly, indicating a slight increase in risk.

Operating revenue to operating property increased moderately, indicating improved profitability.

c. The passenger load factor increased materially, indicating improved profitability.

PROBLEM 12-7

a. 2   c. 1   e. 3
b. 1   d. 5

CASES

CASE 12-1   ALLOWANCE FOR FUNDS

Primary emphasis on "allowance for equity funds used during construction" and "allowance for borrowing funds used during construction". Also, several ratios are included. (The utility industry typically capitalizes interest on construction funds and a rate of return on equity funds used for construction. This can result in reported earnings being substantially different than cash flow from operations. This case also covers construction work in progress and financial ratios that relate to utilities.)

a. The account, allowance for equity funds used during construction, represents an assumed rate of return on equity funds used for construction. The costs that have been added into the cost base have also been added to income, through the account allowance for equity funds.

b. The income statement account, allowance for borrowed funds used during construction, charges to the balance sheet account, construction in progress, the interest on borrowed funds use for construction in progress.
    (Note: In the case, "allowance for borrowed funds used during construction" is called "allowance for borrowing funds used during construction".)

c. Capitalizing interest on borrowed funds prevents this expense from reducing income during the current period. If this interest had not been capitalized, then current income would have been lower.

d. Yes. When interest on borrowed funds is capitalized, then the interest does not reduce income this year, but the interest payments will require funds.

e. Capitalizing allowance for equity funds used during construction increases income during the period of capitalization.

f. Yes. Capitalizing allowance for equity funds used during construction increases income during the period of capitalization, but no funds are provided during this period.

g. Both the capitalization of interest on borrowed funds and the capitalization allowance for equity funds result in the reported income being higher than the cash flow.

h. 1. Operating Ratio = $\dfrac{\text{Operating Expenses}}{\text{Operating Revenues}}$

	1994	1993
	(In Thousands)	
Operating Expenses	$1,946,533	$1,931,035
Operating Revenue	$2,243,029	$2,233,978
	= 86.78%	= 86.44%

The operating ratio increased, indicating an increase in operating expenses in relation to operating revenues.

2. Funded Debt to Operating Property = $\dfrac{\text{Funded Debt}}{\text{Operating Property}}$

	1994	1993
	(In Thousands)	
Funded debt (Long-term debt)	$1,520,488	$1,511,589
Operating Property	$3,716,721	$3,482,501
	= 40.91%	= 43.41%

The funded debt to operating property decreased, indicating a decrease in funded debt in relation to operating property.

3. Percent Earned On Operating Property = $\dfrac{\text{Net Income}}{\text{Operating Property}}$

	1994	1993
	(In Thousands)	
Net Income	$199,426	$190,223
Operating Property	$3,716,721	$3,482,501
	= 5.37%	= 5.46%

There has been a slight decrease in the percent earned on operating property.

4. Operating Revenue To Operating Property = $\dfrac{\text{Operating Revenue}}{\text{Operating Property}}$

	1994	1993
	(In Thousands)	
Operating Revenue	$2,243,029	$2,233,978
Operating Property	$3,716,721	$3,482,501
	= 60.35%	= 64.15%

There has been a decrease in operating revenue in relation to operating property.

5. Times Interest Earned = $\dfrac{\text{Recurring Earnings Before Interest Expense,}}{\text{Interest Expense, Including Capitalized Interest}}$ Tax, Minority Income, and Equity Earnings

	1994	1993
	(In Thousands)	
Operating Income	$296,496	$302,943
Plus: Income Taxes	128,257	121,124
(A)	$424,753	$424,067
Interest:		
Interest On Long-Term Debt	$93,500	$100,777
Other Interest	11,298	9,809
(B)	$104,798	$110,586
(A)/(B)	4.05 times per year	3.83 times per year

Times interest earned improved moderately.
Note: Also, consider a cash flow times interest earned when reviewing a utility.

i. $\dfrac{\text{Construction Work in Progress}}{\text{Net Utility Plant}} = \dfrac{\$374,000}{\$3,716,721} = 10.06\%$ (In Thousands)

There is some risk that not all of the construction work in progress will be allowed in the rate base. There is also a risk as to the rate of return that will be allowed.

CASE 12-2   IN PROGRESS

The utility industry typically capitalizes interest on
construction funds and a rate of return on equity funds used for
construction.   This can result in reported earnings being
substantially different than cash flow from operations.   This
case also covers financial ratios that relate to utilities.

a.   Per the note, allowance for other funds used during
     construction (AFUDC), represents the estimated debt and
     equity cost of funds capitalized as a cost of construction.

b.   The income statement account, allowance for borrowing funds
     used during construction, charges to the balance sheet
     account, construction in progress, the interest on borrowed
     funds use for construction in progress.

c.   Yes.   When interest on borrowed funds is capitalized, then
     the interest does not reduce income this year, but the
     interest payments will require funds.

d.

1.   Operating Ratio = $\dfrac{\text{Operating Expenses}}{\text{Operating Revenues}}$

	1994	1993
	(In Thousands)	
Operating Expenses	$277,668	$277,924
Operating Revenues	$330,035	$329,489
	= 84.13%	= 84.35%

The operating ratio decreased slightly, indicating a decrease in
operating expenses in relation to operating revenues.

2. Funded Debt to Operating Property = $\dfrac{\text{Funded Debt}}{\text{Operating Property}}$

		1994	1993
		(In Thousands)	
Funded Debt:			
Long-Term Debt, Net of Current Maturities		$264,110	$261,100
Long-Term Partnership Obligation, Net of Current Maturities		9,507	12,881
(A)		$273,617	$273,981
Operating Property	(B)	$677,936	$635,869
(A)/(B)		40.36%	43.09%

The funded debt to operating property decreased, indicating a decrease in funded debt in relation to operating property.

3. Percent Earned On Operating Property = $\dfrac{\text{Net Income}}{\text{Operating Property}}$

	1994	1993
	(In Thousands)	
Net Income	$41,025	$39,588
Operating Property	$677,936	$635,869
	= 6.05%	= 6.23%

There has been a decrease in the percent earned on operating property.

4. Operating Revenue To Operating Property = $\dfrac{\text{Operating Revenue}}{\text{Operating Property}}$

	1994	1993
	(In Thousands)	
Operating Revenue	$330,035	$329,489
Operating Property	$677,936	$635,869
	= 48.68%	= 51.82%

There has been a decrease in operating revenue in relation to operating property.

5. Times Interest Earned =

$$\frac{\text{Recurring Earnings Before, Interest Expense, Tax, Minority Income, and Equity Earnings}}{\text{Interest Expense, Including Equity Earnings}}$$

		1994	1993
		(In Thousands)	
Operating Income	(A)	$52,367	$51,565
Interest:			
Interest On Long-Term Debt		$18,604	$18,437
Amortization of Premium, Discount, and Expense on Debt		852	773
Other Interest		1,589	747
(B)		$21,045	$19,957
(A)/(B)		2.49 times per year	2.58 times per year

e.

$$\frac{\text{Construction Work in Progress}}{\text{Net Utility Plant}} = \frac{\text{(In Thousands)}}{\$677,936}\ \frac{\$112,316}{} = 16.57\%$$

There is some risk that not all of the construction work in progress will be allowed in the rate base. There is also a risk as to the rate of return that will be allowed.

f.

	1994	1993	1992
Net Income	$41,025,000	$39,588,000	$36,758,000
	111.61%	107.70%	100%
Earning Per Share of Common Stock	$2.53	$2.44	$2.25
	112.44%	108.44%	100%
Allowance for Other Funds Used During Construction	$3,972,000	$3,092,000	$988,000
	402.02%	312.96%	100%
Allowance for Borrowing Funds Used During Construction	$2,058,000	$1,425,000	$434,000
	474.19%	328.34%	100%

Net income and earnings per share were up moderately. The majority of this increase came from allowance for the cost of funds during construction (AFUDC), which represents the estimated debt and equity cost of funds capitalized as a cost of construction.

CASE 12-3 LOANS AND PROVISION FOR LOANS

(This case provides an opportunity to review the trend in the quality of loans of Sylvania Savings Bank.)

This is an opinion question; therefore, comments will vary. Information on loans can be very significant information. From this footnote, consider the following:

1. Net loans at December 31, 1984, were $175,617,000, an increase of 23% over $142,264,000 at December 31, 1983. In general, this is positive information.

2. During the year, commercial loans increased by 25%, real estate loans increased by 3%, and consumer loans increased by 74%. In general, this is positive information.

3. Net loans represented 68% of total earning assets at December 31, 1984, compared to 64% at December 31, 1983. In general, this is positive information.

4. The average yield on the loan portfolio for 1984 was 13.2%, compared to 12.7% for 1983. In general, this is positive information.

5. Non-earning loans at December 31, 1984, were $2,469,000, as compared to $4,528,000 at December 31, 1983. This is _very_ positive information.

6. During 1984, net loan charge-offs amounted to $1,239,000, compared to $1,414,000 in 1983. This is positive information.

7. The 1984 provision for possible loan losses was $1,430,000, compared to $1,425,000 in 1983. This is positive, considering the reduction in non-earning loans.

8. The reserve for possible loan losses totaled $1,786,000 at December 31, 1984, and $1,595,000 at December 31, 1983. This is positive, considering the reduction in non-earning loans.

9. As a percent of loans less unearned discounts, the reserve was 1.01% in 1984 and 1.11% in 1983. This is probably positive, considering the reduction in non-earning loans.

General Conclusion

This footnote indicates a very good improvement in the quality of the loans.

CASE 12-4 YOU CAN BANK ON IT

(This case includes significant parts of the annual report of the Wells Fargo & Company. It provides an opportunity to review statements of a bank. You may want to consider extending the review beyond the questions included with the case.)

a.

		1998	1997	1996
1.	Net interest income	109.3%	105.2%	100.0%
2.	Provisions for loan losses	309.0%	228.0%	100.0%
3.	Net interest income after provision for loan losses	96.4%	97.2%	100.0%
4.	Total noninterest income	134.8%	119.0%	100.0%
5.	Total noninterest expense	121.3%	103.0%	100.0%

b. 1. Net interest income increased moderately.
    2. Provision for loan losses increased very materially.
    3. Net interest income after provision for loan losses decreased moderately. (The provision for loan losses more than offset the increase in net interest income.)
    4. Total noninterest income increased materially.
    5. Total noninterest expense increased materially. (Notice that the increase in total noninterest income was better than the increase in total noninterest expense.)

c.

	(in millions)	
	1998	1997
Earnings assets:		
Federal funds sold and securities purchased under resale agreements	$ 1,517	$ 1,049
Securities available for sale	31,997	27,872
Mortgages held for sale	19,770	9,706
Loans held for sale	5,322	4,494
Net loans	104,860	103,249
Mortgage servicing rights	3,080	3,048
	$166,546	$149,418

			1998	1997
1.	Earning Assets to Total Assets	$= \dfrac{\text{Total Earning Assets}}{\text{Total Assets}} =$	$\dfrac{\$166,546}{\$202,475}$	$\dfrac{\$149,418}{\$185,685}$
			82.26%	80.47%
2.	Interest Margin to Average Earning Assets	$= \dfrac{\text{Interest Margin}}{\text{Average Earning Assets}} =$	$\dfrac{\$8,990}{\$166,546}$	$\dfrac{\$8,648}{\$149,418}$
			5.40%	5.79%
3.	Loan Loss Coverage Ratio	$= \dfrac{\text{Pretax Income} + \text{Provision for Loan Losses}}{\text{Net Charge - Offs}} =$	$\begin{array}{r}\$3,293 \\ +1,545 \\ \hline \$1,617\end{array}$	$\begin{array}{r}\$4,193 \\ 1,140 \\ \hline \$1,305\end{array}$
			2.99 Times per year	4.09 Times per year
4.	Equity Capital to Total Assets	$= \dfrac{\text{Average Equity}}{\text{Average Total Assets}} =$	$\dfrac{\$20,759}{\$202,475}$	$\dfrac{\$19,778}{\$185,685}$
			10.25%	10.65%
5.	Deposits Times Capital	$= \dfrac{\text{Average Deposits}}{\text{Average Stockholders' Equity}} =$	$\dfrac{\$136,788}{\$20,759}$	$\dfrac{\$127,656}{\$19,778}$
			6.59 Times per year	6.45 Times per year
6.	Loans to Deposits	$= \dfrac{\text{Average Total Loans}}{\text{Average Deposits}} =$	$\begin{array}{r}\$5,322 \\ +\$104,860 \\ \hline \$136,788\end{array}$	$\begin{array}{r}\$4,494 \\ +\$103,249 \\ \hline \$127,656\end{array}$
			80.55%	84.40%

d. 1. Earning assets to total assets increased slightly between 1997 and 1998. This ratio is relatively good, indicating that the bank is putting assets to work effectively.

2. Interest margin to average earning assets declined moderately. This indicates a less profitable situation.

3. The loan loss coverage ratio decreased materially. This represents a substantial decrease in coverage of net charge-offs.

4. Equity capital to total capital declined moderately. Both years appear to be very good.

5. Deposits times capital increased moderately. This implies a modest decrease in the margin of safety.

6. Loans to deposits decreased moderately in 1998. This tentatively indicates decreased risk.

CASE 12-5   PROVED RESERVES

(This case includes part of the Supplementary Oil and Gas Data with the 2001 annual report of Amerada Hess Corporation. These data can be analyzed to gain an insight on important aspects of this oil and gas company.)

a.   Net Proved Developed and Undeveloped Reserves
      Crude Oil, Including Condensate and
      Natural Gas Liquids (Millions of barrels)

	Total	United States	Canada	Europe	Other Areas
December 31, 1999	100.0	29.6	5.8	59.0	5.7
December 31, 2000	100.0	30.7	5.3	57.9	6.1
December 31, 2001	100.0	29.5	4.5	59.3	6.8

Natural Gas (Millions of Mcf)

	Total	United States	Canada	Europe	Other Areas
December 31, 1999	100.0	35.8	22.6	41.6	--
December 31, 2000	100.0	38.8	22.5	38.7	--
December 31, 2001	100.0	41.8	18.7	37.4	2.1

b.   Net Proved Developed Reserves Crude Oil, Including Condensate and Natural Gas Liquids (Millions of barrels)

	Total	United States	Canada	Europe	Other Areas
December 31, 1999	100.0	32.9	7.4	52.7	7.0
December 31, 2000	100.0	33.9	6.5	52.1	7.5
December 31, 2001	100.0	29.1	5.7	57.4	7.8

Natural Gas (Millions of Mcf)

	Total	United States	Canada	Europe	Other Areas
December 31, 1999	100.0	35.1	25.6	39.2	--
December 31, 2000	100.0	37.9	25.2	36.8	--
December 31, 2001	100.0	37.1	22.5	40.4	--

c.   Part (a)

Natural gas liquids, etc.

Europe represents the dominate source of reserves. Canada represents a fairly immaterial source of reserves, and declined significantly.

Natural gas

Europe and the United States represent the major sources of reserves, while the United States increased significantly.

Part (b)

Natural gas liquids, etc.

Europe represents the dominate source of reserves, and it increased materially as a source. The United States and Canada both declined significantly as a source of reserves.

Natural gas

The United States, Canada, and Europe all represent a significant source.

CASE 12-6 HEAVENLY FLYING

(This case provides the opportunity to review the operating results of Delta Air Lines, Inc.)

a.

Delta Air Lines, Inc.
Consolidated Statements of Operations
For the Years Ended June 30, 1998, 1997 and 1996
Vertical Common-Size

	1998	1997	1996
Operating Revenues:			
Passenger	91.8%	92.0%	93.3%
Cargo	4.1	4.1	4.2
Other, net	4.1	3.9	2.5
Total operating revenues	100.0%	100.0%	100.0%
Operating Expenses:			
Salaries and related costs	34.3	33.4	33.8
Aircraft fuel	10.7	12.7	11.8
Passenger commissions	6.9	7.5	8.4
Depreciation and amortization	6.1	5.2	5.1
Contracted services	4.9	4.6	5.7
Other selling expenses	4.8	5.0	4.8
Landing fees and other rents	4.6	4.8	5.0
Aircraft rent	3.9	4.0	4.5
Aircraft maintenance materials and outside repairs	3.5	3.2	3.0
Passenger service	3.2	2.9	3.0
Restructuring and other non-recurring charges	–	.4	6.7
Other	5.1	5.2	4.8
Total operating expenses	88.0%	88.7%	96.3%
Operating Income:	12.0%	11.3%	3.7%

b. 1. Passenger revenues declined in relation to total operating revenue.

2. Other, net revenues increased in relation to total operating revenue.

3. The following items declined moderately:
   a. Aircraft fuel
   b. Passenger commissions
   c. Contracted services
   d. Landing fees and other rents
   e. Aircraft rent

4. The following items increased moderately:
   a. Salaries and related costs
   b. Depreciation and amortization
   c. Aircraft maintenance materials and outside repair

5. There was a substantial charge in 1976 for restructuring and other non-recurring charges.

Chapter 13
Personal Financial Statements and Accounting for
Governments and Not-For-Profit Organizations

QUESTIONS

13- 1. Personal financial statements may be prepared for an individual, a husband and wife, or a larger family group.

13- 2. The basic personal financial statement is the Statement of Financial Condition.

13- 3. No.

13- 4. No.

13- 5. Estimated current value basis.

13- 6. Net worth.

13- 7. Statement of Changes in Net Worth.

13- 8. No.

13- 9. No. Generally accepted accounting principles as they apply to personal financial statements require the accrual basis.

13-10. No. Assets and liabilities are not classified as current and noncurrent. Assets and liabilities are classified in order of liquidity and maturity.

13-11. a. Broker's statements
b. Income tax returns
c. Safe deposit box
d. Insurance policies
e. Real estate tax return
f. Checkbook
g. Bank statements

13-12. Examples would be methods used in determining current values of major assets, description of intangible assets, and assumptions used to compute the estimated income taxes.

13-13. If quoted market prices are not available, then reasonable estimates should be used.

13-14. Note: This is an open-ended question. The responses here are merely suggestions.
1. Dues will not increase
2. A monthly magazine will be started
3. Add 100 new members
4. Retain a minimum of 90% of the current members

13-15. No. Not-for-profit organizations are not allowed to use fund accounting.

13-16. No. The accounting for a profit-oriented business is centered on the entity concept and the efficiency of the entity. The accounting for governments does not include a single entity concept or efficiency.

13-17. a. General fund - All cash receipts and disbursements not required to be accounted for in another fund.

b. Proprietary fund - Intention is to maintain the fund's assets through cost reimbursement by users or partial cost recovery from users and periodic infusion of additional assets.

c. Fiduciary fund - The principal of a fiduciary fund must remain intact. Typically, revenues earned may be distributed.

13-18. The number of funds that will be utilized will depend upon the responsibilities of the particular state or local government and the grouping of these responsibilities.

13-19. When the representatives of the citizens approve the budget, then the individual expenditures become limits. An increase in an approved expenditure will require approval by the same representatives of the citizens. Thus, the representatives of the citizens set up a legal control over expenditures.

13-20. Government Finance Officers' Association.

13-21. No. Industrial revenue bonds are not backed by the full faith and credit of the governmental unit.

13-22.

13-22. Budgeting by objectives and/or measures of productivity can be incorporated into the financial reporting.

13-23. No. The accounting for a profit enterprise is centered on the entity concept and the efficiency of the entity. Fund accounting is centered on a self-balancing set of accounts. Fund accounting would not be a reasonable method for a profit enterprise.

TO THE NET

1. The mission of the Governmental Accounting Standards Board i
   to establish and improve standards of state and local
   governmental accounting and financial reporting that will
   result in useful information for users of financial reports
   and guide and educate the public including issuers, auditors
   and users of those financial reports.

2. **Introduction to Performance Measurement**

   The assessment of a governmental entity's performance
   requires more than information about the acquisition and use
   of resources. It also needs information but also about the
   outputs and outcomes of the services provided and the
   relationship between the use of resources and the outputs a
   outcomes of government services. Employing a variety of
   measures of inputs, outputs and outcomes, measures that
   relate efforts to accomplishments, and additional explanato
   material will assist users of general purpose external
   financial reporting to assess governmental performance more
   fully.

   Performance measurement reporting is tied directly to the
   concept of <u>managing for results</u>. Performance information i
   needed for:

   1. setting goals and objectives

   2. planning program activities to accomplish these goals a
      objectives

   3. allocating resources to programs

   4. monitoring and evaluating results to determine if
      progress is being made toward achieving the goals and
      objectives and

   5. modifying program plans to enhance performance.

   Performance measures organize information for use by the
   decision-makers engaged in those activities. Through the
   measurement, analysis, and evaluation of SEA data, public
   officials can identify ways to maintain or improve the
   efficiency and effectiveness of activities and provide the
   public with objective information on their results.

Categories of Service Efforts and Accomplishment Indicators

The types of performance indicators defined below reflect common elements that are used in current practice in most performance measurement systems. The four categories of service efforts and accomplishment indicators displayed here are the basic building blocks of many performance measurement systems. These measures report what services the entity has provided, whether those services have achieved the objectives established, and what effects they have had upon the recipients and others (service accomplishments). This information, when compared to service efforts (inputs), also provides a basis for assessing the efficiency of the entity's operations.

These definitions provide a basis for understanding what a performance indicators is designed to measure.

A. Indicators of Service Efforts

1. Inputs-Dollar costs of the service during the period:
   a. In "current" dollars
   b. In "constant" dollars (that is, adjusted for price level changes)
   c. Per household or per capita, in either current or constant dollars

2. Inputs-Amounts of nonmonetary resources expended, especially the amount of work time expended during the period (for the service). These might be expressed in such units as full-time-equivalent years or employee hours.

B. Indicators of Service Accomplishments

1. Outputs-Amount of workload accomplished

2. Outcomes-A numerical indicator of program results. This category includes indicators of service quality (such as timeliness), effectiveness, and the amount or proportion of "need" that is (or is not) being served.

C. **Indicators that Relate Service Efforts to Service Accomplishments**

These can also be labeled <u>efficiency indicators</u>@, which include both input/output and input/outcome indicators. The term "productivity indicator" is sometimes used instead of efficiency indicator. Productivity is usual defined in the productivity literature as "output divide by input," the reciprocal of "input divided by output."

1. <u>Amount of input related to (divided by) amount of output</u>. "Input" can be any of the variations included under section A, and "output" refers to B.

2. <u>Amount of input related to (divided by) amount of outcomes or results</u>. Again, "input" can be any of the variations noted in section A. "Outcome" refer to B.2.

3. <u>Productivity (or efficiency) *indexes*</u>. These traditionally have been used in reporting national productivity trends. Indexes are calculated by relating the ratio of productivity in the current year to that of a preselected base year. These indexes have an advantage in that the productivity ratios for different activities of a service, or across services, can be combined by weighting each ratio by the amount of input for each activity.

D. **Explanatory Information**

This is a term used to cover a variety of information relevant to a service that helps users understand the performance indicators and factors affecting an organization's performance. The explanatory informatic should be grouped into two categories:

1. Elements substantially outside the control of the public agency, such as demographic characteristics

2. Elements over which the agency has significant control, such as staffing patterns.

PROBLEMS

PROBLEM 13-1

a. $ 80,000 Purchase price
       10,000 Improvements
       90,000
        1.40 Increase in inflation rate
      126,000
       20,000 Less mortgage
      $106,000

   Note: An appraisal would likely be preferable to this
   computation.

b. $9,000.   The average selling price for this model of car.

c.   Estimated current value of the IRA:

          IRA $20,000
          Less Taxes:
          1.   10% IRS penalty for early withdrawal   <$ 2,000>
          2. $20,000 x 30%   < 6,000>

                                                        <$ 8,000>
          Estimated current value of the IRA $12,000

d.   The guarantee should not be presented as a liability.   It
      should be disclosed in a footnote, if material.

e.   If the offer to buy back the mortgage is still outstanding,
      the estimated current value of the debt would be $40,000.   If
      the buy-back offer has expired, then the estimated current
      value of the mortgage is $45,000.

PROBLEM 13-2

a.   Ree's:
        1,000 shares x $20 = $20,000
        Less commission   148
                             $19,852
      Bell's:
        2,000 shares x $8 = $16,000
        Less commission   170
                             $15,830

349

b. Certificate of deposit $10,000
    Accrued interest   500
                                                             10,500
    Less early withdrawal penalty   300
                                                            $10,200

c. Present selling price per share $ 25
    Option price per share   20
    Estimated value of options per share (A)   5
    Number of options (B)   500
    Total estimated value of options [A x B] $2,500

d. Cash value $50,000
    Less loan outstanding   20,000
    Estimated current value $30,000

e. $90,000 estimate of current value
     4,500 broker fee (5% x $90,000)
    $85,500

    Note: It would be better to get an independent appraisal of
    the home than to use Larry's estimate.

PROBLEM 13-3

a. Marketable securities $5,000   x 28% = $1,400
   Residence   25,000   x 28% = 7,000
                                              $8,400

b.   **Bob and Carl**
                Statement of Financial Condition
                      December 31, 2001

   Assets
     Cash $ 20,000
     Marketable securities   50,000
     Life insurance   50,000
     Residence   125,000
     Furnishings   25,000
     Jewelry   20,000
     Autos   12,000
                                             $302,000

   Liabilities
     Mortgage payable $ 90,000
     Note payable   30,000
     Credit cards   10,000
       Total liabilities   130,000

   Estimated income taxes on differences
     between estimated current value of
     assets and their tax basis   8,400*
   Net worth   163,600
                                             $302,000

*($5,000 + $25,000) x 28% = $8,400

c. 1. The net worth is $163,600. Many would consider this a
        relatively high amount.

   2. Liquid assets total $70,000 (cash, $20,000; and marketable
        securities, $50,000).

   3. The majority of the liabilities are long-term (mortgage
        payable, $90,000).

   4. Comparison of specific assets with related liabilities:

        Residence:
         Current value $125,000
         Mortgage payable   90,000
         Net investment $ 35,000

PROBLEM 13-4

a. Marketable securities: $20,000 x 28% = $ 5,600
    Options: $30,000 x 28% =   8,400
    Residence: $50,000 x 28% = 14,000
    Royalties: $20,000 x 28% =   5,600
                                              $33,600

b.
Mary Lou and Ernie
Statement of Financial Condition
December 31, 2001

Assets	
Cash	$ 20,000
Marketable securities	100,000
Options	30,000
Residence	150,000
Royalties	20,000
Furnishings	20,000
Auto	15,000
	$355,000

Liabilities	
Mortgage	$ 70,000
Auto loan	10,000
Total liabilities	80,000

Estimated income taxes on differences between estimated current value of assets and their tax basis	33,600*
Net worth	241,400
	$355,000

*($20,000 + $30,000 + $50,000 + $20,000) x 28% = $33,600

c. 1. The net worth is $241,400.

   2. Liquid assets total $120,000 (cash, $20,000; marketable
       securities, $100,000).

   3. Most of the liabilities appear to be long-term (mortgag
       payable, $70,000).

4. Comparison of specific assets with related liabilities:

Auto		Residence	
Current value	$15,000	Current value	$150,000
Auto loan	10,000	Mortgage	70,000
Net investment	$ 5,000	Net investment	$ 80,000

PROBLEM 13-5

a.

Bob and Sue
Statement of Changes in Net Worth
For the Year Ended December 31, 2001

Realized increases in net worth		
Salary		$ 60,000
Dividend income		2,500
Interest income		2,000
Gain on sale of marketable securities		500
		65,000
Realized decreases in net worth		
Income taxes		20,000
Interest expense		6,000
Personal expenditures		29,000
		55,000
Net realized increases in net worth		10,000
Unrealized increases in net worth		
Stock options		3,000
Land		7,000
Residence		5,000
		15,000
Unrealized decreases in net worth		
Boat		3,000
Jewelry		1,000
Furnishings		4,000
Estimated income taxes on the differences between the estimated current values of assets and the estimated current amounts of liabilities and their tax bases		15,000
		23,000
Net unrealized decreases in net worth		8,000
Net increase in net worth		2,000
Net worth at the beginning of year		150,000
Net worth at the end of year		$152,000

b. 1. Most of the realized increases in net worth came from salary ($60,000).

2. The major decreases in realized net worth were income taxes ($20,000) and personal expenditures ($29,000).

3. Net realized increases in net worth, $10,000.

4. Land had the most material increase in unrealized net worth ($7,000).

5. Principle unrealized decreases in net worth was the estimated income taxes on the difference between the estimated current values of assets and the estimated amounts of liabilities and their tax bases ($15,000).

6. Net unrealized decreases in net worth ($8,000).

7. Net increase in net worth ($2,000).

8. Net worth at the end of year ($152,000).

PROBLEM 13-6

a.

Jim and Carl
Statement of Changes in Net Worth
For the Year Ended December 31, 2001

Realized increases in net worth		
Salary		$ 50,000
Interest income		6,000
		56,000
Realized decreases in net worth		
Income taxes		15,000
Interest expense		3,000
Personal property taxes		1,000
Real estate taxes		1,500
Personal expenditures		25,000
		45,500
Net realized increases in net worth		10,500
Unrealized increases in net worth		
Marketable securities		2,000
Land		5,000
Residence		3,000
Stock options		4,000
		14,000
Unrealized decreases in net worth		
Furnishings		3,000
Estimated income taxes on the differences between the estimated current values of assets and the estimated current amounts of liabilities and their tax bases		12,000
		15,000
Net unrealized decreases in net worth		1,000
Net increase in net worth		9,500
Net worth at the beginning of year		130,000
Net worth at the end of year		$139,500

b. 1. Net increase in net worth was $9,500, which brought the net worth at the end of the year to $139,500.

2. The major increase in realized net worth was salary ($50,000).

3. The major realized decrease in net worth was personal expenditures ($25,000).

PROBLEM 13-7

a. Revenues:
Income taxes	51.1
Property taxes	5.1
Special assessments	7.1
Licenses and permits	.9
Intergovernmental services	21.5
Charges for service	4.1
Investment earnings	2.6
Fines and forfeitures	1.6
All other revenue	.9
Total revenues	94.8

Expenditures:
Current:
General government	6.4
Public service	8.9
Public safety	43.2
Public utilities	1.0
Community environment	7.3
Health	6.6
Parks and recreation	1.8
Capital outlay	15.0

Debt service:
Principal retirement	4.8
Interest and fiscal charges	5.0
Total expenditures	100.0

b. The most significant revenue item is income taxes. The most significant expenditure item is public safety.

PROBLEM 13-8

a. **City of Toledo**

Income Tax Revenues
Horizontal Common-Size Analysis

Fiscal Year	(%) Common-Size Analysis
1988	100.0
1989	97.4
1990	98.6
1991	95.7
1992	100.8
1993	105.7
1994	114.1
1995	118.5
1996	126.4
1997	130.3

b. Income tax revenues were down, between 1988 and 1992.   There
   have been significant increases in income tax revenues between
   1991 and 1997.

PROBLEM 13-9

a. Assessed value increased from $3,091,093,000 in 1988 to
   $3,450,882,000 in 1997, an increase of $359,789,000.

b. Net general bonded debt increased from $68,794,000 in 1988 to
   $105,349,000 in 1997, an increase of $36,555,000.

c. Assessed value increased 11.6%, while net general bonded debt
   increased 53.1%.   Debt went up much more than the increase in
   assessed value.

PROBLEM 13-10

a. Combined fund balance increased from $15,761,000 in 1997 to
   $17,975,000 in 1998, an increase of $2,214,000.

b. Institute of Management Accountants, Inc. and Affiliates
   Combined Statement of Activities and Changes in Net Assets
   Horizontal Common-Size Analysis
   Years Ended June 30, 1998 and 1997
   (Revenues and Support, and Expenses)

	In Percentage	
	1998	1997
Revenues and support:		
Membership dues and fees	96.1	100.0
Education programs	104.4	100.0
Annual conference	95.4	100.0
Advertising and sales of publications	103.9	100.0
CMA/CFM examination fees	79.5	100.0
Interest income	113.8	100.0
Other	75.0	100.0
Total revenues and support	99.0	100.0
Expenses:		
Payments to chapters	97.7	100.0
Chapter and member services	95.3	100.0
Education programs	103.5	100.0
Marketing	103.4	100.0
Annual conference	108.3	100.0
Publications and information center	110.0	100.0
CMA/CFM program	80.8	100.0
Research expenditures	22.8	100.0
Administration and occupancy costs	90.3	100.0
Asset valuation charge	0.0	100.0
Other	72.7	100.0
Total expenses	90.9	100.0

c. Institute of Management Accountants, Inc. and Affiliates

Combined Statement of Activities
Vertical Common-Size Analysis
Years Ended June 30, 19985 and 19974
(Total Revenue and Expenses)

In Percentage

	1998	1997
Revenues and support:		
Membership dues and fees	40.8	42.1
Education programs	8.1	7.7
Annual conference	3.5	3.6
Advertising and sales of publications	12.6	12.0
CMA/CFM examination fees	8.0	7.9
Investment income	24.6	21.4
Other	4.1	5.4
Total revenues and support	100.0	100.0
Expenses:		
Payments to chapters	5.3	5.4
Chapter and member services	10.3	10.7
Education programs	10.0	9.6
Marketing	2.7	2.6
Annual conference	3.1	2.8
Publications and information center	13.8	12.4
CMA/CFM program	8.2	10.0
Research expenditures	.8	.6
Administration and occupancy costs	30.3	33.2
Asset valuation charge	--	3.5
Other	4.0	5.4
Total expenses	88.4	96.2

d. Horizontal
1. Very significant decrease in CMA/CFM examination fees.
2. Very significant decrease in other revenues.
3. Significant increase in investment income.
4. Significant increase in publications.
5. Very significant increase in administration and occupancy costs.
6. Asset valuation charge eliminated.
7. Very significant decrease in other expenses.

Vertical
1. Asset valuation charge eliminated.
2. Significant decrease in total expenses.

CASES

CASE 13-1 GOVERNOR LUCAS - THIS IS YOUR COUNTY

a.

1997 Totals

Memorandum Only

Assets and other debts:

	1997 Totals Memorandum Only
Pooled cash and cash equivalents	5.8%
Investments	16.7
Segregated cash accounts	4.5
Receivables	
Taxes	12.5
Accounts	.6
Special assessments	2.4
Accrued interest	.2
Loans	.1
Due from other funds	.1
Due from other governments	1.7
Inventory: materials and supplies	.1
Property, plant and equipment	
Land	2.3
Land improvements	12.7
Buildings, structures and improvements	19.1
Furniture, fixtures and equipment	6.1
Less: accumulated depreciation	(6.4)
Construction-in-progress	2.6
Amount available in debt service fund	1.1
Amount to be provided for retirement of general long-term obligations	17.8
Total assets and other debit	100.0

b.   1.   Special revenue
      2. $40,788,000
      3. $21,845,000

c.   1.   General Fund: This fund accounts for the general operating revenues and expenditures of the County not recorded elsewhere. The primary revenue sources are sales and use taxes, property taxes, state and local government fund receipts, investment earnings, and charges for services.

2. Special Revenue Funds: These funds are used to account for specific governmental revenues (other than major capital projects) requiring separate accounting because of legal or regulatory provisions or administrative action. These funds include: Public Assistance, the Board of Mental Retardation, and the Motor Vehicle and Gas Tax funds, which are major funds of the County.

3. Capital Projects Funds: These funds are used to account for the acquisition or construction of capital assets. Revenues and financing sources are derived from the issuance of debt or receipts from the General Fund and Special Revenue funds.

d. Basis of Accounting: All financial transactions for Governmental and Fiduciary Funds are reported on the modified accrual basis of accounting.

   e. (1) Revenues are recorded when received in cash (budget) as opposed to when susceptible to accrual (GAAP).

   (2) Expenditures are recorded when encumbered, or paid in cash (budget), as opposed to when susceptible to accrual (GAA).

   f. 1. Depreciation is not provided for the General Fixed Assets Account Group.

   2. Depreciation for the Proprietary Funds is determined by allocating the cost of fixed assets over their estimated useful lives on a straight-line basis. A full year of depreciation expense is taken in the year of acquisition, and none in the year of disposal.

g.

	1.	2.	
	Total		Total
Fiscal	Nominal	Fiscal	Real
Year	Expenditures	Year	Expenditures
1988	100.0	1988	100.0
1989	108.0	1989	105.3
1990	114.8	1990	105.0
1991	123.4	1991	109.3
1992	120.7	1992	103.8
1993	128.2	1993	107.0
1994	143.2	1994	116.6
1995	147.1	1995	116.5
1996	169.1	1996	130.1
1997	181.6	1997	136.6

3. Total real expenditures increased substantially less than total nominal expenditures. Total real expenditures consider inflation.

4. 1977

181.5 / 480.8 x $341,414 = $128,882

Note: Difference between table amount and computed amount due to rounding.

h. 1.

	General	Tangible	Property	County
Fiscal	Property	Personal	Transfer	Sales
Year	Tax	Tax	Tax	Tax
1988	100.0	100.0	100.0	100.0
1989	112.1	102.4	95.0	102.0
1990	119.9	105.0	83.7	97.9
1991	122.1	100.1	181.1	99.5
1992	129.8	98.2	249.7	133.4
1993	144.0	96.3	293.9	130.2
1994	145.5	100.1	302.8	174.7
1995	148.4	102.2	331.4	162.0
1996	169.2	116.8	360.3	167.9
1997	173.6	119.3	389.0	178.7

2. Property transfer tax had the biggest percentage increase. Tangible personal property had the least increase.